MORE WITH LESS

MORE WITH LESS

Maximizing Value in the Public Sector

Bernard Marr

Chief Executive and Director of Research, Advanced Performance Institute

James Creelman

Performance Management Researcher and Advisor and a Fellow of the Advanced Performance Institute

First published 2011 by
PALGRAVE MACMILLAN

Palgrave Macmillan in the UK is an imprint of Macmillan Publishers Limited,
registered in England, company number 785998, of Houndmills, Basingstoke,
Hampshire RG21 6XS.

Palgrave Macmillan in the US is a division of St Martin's Press LLC,
175 Fifth Avenue, New York, NY 10010.

Palgrave Macmillan is the global academic imprint of the above companies
and has companies and representatives throughout the world.

Palgrave® and Macmillan® are registered trademarks in the United States,
the United Kingdom, Europe and other countries

ISBN 978-0-230-28356-5   hardback

This book is printed on paper suitable for recycling and made from fully
managed and sustained forest sources. Logging, pulping and manufacturing
processes are expected to conform to the environmental regulations of the
country of origin.

A catalogue record for this book is available from the British Library.

A catalogue record for this book is available from the Library of Congress.

10   9   8   7   6   5   4   3   2   1
20   19   18   17   16   15   14   13   12   11

Printed and bound in Great Britain by
CPI Antony Rowe, Chippenham and Eastbourne

James Creelman:
To the memory of my sister Margaret (Margo) Kyle Murray Creelman
(1957–2006)

Bernard Marr:
To Claire, Sophia and James (who make me so happy every day)

CONTENTS

ABOUT THE AUTHORS

Bernard Marr

Bernard Marr is a leading global expert and best-selling author on organizational performance. In this capacity he regularly advises companies, organizations and governments around the globe, which makes him an acclaimed and award-winning keynote speaker, consultant and teacher. Bernard Marr is acknowledged by the *CEO Journal* as one of today's leading business brains.

Bernard has written a number of seminal books and over 200 high profile reports and articles on managing organizational performance. This includes the best-sellers *Managing and Delivering Performance, The Intelligent Company*, and *Strategic Performance Management*, as well as a number of Gartner Reports and the world's largest research studies on Government Performance.

Bernard Marr is one of the most experienced government advisors in the area of performance management and frequently helps central and local government organizations across the world improve their performance management practices. His clients include, among others, central governments and administrations, central auditing organizations and regulators, central banks, ministries, as well as many local government organizations including councils, police forces, fire services, housing associations, and health services. For example, he has worked with the Ministry of Defense, the Home Office, the Bank of England, the NHS, HM Revenue & Customs, Government of Victoria, the Department of Culture, Arts and Leisure, Audit Scotland, the Health & Safety Executive, the Army, the Air Force and many more.

At present, Bernard heads up the famed Advanced Performance Institute (API). Prior to this he held influential positions at the University of Cambridge and at Cranfield School of Management. Today, he holds a number of visiting professorships and fellowships and he serves on the editorial boards of many leading journals and publications in the field. Bernard's expert comments on organizational performance regularly appear in high-profile publications such as the *Financial Times*, the *Sunday Times*, *Financial Management*, the *CFO Magazine* and the *Wall Street Journal*.

Bernard can be contacted via e-mail at: bernard.marr@ap-institute.com

James Creelman

James Creelman is a fellow at the Advanced Performance Institute (API). He is a recognized global authority on the Balanced Scorecard and Enterprise Performance Management (EPM). James is the author of 20 books and reports on the topic, including "Managing Business in Asia: Succeeding with the Balanced Scorecard" (a best-seller in Asia) and "Reinventing Planning and Budgeting for the Adaptive Enterprise."

As well as advising organizations on their Balanced Scorecard and EPM initiatives, James also leads workshops and training seminars throughout the world.

ABOUT THE API

The Advanced Performance Institute (API) is the world's leading independent research and advisory organization specializing in organizational performance. The institute provides expert knowledge, research, consulting and training on concepts such as Strategic Performance Management, Balanced Scorecards, Performance Indicators, Business Intelligence, and Performance Improvement.

The aim of the API is to provide today's performance-focused organizations with insights, advice and services that help them deliver superior performance. Customers of the API are wide ranging and include many of the world's leading blue chip companies as well as public sector organizations, governments and not-for-profit organizations around the globe.

Some of the services API could offer your organization are:

- *Consulting* – The API are experts in helping public sector organizations perform better. We do this through the implementation of strategic performance management systems which are perfected through real-life implementation experience across many industries. The institute is able to facilitate each step to ensure clearly articulated and prioritized strategies, state of the art strategy maps, meaningful performance indicators as well as lean and aligned processes.
- *Training* – The API specializes in customized in-house training and coaching programs on organizational performance. This includes training and up-skilling of internal performance management teams, workshops on specific issues such as KPI design, performance reporting, analytics or dashboard design as well as coaching for executive teams and management boards on driving performance improvements.
- Best-Practice – The API conducts internationally recognized research with the aim of understanding and sharing the latest trends and best practices in the field of managing and measuring organizational performance. A wide selection of case studies, research reports, articles and white papers can be downloaded free from the API website.

For more information please visit: www.ap-institute.com

LIST OF FIGURES AND TABLES

FIGURES

TABLES

ACKNOWLEDGEMENTS

Our work at the Advanced Performance Institute has given us ample opportunities to work with and learn form some of the leading public sector organizations across the world. Of course, there are so many individuals who have influenced our thinking and we hope they all know who they are and how much we have valued any input and dialog over the years. In particular, this book would not have been possible without the assistance of the following people, all of whom we gratefully acknowledge. Diane McGiffen, Audit Scotland; His Excellency (HE) Fahmi Bin Ali Al-Jowder, Raja Al Zayani, Mark Ranford, Atif Adeel, Farah Ebrahim Al-Majed, Fareed Karaymeh, Jennifer Zhang, Hana Jassim, Ministry of Works, Bahrain; Ronan Cregan, Emer Husbands, Gerry Millar, Belfast City Council; Peter Ryan, Christchurch City Council; Richard Ryder, Kay McNeil, Information Managing Section, Her Majesty's Revenue and Customs; Bill Barberg, Insightformation; Andrea Smith, International Baccalaureate; Michelle McCusker, North WestCollaborative Commercial Agency; Patricia Bush, The Palladium Group; Maurice Atkinson, Regulation and Quality Improvement Authority (Northern Ireland). We would like to extend a special thank you to Dr David Norton, The Palladium Group, for providing a foreword to this work.

FOREWORD

The subject of *performance management* (PM) has received considerable attention in the literature of late. References like Enterprise performance management (EPM), Corporate performance management (CPM) and Business performance management (BPM) abound with no clear consistency of meaning. My personal definition of PM is *"the execution of the organization mission through the coordinated effort of others."* PM is a system and a process that impacts everyone in the organization. You can argue that performance management is the most important job of a manager. In fact, you could argue that the execution of the organization mission through the coordinated efforts of others is the only job of management.

Since Bob Kaplan and I introduced the Balanced Scorecard (BSC) approach to performance management almost 20 years ago, the use of such BSC-based systems has grown in both scale and complexity. From simple business units to complicated conglomerates, the BSC approach to performance management has been used in organizations of every size and type. These organizations share one common trait – COMPLEXITY. Thousands of people working in different functions and locations must somehow make decisions on a daily basis that are consistent with the goals of their organization. The more complex the environment, the more difficult it is to manage performance. Complexity is the enemy.

While all organizations are inherently complex, public sector organizations present the greatest challenge for effective performance management. Two structural features contribute to this. First, performance is seldom confined to a single, formal organization. The role of government is generally an *intermediary* in a process of prioritization and resource allocation. The boundaries of a performance management process must include the organization, as well as numerous stakeholders and numerous resource providers. Performance management processes must be designed for *virtual organizations*.

Secondly, performance management takes place in an *adversarial* structure that intentionally pits different coalitions against one another (in a two-party or parliamentary system.) It is said that democracy is messy. Managing performance in an adversarial environment requires a *balancing* of divergent views. *Consensus* building is the goal of the performance management process.

The BSC approach to performance management provides a solution to this challenge: SIMPLICITY. It begins with a philosophy: having executives who are focused and can mobilize their people, strategies that are measured, organizations that are aligned, people who are motivated, and governance that is strategic. This philosophy is embedded in a strategy management system that facilitates change in a purposeful, coordinated way.

The authors of this excellent work are to be congratulated for tailoring the classic architecture of the Balanced Scorecard performance management system to the unique challenges posed by public sector organizations. This is an excellent reference for those in the public sector who are responsible for good performance management. As a consumer of public sector services, I will be the ultimate beneficiary of this work.

David P. Norton
Boston, MA, USA
July 2010

1

BOTH EFFICIENT AND EFFECTIVE: THE NEW PUBLIC SECTOR PERFORMANCE AGENDA

*We can no longer afford to sustain the old ways when we know
there are new and more efficient ways of getting the job done.*

Barack Obama

INTRODUCTION

It is fair to say that the collapse of the financial markets in 2007/2008 was an epoch making event. As well as popularizing the then obscure term "credit crunch," commentators watched in disbelief as long-established and venerable companies such as Lehman Brothers went out of business and other household names such as Citibank in the US and the Royal Bank of Scotland in the UK were saved from extinction only through massive financial interventions from their national Governments.

Few industries and sectors were unscathed by the global economic recession that was triggered by the collapse of the financial markets. From construction to publishing, from property to computing, organizations were forced to hurriedly batten down the hatches and wait while the recessionary hurricane passed by. Although we have avoided the deep "depression" that was widely predicted at the turn of 2009, the recession can still be seen as a massive economic catastrophe and it is safe to claim that the road to full recovery will be long and treacherous and many more well known organizations may well die en route.

1

THE AMERICAN RECOVERY AND REINVESTMENT ACT

Financing the recovery will place enormous demands on public purses that, due to demographic and other influences, have already been stretched in recent years. Perhaps the most powerful measure of the cost of recovery can be gleaned by considering the price tag on The American Recovery and Reinvestment Act (ARRA) of 2009. Largely based on proposals made by President Barack Obama, the Act introduced measures intended to stimulate the US economy that together will cost about US$787 billion. The range of measures include federal tax cuts, expansion of unemployment benefits and other social welfare provisions as well as domestic spending on education, healthcare and infrastructure projects. And bear in mind that ARRA spending is on top of significant amounts of money that have already been pumped into the US economy by the Government (and that was replicated in other nations such as the UK) to shore up the banking sector as well as the cost of other recession-busting and depression-avoiding interventions.

TRANSPARENCY AND ACCOUNTABILITY

When looked at strictly from a performance management perspective ARRA is nothing short of groundbreaking. For many years, those of us working to improve performance management within the Government and public sectors (which, for ease of reading, together we will refer to as the public sector) have been actively promoting the establishment of mechanisms that substantially improve performance accountability and transparency, which we have long argued must be at least on par with that expected in the commercial sector.

Therefore it is heartwarming to note that an ARRA provision called for "a website on the internet to be named Recovery.gov, to foster *greater accountability and transparency* (authors' italics) in the use of funds made available in this Act."[1] Recovery.gov is operated by the Recovery Transparency and Accountability Board, which was also created by the Act.

Unprecedented in the levels of performance transparency and accountability (indeed the words "Track the Money" are emblazoned across every webpage) the website tracks areas such as:

– Are the public benefits from the use of the Recovery funds being reported clearly, accurately and in a timely manner?
– Are Recovery projects avoiding unnecessary delays and cost overruns?
– Do Recovery programs meet specified goals and targets?

FEDERAL DIRECTOR OF PERFORMANCE

Although the ACCA can be viewed as a short-term response to a desperate situation (even though some of the funding is earmarked for longer-term economic developments) the Act should be understood within a broader performance improving agenda that beats at the heart of the Obama administration. For example, in June 2009 the President appointed Jeffrey D. Zients (an American CEO, management consultant and entrepreneur) as the United States Chief Performance Officer. Zients is also Deputy Director for Management of the Office of Management and Budget in the federal government of the United States. According to President Obama, Zients' assignment is to help "streamline processes, cut costs, and find best practices throughout the US government."[2]

Zients replaced Nancy Killefer who withdrew from her nomination to this position in February 2009 to avoid controversy about her personal income taxes.

On announcing the new position of Chief Performance Officer, Obama made a statement that accurately describes the need for reform in public sector performance management across the globe, "We can no longer afford to sustain the old ways when we know there are new and more efficient ways of getting the job done," he said, adding that, "Even in good times, Washington can't afford to continue these bad practices. In bad times, it's absolutely imperative that Washington stop them and restores confidence that our Government is on the side of taxpayers and everyday Americans."

Although the two just-cited examples relate to the USA, throughout the world we are witnessing a radical refocusing of how the public sector is spending its money, with words such as transparency, accountability, efficiency and effectiveness peppering the uncountable performance dialogs that are taking place from the UK to New Zealand, from Canada to Singapore.

A PUBLIC SECTOR HISTORY OF PERFORMANCE IMPROVEMENT

Although the discussions have become heightened, the quest to radically improve performance is hardly a new concept in the public sector. Over the preceding two decades there have been repeated attempts to remove waste, bureaucracies and the inward foci from public sector agencies. For instance in 1993 the then US President Bill Clinton introduced the Government Performance Results Act (GPRA), which set out to improve agency program performance and accountability, thus improving the public's confidence in Federal Agencies. Key program goals included:

– Initiate program performance reforms with a series of pilot projects in setting program goals, measuring program performance against those goals, and reporting publicly on their progress.
– Improve Federal program effectiveness and public accountability by promoting a new focus on results, service quality and customer satisfaction.

As the result of this Act, the head of each Government agency has to submit to the US congress a strategic plan detailing the strategic aims and performance indicators. The key performance results are then aggregated into an executive branch management scorecard, which is published for everybody to see.

Note the use of terms such as measurement, goals, reporting and accountability, which all feature strongly in the words that have been coming out of ARRA and the importance of transparency.

Switching our attention to the UK, a catalog of programs and initiatives has been launched in recent years with the clear goal of improving public sector performance. For example the "best value" scheme that requires local authorities to deliver service to clear standards by the most economic, efficient and effective means available was first launched in 1999 and has evolved since. Other UK-based Government initiatives that have been in place for some time include the use of national league tables for National Health Services trust and primary and secondary schools. Although controversial (critics claim that local factors are not taken into account and that the emphasis should be on celebrating and sharing best practice rather than naming and shaming poor performers) league tables have delivered some benefits in that they have catapulted performance issues onto the agendas of health trusts and school managers as well as raising public awareness of the distance that separates the best from the worst performers.

THE EFFICIENCY PRIORITY

But although we have witnessed concerted attempts to improve public sector performance through the last decade of the last century and the first of this, as we enter the second decade of the 21st century there is no doubt that there is a new performance imperative to contend with.

The fact is, as a result of the recession that followed the credit crunch public sector leaders have to do a lot more than ever before but with much smaller public purses. In essence, public sector bodies have little option but to focus squarely onto cost savings and efficiency gains.

Scottish example

As just one indication of the scale of the challenge that is facing public sectors leaders throughout the world, Audit Scotland (which is a case study in this book) released a report in November 2009 that painted a worrying picture of Scotland's future public sector finances. The report noted that although it was commendable that Scottish Ministers had committed to a 2% annual efficiency saving to 2011 (Audit Scotland itself has internally embraced this target) that this would be insufficient to fill the shortfall that will see the Scottish budget fall between 7% and 13% in real terms by 2013–2024. This shortcoming, it commented, was caused primarily by falling government revenues, rising unemployment, ever-increasing demands for improved public services and an aging population.

To contend with this shortfall, the Scottish Auditor General Robert Black noted that difficult decisions would be needed to find other ways to reduce public spending. Black highlighted an "urgent need" to improve the efficiency and productivity of public services in Scotland, alongside better information linking spending with actual service delivery, costs and performance. Put in stark terms, the Audit Scotland report warned that "severe spending constraint is on the way."[3]

Of course Scotland is not the only nation facing spending constraints, the same holds true for public sector funding in just about every other developed nation. Without significant efficiency gains, public sector bodies will simply not be able to properly deliver their services in the next decade.

A DELAY IN IMPACT

As a result, the need to become efficient has become perhaps the key performance imperative for public sector bodies. What's more as there is a delay from the time commercial organizations emerge from recession and public funds recovering, the aftermath of the current recession will continue to hurt the public sector long after the present downturn ends.

Basically, while most private businesses can just get on with the job after money starts flowing more freely, governments have to deal with the huge debt burdens, they still own major stakes in banks that need to be restructured and they have to cope with the reduced tax income. While budgets are often set for three or five years, the next budget round will mean reduced budgets for most government organizations – be it central government departments, agencies, education institutions, schools, NHS organizations, police forces, fire and emergency services, justice organizations, local authorities, etc. All of those will be forced to cut costs and become leaner and more efficient, which is a trend that is likely to continue for many years until the massive debts are repaid and public purses look more healthy again. The fact is over the coming years public sector bodies are facing harsh economic realities, the likes of which has not been seen since the end of World War 2.

IMPROVING EFFECTIVENESS

But note. Although there will be massive pressure on public sector bodies to deliver quantifiable and significant cost savings in the coming years there is a wider and more complex performance challenge facing public sector leaders. They will have to achieve the potentially large-scale cost reductions without negatively impacting citizen-facing performance. Indeed as the public gets more demanding of performance, public sector bodies might be expected to improve service outputs with the same or fewer resources. While this might be achievable in some large and inefficient departments, it's a lot harder for some organizations that are already lean. Basically efficiency savings are on a logarithmus scale and will become exponentially more difficult.

So here's the rub. Public sector bodies are being asked to become both more effective *as well as* more efficient (not therefore becoming efficient at the expense of being more effective). Often seen as interchangeable words, we can define efficiency as "doing things right," and effectiveness as "doing the right things."

In essence, from an effectiveness perspective the general public of developed nations are demanding that their public sector agencies perform to the same level of customer-centricity that they now expect from their commercial sector suppliers. Indeed over the last 20 years or so (perhaps measurable from the early 1980s when total quality management principles were first introduced into Western organizations with their focus on increased efficiencies through tight process management as well as the inculcation of greater customer focus – see Chapter 3) as the performance of private sector companies improved, consumers began to use the standards of the best companies as the benchmark for all of their service providers – commercial or public. The performance of the public sector was generally found wanting which led to an interesting cycle: private citizens vented their frustrations regarding public sector performance on elected officials. These officials then passed this anger straight back to public sector managers, with the non-negotiable order to demonstrate substantial service performance improvement. Fast forward to today, this means that as public sector bodies look to (and are forced to) cut costs they will not be allowed to trade this with any measurable and sustained degradation of service. However unfair it might seem to beleaguered public sector leaders, the general public will not stand for poorer performance from public sector bodies and therefore neither will their elected officials.

EFFICIENCY AND EFFECTIVENESS: AUDIT SCOTLAND CASE EXAMPLE

In short, the expectation of public sector leaders is that they deliver "more value for less money." As a best practice example of this promise consider our case organization: Audit Scotland. Its vision is that: "On behalf of the Auditor General and the Accounts Commission, we will provide assurance to the people of Scotland that their money is spent appropriately and we will help public sector organizations in Scotland to improve and perform better." This vision speaks directly to the efficiency (value for money) and effectiveness (performance improvement) strands of Audit Scotland's responsibilities. Diane McGiffen, Audit Scotland's Director of Corporate Services notes that, "The vision we have now captures the essence of the priorities that our stakeholders and clients have identified for the next five years," therefore stressing the fact that their customers anticipate improvements to both efficiency and effectiveness performance strands – not one or the other.

As well as an external performance improvement focus, Audit Scotland pays equal attention to improving the efficiency and effectiveness of its own performance. To help achieve both its external and internal goals and bring these together in one document, Audit Scotland, as with all of the other case organizations in this book, uses a Balanced Scorecard as it core management framework.

A BALANCED SCORECARD

Described in detail in Chapter 2, a Balanced Scorecard is essentially a strategic management framework that comprises both financial and non-financial performance perspectives. First popularized in the early 1990s by Harvard Business Professor Dr Robert Kaplan and management consultant Dr David Norton, a "classic" Balanced Scorecard (that is as defined by Kaplan and Norton) comprises learning and growth, internal process and customer perspectives in addition to the financial perspective. These perspectives are collocated within a Strategy Map and an accompanying scorecard of indicators, targets and initiatives.

A number of variations to the Balanced Scorecard have evolved since the Kaplan/Norton framework was first introduced. Indeed the term Balanced Scorecard today most accurately relates to a broad range of performance management systems or frameworks that comprise financial and non-financial performance dimensions.

VALUE CREATION MAP

Alongside the "classic" Balanced Scorecard, this book also outlines how organizations have amended and changed the Balanced Scorecard concept to make it work for their organization. Bob Kaplan and Dave Norton make it very clear that organizations shouldn't see the "classic" scorecard template as a straight jacket and encourage organizations to change the standard templates to better reflect their unique strategies. One such evolution is the Value Creation Map that is used by Audit Scotland and many of the other case studies that we profile. The Value Creation Map is also described in detail within the next chapter. But as a quick description, a Value Creation Map describes the strategic objectives, initiatives and supporting key performance questions and key performance indicators that an organization must master in order to deliver to its vision or mission. Figure 1.1 provides a diagrammatic overview of a Strategy Map of a "classic" Balanced Scorecard and a Value Creation Map (which throughout this book we will also refer to as a Strategy Map). The process of strategy mapping (the most important phase in any Balanced Scorecard creation) is described fully in Chapter 4.

PERFORMANCE PRIORITIZATION IN THE PUBLIC SECTOR

Although the original Kaplan/Norton Balanced Scorecard was designed for deployment within commercial organizations (and indeed emerged

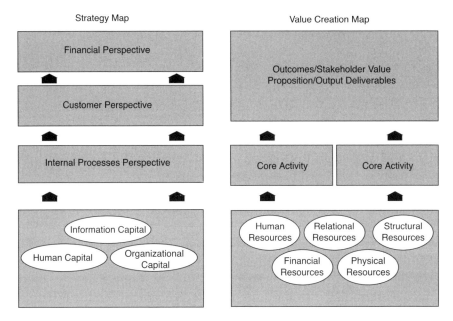

Figure 1.1   **Balanced Scorecard Strategy Map and a Value Creation Map**

from a 1990 study involving 12 large listed organizations that were looking at better ways to measure performance than could then be achieved through reliance on financial metrics alone[4]) Balanced Score-cards have perhaps become even more popular and enduring in public sector organizations. A key reason for this popularity is that a Balanced Scorecard enables public sector leaders to successfully contend with a challenge that is normally far tougher for them than their private sector counterparts – prioritizing where to spend money (which of course has today taken on a significantly more important focus than has previously been the case).

Simply put, whereas commercial organizations can boil every-thing down to some form of shareholder value focus (be that as a publicly traded or family owned enterprise) for public sector bodies there's a requirement to deliver equal value to a range of stakeholders: funders, consumers and partners, as examples. This can confuse the public sector leaders as to where they should prioritize attention and resources. Peter Ryan, Manager, Planning and Performance at our case study organization Christchurch City Council puts it well: "The leaders of public sector bodies have a great deal of difficulty in knowing what they're there to produce in terms of outcomes and what they need to support that," he says. "So their greatest short-coming is that they lack a real sense of what their business is."

Ryan continues that, "It's not like a private company where you're just pitching it at a profit measure which is a nice, simple thing to have as a prime directive. Public sector organizations have so many things that they're seeking to deliver that they end up not knowing what they're supposed to do."

He asks: "How can they set realistic and useful performance objectives and targets and prioritize performance when they're not sure what they're supposed to do in the first place?"

Ryan, along with other practitioners and thought leaders that we interviewed for this book states that a Balanced Scorecard is an ideal tool for those public sector leaders that want to properly understand what they should be doing and where to prioritize their spending. And usefully, given that public sector organizations are not subjected to the commercial sensitivities that exist in the private sector, they have been much more willing over the years to share the content of their Balanced Scorecards with other organizations. As a consequence, a substantial body of best practices and learning has emerged and been made freely available, which has been much less evident in the commercial sector. The best of these practices and learnings are reported in this book.

LEAN METHODOLOGIES

Throughout this book we also provide best practices in learnings as to how public sector organizations have used "Lean" methodologies to drive significant efficiency gains. Essentially Lean is a collection of methodologies and approaches (of which Six Sigma is perhaps the most popular) that are used to systematically identify and drive waste out of organizational activities and processes. Long-established and proven within the commercial sector, leaders within the public sector are waking up to the cost-saving potential of Lean within their own setting. As we explain throughout this book, Lean methodologies work extremely well when deployed as part of a Balanced Scorecard implementation. When Lean is used as part of a scorecard effort, organizations can ensure that they identify the most impactful organization-wide efficiency opportunities while making sure that the effectiveness performance dimension is not compromised. It also ensures that efficiency programs are tied to the organization's longer-term strategic agenda. Although the role of Lean within a scorecard implementation is described in many parts of the book, we describe Lean in detail within Chapter 3 and explain its key role in the identification of strategic initiatives in Chapter 6.

CONCLUSION

This chapter has explained that as a result of the economic downturn public sector organizations are under intense pressure to become much more efficient in their usage of scarce financial and other resources. But we also explained that they will be under huge pressure to remain effective; that is continuing to deliver (and improve upon) the required standards of service to an ever-demanding and increasingly unforgiving citizen-base: that is delivering "more value for less money."

The remainder of this book explains how public sector leaders can properly deliver these efficiency/effectiveness requirements. This begins with building a Balanced Scorecard, which as we describe in the next chapter is much more than simply choosing a bunch of financial and non-financial performance metrics (as we also explain, too many public sector bodies have become "obsessed" with measurement in recent times, largely as a consequence of externally mandated target-setting). Rather it is about public sector bodies using Balanced Scorecard principles and methodologies to place a robust strategic performance management framework, which includes a measurement component. In essence, this is about identifying *what matters*, measuring this and then managing it so to improve the effectiveness, efficiency and overall performance of an organization. Such an approach beats at the heart of the new public sector performance agenda.

SIDEBAR

Global study of performance management in the public sector

Recently the Advanced Performance Institute (API) conducted the research project, *Strategic Performance Management in Government and Public Sector Organizations – a Global Survey*, which, with more than 1100 responses is the largest and most comprehensive global study of Government and public sector Performance Management to date.[5]

These findings, alongside an extensive review of academic and practitioner literature on performance measurement and performance management, and from a consultation with a panel of leading academics and practitioners in this field – enabled the identified best practices and from this tested ten principles of good performance management for government and public sector organizations.

We questioned public sector respondents about their Performance Management practices in this light, tested the impact of these principles on organizational success using the latest statistical tools, determined how widespread these approaches are, and how effective they are when used. We found that organizations which have these principles in place are able to:

1. Create clarity and agreement about the strategic aims.
2. Collect meaningful and relevant performance indicators.
3. Use these indicators to extract relevant insights.
4. Create a positive culture of learning from performance information.
5. Gain cross-organizational buy-in.
6. Align other organizational activities with the strategic aims outlined in the Performance Management system.
7. Keep the strategic objectives and performance indicators fresh and up-to-date.
8. Report and communicate performance information well.
9. Use the appropriate IT infrastructure to support their Performance Management activities.
10. Give people enough time and resources to manage performance strategically.

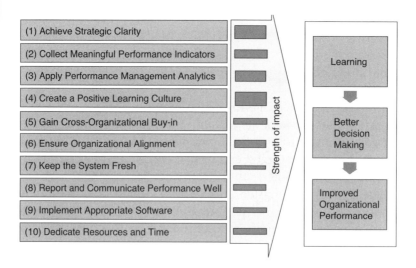

Figure 1.2   **10 Principles of Good Performance Management**

The principles with the strongest individual impact on performance improvement were confirmed to be: (1) creating clarity about the strategy with agreement on intended outcomes, outputs and necessary enablers, and (4) creating a positive culture of learning and improvement (see Figure 1.2).

Both (1) and (4) are prerequisites for succeeding with a Balanced Scorecard. That said, where all ten principles were found to be in place, the improvement was particularly substantial, confirming that the combined effect is far greater than the sum of the parts. It is notable that most of the case studies within this book would score highly for the deployment of all ten principles. Throughout this book we report the key findings from this study.

2

BALANCED SCORECARDS: THE JOURNEY FROM MEASUREMENT TO STRATEGIC PERFORMANCE MANAGEMENT

What's the use of running if you are not on the right road?
German proverb

INTRODUCTION

There is a well-known adage that "What get's measured gets done."[1] In recent years many organizations from both the commercial and public sectors have been diligently measuring just about everything that moves in the belief that the simple act of doing so will somehow substantially improve performance.

As public sector leaders come under intense pressure to deliver step-change efficiency gains, we can be sure that many will redouble their measurement efforts. What's more, some of their key stakeholder groups, such as central Government, are likely to demand as much. Indeed there is a real possibility that the requirements for increased transparency and accountability around public sector performance will translate into even more of the large-scale target setting from central Governments that have become the norm in many countries over recent years, although the recently elected UK Government has at least indicated that this will not be the case. The belief being that strict targets and the reporting of performance to those targets is *all* that is needed to move the public sector organization toward heightened performance. As we explain in this chapter, such a belief is both a dangerous and erroneous proposition.

While we agree that it is true that measurement is crucial to the galvanizing and monitoring of public sector performance, and that the introduction of metrics can positively change behavior (although it oftentimes leads to the exact opposite – the encouragement of negative behaviors), it is not an end in itself. Metrics are but one part of a larger performance management system: a system that must start with strategy.

CLARITY OF STRATEGIC AIMS

As we explained in Chapter 1, a study of more than 500 public sector bodies (comprising more than 1100 individual responses) across the globe for the Advanced Performance Institute (API) report, *Strategic Performance Management in Government and Public Sector Organizations*[2] (the largest such study every conducted) found that "Create clarity and agreement about the strategic aims," was the single greatest contributor to superior performance.

Simply put, securing great results begins with (and is largely dependent on) a full and proper understanding of the organization's strategic context. As the opening paragraph of the API report notes, "Public sector organizations may have the most ambitious plans for transforming services and delivering against government targets, but if they don't keep day-to-day activities tightly aligned to what actually matters, they'll find themselves getting nowhere fast."

What actually matters is the delivery of strategic goals. In the Balanced Scorecard methodology that we describe within this book, the first step is the creation of a Strategy Map that clearly articulates the strategic goals of the organization. The main goal of creating such a map is that it creates clarity and agreement about the strategic aims. Then, *and only then,* should the organization think about metrics. Disappointingly the API research found that public sector organizations are overly concerned with, and focused on measurement.

BEING OUTPUTS-FOCUSED

As well as being metrics-focused the report found that public sector bodies are typically not paying attention to the measures that are more likely to drive breakthrough performance improvements. Mostly, public sector bodies collect data on "outputs," that are typically things that are easy to measure (e.g., the number of flyers dropped through doors promoting the use of carbon monoxide detectors in homes), instead of "outcomes," which are the ultimate goals of the organization in question (relating to the previous example, measuring the number of deaths from carbon monoxide poisoning in a community might be the corresponding outcome). Being "output" as opposed to "outcome," focused drastically reduced the potential of driving efficiency gains and performance improvement, the report noted.

Figure 2.1 shows the components of strategy, with enablers at the base, rising through outputs, outcomes and overall aim (or mission) at the apex. Note therefore that we are not saying that public sector organizations should not focus on outputs (indeed at deeper operational levels this will be required); rather we are stating that an output-based focus should support an outcome-based perspective, and that the latter should always take precedence.

Therefore we should be cheered that the API research found that most respondents (68%) agreed that articulating outcomes (the overall goals, for example "improving service delivery") was more important than articulating outputs ("You must hit target X this month"), and that, above all, they needed to understand and clarify the key enablers (94%) if they want to have a real impact on performance. However, most organizations were found to articulate their output objectives quite well, while only just over half clearly articulated their outcome objectives (Figure 2.2). Moreover, just 4% of participants said that they

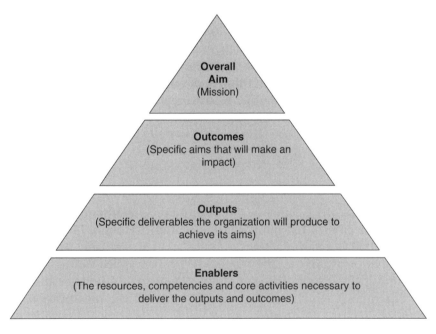

Figure 2.1   **Components of a Strategy**

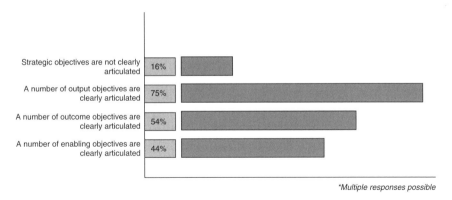

*Multiple responses possible

Figure 2.2   **How Well Strategic Goals are Articulated**

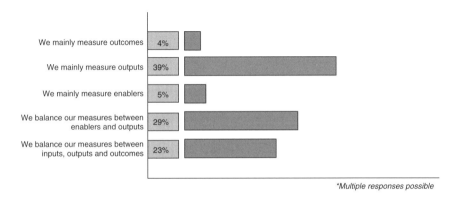

*Multiple responses possible

Figure 2.3   **Measuring Outcomes or Outputs**

"mainly measure outcomes" while 39% said they "mainly measure outputs." (Figure 2.3)

Reasons for being output-focused

And a key reason for being output-focused, the report found, was a lack of a clearly mapped strategy. Given that fact evidence shows that step-change performance improvement is achieved when metrics support strategic goals, it is worrisome that just 15% of survey respondents stated that this is the case in their organization, and even less (6%) believe that all of their performance indicators are relevant and meaningful – perhaps not surprising given that 16% of organizations stated that their objectives are not clearly articulated at all (Figure 2.2).

A target-centric central government mindset

But to be fair, it is obvious why so many public sector organizations have become so preoccupied with output-focused metrics. As we make much of in this book, and highlighted at the start of this chapter, in recent years public sector bodies have been bombarded with central Government imposed performance targets, the attainment of which has become *the* overriding priority for agency leaders.

The pervasive use of performance league tables in the UK for instance (most notably for hospitals and schools) is perhaps the best illustration of this target-setting mentality and regime. With league tables published to the wider community and stakeholder groups and funding levels oftentimes dependent on the league position achieved, it is understandable that the leaders of stretched public sector organizations place their attention and resources onto delivering to the output-focused measures that typically inform the tables. Although we argue target-based league tables have led to some benefits in that at least it has put performance management on the public sector agenda, it has also led to the institutionalizing of widespread dysfunctional behavior where the goal is achieving the target and not a strategic outcome.

As a powerful and disturbing example, the 2010 report into appalling failings in patient care at the UK's Stafford Hospital (where between 400 and 1200 more people died between 2005–2008 than would have been expected) found that amongst the reasons why patients were routinely neglected was that the management team had become preoccupied with cost-cutting and hitting predefined targets. This is perhaps an extreme example of how external targets that are supposed to improve performance, can have the diametrically opposite effect than intended, but still provide a chilling warning as to what might happen in public sector organizations when the upcoming cost-cutting agenda takes hold.

With pressure to hit externally imposed targets, it is therefore far from surprising that according to API's *Strategic Performance Management* survey fully 68% of organizations believed that some performance data had been fabricated.[3] This means that some systems can't be trusted and that they therefore provide invalid input into the decision-making process, possibly leading to the wrong or counterproductive decisions and resource allocation, and ultimately failing to improve public accountability.

BEING OUTCOME FOCUSED

Yet we are beginning to witness a gradual shifting away from output to outcome-based performance management and measurement within the public sector; or put another way from a narrow measurement/ target setting view to a broader strategic performance management perspective. This is more evident is some countries than others.

Christchurch City Council case example

As a leading example, we can point to New Zealand, which has one of the most advanced approaches in the world for ensuring outcome-based strategic public sector performance management. As one sector example, as a consequence of the New Zealand Local Government Act of 2002, local authorities are mandated to set community outcomes and supporting performance metrics that must be identified and agreed upon through an extensive, heavily participative and legally mandated consultation program with local residents and other groups.

Community outcomes

Community outcomes are reviewed every six years. The present outcomes for Christchurch City Council (a best practice case study that we point to throughout this book) which take the city to 2012 are a safe city; a city of people who value and protect the natural environment; a well governed city; a prosperous city; and a healthy city.

These outcomes are shown with supporting performance indicators in Figures 2.4 and 2.5. Note how the goals and indicators are articulated using outcome – as opposed to output-based language. For instance, the ultimate strategic outcome, a Safe City, is defined as "We live free from crime, violence, abuse and injury. We are safe at home and in the community. Risks from hazards are managed and mitigated." In turn, City of Christchurch knows it is getting there by "outcome goals" such as a decline in levels of crime and injury and that "people feel safe at all times in the city." Key performance indicators include "hospital treatment for accidents" and "road casualty statistics."

As a further example, the community outcome "a well governed city" is defined as "Our values and ideas are reflected in the actions of our decision-makers. Our decision-makers manage public funds responsibly, respond to current needs and 'plan for the future' includes goals such as 'everybody participating in public decision-making,'" and

Community Outcome	We will know we are using these key indicators	Progress will be measured using these key indicators
A safe city		
We live free from crime, violence, abuse and injury. We are safe at home and in the community. Risks from hazards are managed and mitigated.	• Rates of crime and injury decline. • People feel safe at all times. • We have excellent safety networks, support people and services.	• Hospital treatment for accidents • Total offences • Notifications to CYF • Perceptions of safety • Road casualty statistics
A city of inclusive and diverse communities		
Our diversity is seen, heard, valued and celebrated. All people feel a sense of belonging and participate in the community.	• Our city is built on strong communities. • A diverse range of people feel at home. • Everybody is able to participate, particularly those who are most vulnerable.	• Deprivation Index • Income gap between low and high income earners • Perceptions of ethnic diversity • Maori language speakers • Perceptions of quality of life • Perceptions of community • Support
A city of people who value and protect the natural environment		
Our lifestyles reflect our commitment to guardianship of the natural environment inland around the city of Christchurch. We actively work to protect, enhance and restore our environment for future generations.	• Everybody takes responsibility for their impact on the natural environment. • Biodiversity is restored, protected and enhanced. • We manage our city to minimize damage to the environment.	• Tonnes of waste to landfill • Liquid waste • Total ground water use • Renewable versus nonrenewable energy, consumption • Waste recycling • Recreational water quality • Number and area of ecological heritage sites

Figure 2.4   **Christchurch City Council's Long Term Community Outcomes
and Supporting Performance Indicators**

"everybody feels represented by their decision-makers" and has key performance indicators such as "confidence in council decision-making" and "voter turnout at council elections."

These community outcomes were arrived at through a number of participative processes that were conducted during a year period, including:

- Results from monitoring trends and other information (more than 500 measures);
- Reviews of prior consultations (5000 submissions, 54 reports);
- Reviews of reports and literature (300 reports);
- Reviews of government strategies (187 strategies);
- Review of existing Council strategies and Community Board statements;
- Stock-take of existing services and funding from the Council and government agencies;

Community Outcome	We will know we are using these key indicators	Progress will be measured using these key indicators
A well governed city		
Our values and ideas are reflected in the actions of our decision-makers. Our decision-makers manage public funds responsibly, respond to current needs and plan for the future.	• Everybody actively participates in public decision-making. • Everybody feels represented by their decision-makers. • Our decision-makers plan for a sustainable.	• Confidence in council decision-making • Representation on school boards of trustees • Census response rates • Voter turnout at council elections • Voter turnout at general elections
A prosperous city		
We have a strong economy that is based on a range of successful and innovative businesses. We value sustainable wealth creation, invest in ourselves and in our future.	• Has a strong, healthy economy. • Standards of living improve for everyone. • Our economic development prioritizes future well-being.	• Economic Activity Index • Full and part time employment rates • Unemployment rate • Personal, family and household income • Volume of commercial waste • Recycling
A healthy city		
We live long, healthy and happy lives.	• We all have access to affordable health services that meet our needs. • More people live healthy lifestyles. • Our city environment supports the health of the community.	• Self reported health status • Life expectancy • Frequency of physical activity • Type 2 diabetes rates • Barriers to accessing GPs • Number of days exceeding air quality guidelines

Figure 2.5 **Christchurch City Council's Long Term Community Outcomes and Supporting Performance Indicators**

- Interviews with key stakeholders;
- Interviews and workshops with elected members;
- Research with key groups such as people with disabilities, Maori and Pacific people;
- Discussion papers developed with external stakeholders and reference groups;
- Feedback on the 2004 to 2014 Long-Term Council Community Plan (LTCCP) and the Community Outcomes developed in 2004;
- Feedback from a specially designed section on the Council's website.

How the Christchurch City Council delivers these community outcomes is described in great detail within their LTCCP. This is the council's "contract with the community," describing how it intends to deliver and to achieve the outcomes as well as the other long-term goals of the city. "The shift from community outcomes to the LTCCP means a move from the conceptual to the highly concrete," explains Peter Ryan, Christchurch City Council's Planning and Performance Manager.

The LTCCP covers a period of ten consecutive financial years, though it is reviewed every three years; the most recent preparation being in 2008 for the timeframe of 2009–2019. This allows the Council to take a long-term view while enabling it to adjust for constantly changing financial and other factors and keep its accounting and budgets up-to-date.[4]

So to further sharpen its strategic focus, the Christchurch City Council underpins its outcome-based management approach with a Balanced Scorecard Strategy Map (we describe their approach in Chapter 3). Through their Balanced Scorecard (which they simply call a "plan on a page,") Christchurch City Council identifies the critical few relationships and capabilities that will truly make the difference in delivering the long-term outcomes and to more firmly tie operational performance to strategic goals.

THE BALANCED SCORECARD

This brings us to a description of the Balanced Scorecard. As we explained in the introductory chapter, the term Balanced Scorecard has come to represent any performance management framework that comprises both a financial and non-financial perspectives. These range from systems that simply comprise a "balance" of KPIs to fully developed strategic performance management frameworks. In describing the Balanced Scorecard we will focus attention on the "classic" scorecard model as well as a slightly amended version:

1. The "classic" Balanced Scorecard as described and evolved by Harvard Business School Professor Dr. Robert Kaplan and management consultant Dr. David Norton. This comprises a Strategy Map and a scorecard of measures, targets and initiatives.
2. The Value Creation Map, as developed by the Advanced Performance Institute. This generally comprises a Strategy Map, strategic initiatives and supporting key performance questions, key performance indicators, and a value narrative.

It is important to note that these two approaches are not competing frameworks as they follow exactly the same logic and underpinning principles. What it does, however, illustrate is that there is flexibility in the way Balanced Scorecards are developed. However, in both versions the most important component is the creation of a Strategy Map.

The "classic" Balanced Scorecard

We shall describe the "classic" Balanced Scorecard by briefly summarizing the five books written on the topic by Kaplan and Norton. It is important to do this as each book represents an evolution of their thinking and of the framework.

The Balanced Scorecard: Translating strategy into action

The first book *The Balanced Scorecard: Translating Strategy into Action*,[5] was released in 1996 but developed out of a series of Harvard Business review articles written by the authors, that began with an article that appeared in the January/February 1992 edition of *Harvard Business Review*.[6] Within that article Kaplan and Norton made a simple proposition: that the financial model of business alone as the primary means of managing performance was no longer adequate. The financial model was useful, they said, for providing detail on what happened yesterday, but was of little use in managing the future development of the business.

The *Harvard Business Review* article basically reported the findings of a 1990 study by Kaplan and Norton of about ten companies including Cigna, Apple Computer and Hewlett Packard, that set out to address the growing awareness amongst corporate leaders of the inadequacy of financial metrics. The purpose of their study was to solve this narrow measurement problem and the research focused on how the participating companies were dealing with this issue.

As part of this review, Kaplan and Norton looked at Analog Devices. The company's then vice-president of quality improvement and productivity, Art Schneiderman explained to the study group how Analog Devices was successfully using what it called "a corporate scorecard" to monitor its performance. This scorecard included performance measures relating to customer delivery times, quality and cycle times for manufacturing processes, and effectiveness of new product development, as well as financial measures. The "scorecard" was therefore a balance of financial and non-financial metrics.

Consequently, on the basis of this program of research, Kaplan/Norton formulated the first Balanced Scorecard, having adopted Analog Device's "scorecard" term.

Of course, Kaplan and Norton were far from the first people to question the continued efficacy and appropriateness of only looking at performance through a financial lens. Indeed their study took place during a time of heightened focus on "balancing" financial and non-financial performance dimensions, largely triggered by the success of Japanese companies in taking large chunks of western market shared through the deployment of Total Quality Management (TQM) and related disciplines (Lean methodologies, which we focus great attention on within this book, grew out of the TQM movement). In attempting to drive a TQM mindset into US organizations the US Government launched the Malcolm Baldrige Framework and Award in 1987, which is based on seven criteria: leadership, strategic planning, customer and market focus, measurement analysis and knowledge management, human resource focus, process management and business results. 1992 (and therefore the same year as the scorecard was introduced through the first HBR article) saw the introduction of The EFQM Business Excellence model (see Figure 2.6), which comprises nine criteria areas, categorized as enablers and results. Each criteria has a weighting to designate its overall importance. Enablers are leadership (with a 10% weighting), people (9%), policy and strategy (8%), partnership and resources (9%), and processes (14%). The results areas are people (9%), customer (20%), society (6%) and key performance results (15%).

The Malcolm Baldrige Model and the EFQM Framework have spurred the development of a number of regional frameworks, such as the Australian Business Excellence Model and The Singapore Business Excellence Model, amongst others. Christchurch City Council uses the New Zealand version of the Malcolm Baldrige Award (Performance Excellence Study Award – PESA) alongside the Balanced Scorecard. The council was a PESA award winner in 2006.

Positioned at this stage as a measurement system, the classic Balanced Scorecard (as first described in 1992) set out to capture performance

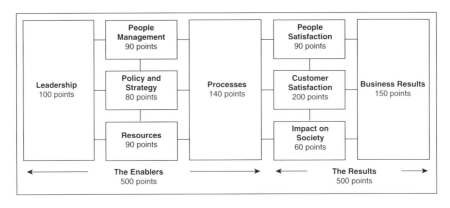

Figure 2.6 **EFQM Model**

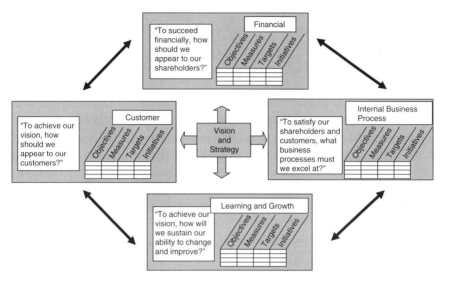

Figure 2.7 **Balanced Scorecard 4 Box Model**

from four perspectives: one financial and three non-financial: customer, internal process and learning and innovation (subsequently redefined as learning and growth when Kaplan and Norton realized that innovation correctly belonged within the internal process perspective). Figure 2.7 is a schematic of the Balanced Scorecard, showing how it supports a central vision and strategy. Around this hub is built the four perspectives with their own strategic objectives, measures, targets and initiatives.

Although organizations gained substantial value from the first generation Balanced Scorecard, some of the early adopters such as Cigna Property & Casualty, Mobil Oil and Brown & Root, found that the Balanced Scorecard worked best not when used simply as an extension of the financial measurement system, but when it was hardwired to strategy and deployed as a strategic implementation framework.

Strategy maps

What these pioneering organizations found to be missing in such an achievement was a mechanism for showing the cause-and-effect relationship between, and within, the strategic objectives housed within the four perspectives. Thus was born the idea of Strategy Maps, which would eventually become the topic of Kaplan and Norton's third book, called "Strategy Maps."[7]

Although the third of Kaplan and Norton's books we will discuss the Strategy Maps book before the second book. This is because Strategy Maps are the most important component of a Balanced Scorecard system and should be understood before we consider strategy-focused organizations (which was the subject of book two, and which included, rather than focused on, Strategy Maps). But note that in early versions, Strategy Maps were generally referred to as Linkage Models. A public sector Strategy Map, this one for the City of Brisbane (another early scorecard adopter and at which Peter Ryan led the scorecard implementation effort) is shown in Figure 2.8 About the evolution of Strategy Maps, Ryan makes this insightful observation, which partly explains why many companies still wrongly see the Balanced Scorecard being about measurement and not strategy. "While at Brisbane City Council, the biggest challenge I faced with working with the Balanced Scorecard was when the model and emphasis switched from a four quadrant KPI view of the world to one driven by a causal

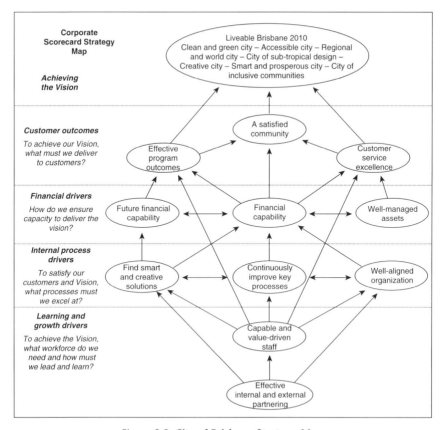

Figure 2.8 **City of Brisbane Strategy Map**

Strategy Map," he says. "Worldwide, the thinking and literature moved on early in the final years of the 1990s, but many people did not."

He continues that once people see the Balanced Scorecard as KPIs in four boxes, moving them to strategy and mapping strategy is incredibly difficult. "So I found myself in the odd position of having the biggest resistors to contemporary scorecard thinking being those who believe themselves to be scorecard enthusiasts. It took a lot of work to undo that." Undoing this work has been an ongoing task for all of us involved with the Balanced Scorecard.

An important point to bear in mind is that the four perspectives are not mandatory, nor for that matter the perspectives order (which in commercial organizations normally has finance/shareholder at the top and then followed by customer, internal process and learning and growth). It was left to organizations to create the number and hierarchical sequence of perspectives that best described how they should implement their strategy.

Not mandating the number of perspectives (and perhaps more importantly the order) had important ramifications for the public sector. Although the Balanced Scorecard was originally developed for use in the private sector, the potential for deployment in the public sector soon became evident to pioneering leaders of not-for profit bodies. Indeed amongst the early private sector scorecard adopters that used Strategy Maps, we find an exemplary example from the public sector: and one that would have a far-reaching impact on the scorecard movement.

City of Charlotte case study

With a population of just over 500,000 the City of Charlotte in North Carolina, USA was perhaps the first public sector body in the world to successfully adopt the scorecard, when it did so in 1996.

In the early 1990s, Charlotte developed a strategy to concentrate on five "focus areas" deemed critical to delivering outstanding local services. The focus areas being:

- City within a city
- Economic development
- Transportation
- Community safety
- Restructuring government

With the five focus areas agreed, the management team started to look for an effective mechanism for measuring, monitoring, improving and communicating progress against these areas. After reading the early scorecard articles in Harvard Business Review, they settled on the Balanced Scorecard as the most promising framework.

Central to the scorecard creation were Charlotte's vision and mission statements. Under the banner "public service is our business" its vision statement reads: "The City of Charlotte will be a model of excellence that puts the citizens first. Skilled, motivated employees will be known for providing quality and value in all areas of service. We will be a platform for vital economic activity that gives Charlotte a competitive edge in the market place. We will partner with citizens and businesses to make this a community of choice for living, working and leisure activities."

When building its corporate scorecard, the first line of Charlotte's vision "The City of Charlotte will be a model of excellence that puts the citizens first," was of particular importance and did, at first, cause some design problems. The solution would later prove valuable to other public sector bodies taking the scorecard route.

"We first tried to create the scorecard along the traditional format of the non-financial perspectives interacting through cause and effect relationships to impact the financial perspective," explains budget manager, Lisa Schumacher, who facilitated the creation of the Balanced Scorecard within the City of Charlotte. "However, we had real problems with this because it just didn't fit the way we work." She adds that although financial responsibility is of course important to the City of Charlotte, the customer is more important. "Therefore we changed the order of importance and put the customer at the top," she says, adding that just making this small change made a huge difference.

The process of creating the corporate scorecard took about three months, comprising of half-day workshops every two weeks. At the end of the process, the City of Charlotte created a Balanced Scorecard consisting of customer, financial accountability, internal process and learning and growth perspectives. Figure 2.9 shows the City of Charlotte's Strategy Map (or linkage model as it was then called).

In Chapter 3 we describe how placing customer at the top of the Strategy Map has been commonplace in the public sector (as also shown in the Brisbane City Council example). But there are other alternatives, as we will explain.

The City of Charlotte was particularly innovative in creating tailored scorecards for the five focus areas. Just as the corporate scorecard translates the five focus areas into strategic themes, each focus area has goals and measures addressing the four Balanced Scorecard perspectives. And each focus area has its own mission statement. As examples,

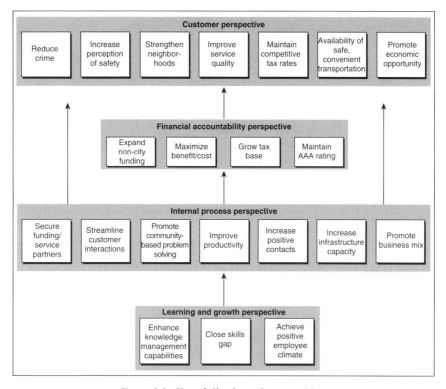

Figure 2.9 **City of Charlotte Strategy Map**

the mission for the focus area economic development is, "To support a business environment that fosters economic opportunity for citizens and businesses."

"Creating scorecards for the focus areas required management to choose or affirm objectives and decide how success would be determined," says Schumacher. "This process involved many hours of brainstorming and debating. The conversations on mission, roles and impacts on issues were excellent and at the conclusion staff had a consensus on the strategy and the impact desired."[8]

A strategy-focused organization

With the Balance Scorecard being gradually repositioned during the 1990s as strategy – as opposed to measurement-focused, Kaplan and Norton's second scorecard book, published in early 2001, set out a step-by-step process for creating a strategy-focused organization.[9]

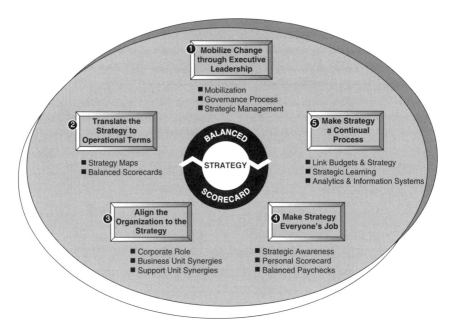

Figure 2.10 **Principles of a Strategy Focused Organization**

The authors specified five principles for creating a strategy-focused organization (Figure 2.10). These principles were not arbitrarily chosen. Rather they emerged from their observation of the interventions deployed by the most successful scorecard adopters, such as Charlotte and Brisbane.

In doing so, they positioned the Balanced Scorecard as a strategic management framework that acted as a focal point for all of an organization's activities. The importance of this shift should not be understated. As Balanced Scorecards developed through the first decade of this century they became the central framework to which all other strategic and operational activities and improvement programs could be aligned (such as budgeting and planning, knowledge management, six sigma and Lean, all of which we consider in later chapters). We explain in Chapter 9 how functions such as the Office of Strategy Management have emerged to coordinate the alignment of these activities and programs. The six principles of the Strategy-Focused Organization are:

Principle 1: Translate the strategy into operational terms

This principle comprises two sub-components: Strategy Maps and Balanced Scorecards that together describe the strategy and its implementation. It is by translating strategy into the logical architecture of a

Strategy Map and a Balanced Scorecard that organizations create a common, understandable point of reference for everyone.

Principle 2: Align the organization to the strategy

Synergy is the overarching goal of organization design. Organizations consist of numerous sectors, business units and specialized departments, each with its own strategy. For organizational performance to become more than the sum of its parts, individual strategies must be linked and integrated. The corporation defines the linkages expected to create synergy and ensures that those linkages actually occur.

Principle 3: Make strategy everyone's everyday job

To move strategy out of the boardroom into the office and shop-floor and make it "everyone's everyday job" is the pre-eminent challenge for organizations and this principle considers personal scorecards and a "balanced paycheck."

Principle 4: Make strategy a continual process

Putting the Balanced Scorecard at the heart of the organization's management system involves creating links from strategy to budgets and also calls for a robust learning process. An important sub-component of this principle is "analytics and information systems."

Principle 5: Mobilize change through executive leadership

Kaplan and Norton emphasize the make-or-break influence of top management: "If those at the top are not energetic leaders of the process, change will not take place." Simply, if the CEO does not want the scorecard then don't try to do it, the scorecard effort will fail.

As we progress through this book we will explain how these principles and their sub-components are being implemented within public sector organizations, in the various scorecard systems in use.

ALIGNMENT

Kaplan and Norton's fourth book *Alignment: Using the Balanced Scorecard to Create Corporate Synergies* took the scorecard concept to a new level, and was essentially a broader description of their SFO Principle 2. They presented the idea of a Corporate Strategy Map and Balanced Scorecard that sits atop more common scorecards at Strategic Business Unit (SBU) and devolved levels.[10]

Alignment checkpoints

The vision is that the whole enterprise can be aligned from the corporate level down and out to board of directors and customers and vendors. This organizational alignment is described through eight alignment checkpoints:

1. Enterprise (or corporate) strategy update: most of the alignment process flows from here.
2. Align the enterprise Strategy Map with the board of directors' Strategy Map.
3. Align the enterprise Strategy Map with support unit strategy maps.
4. Align enterprise strategy update with strategic business unit (SBU) strategy update.
5. Align SBU strategy update with support unit strategy update.
6. Align SBU strategy updates with customers.
7. Align SBU Strategy updates vendors/alliances.
8. Align corporate functional strategy update with SBU support unit updates.

The corporate scorecard depicts how the organization creates value through synergy. The focus on synergy signals a crucial difference from a conventional SBU scorecard in that the corporate scorecard does not include a perspective that is concerned with how success looks like in the eyes of the customer. Indeed it *owns* the business units.

THE EXECUTION PREMIUM

In their most recent book: *The Execution Premium: Linking Strategy to Operations for Competitive Advantage,*[11] Kaplan and Norton introduce the six steps "execution premium" model to align operational performance with strategy management. Shown in Figure 2.11 these steps are: 1 Develop the Strategy; 2 Translate the Strategy; 3 Align the Organization; 4 Plan Operations; 5 Monitor and Learn; 6 Test and Adapt.

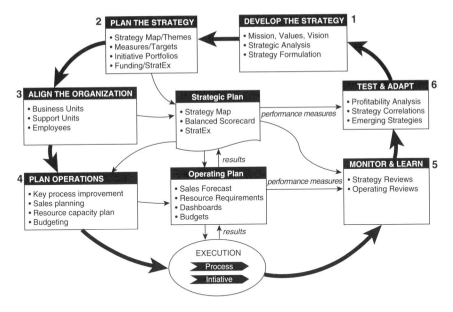

Figure 2.11 **The Execution Premium Management System**

Stage 1: Develop the strategy

At this stage organizational leaders address three questions.

1. *What business are we in and why (clarify mission, values and vision)?* The MVV statements establish guidelines for formulating and executing the strategy.
2. *What are the key issues (conduct strategic analysis)?* Managers review the situation on their competitive and operating environments since they last crafted their strategy.
3. *How can we best compete (formulate the strategy)?* This considers areas such as the customer value proposition, key processes required to create the differentiation in the strategy, and human capital and technological requirements to enable the delivery of the strategy.

Stage 2: Plan the strategy

In this stage, managers plan the strategy by developing strategic objectives, measures, targets, initiatives and budgets that guide action and resource allocation. Companies typically address five questions at this stage.

33

1. *How do we describe our strategy (create Strategy Maps)?* This describes the objectives required to deliver to the strategy. It is now common for organizations to cluster related objectives according to, perhaps five or six strategic themes. This makes it easier for managers to separately plan and manage each of the key components of the strategy but still have them operate coherently.
2. *How do we measure our plan (select measures and targets)?* In this stage, managers convert the objectives defined in the Strategy Map into a Balanced Scorecard of measures, targets and gaps (that must be closed over the lifetime of the plan).
3. *What action programs does our strategy need (choosing strategic initiatives)?* The initiatives and action programs aimed at achieving targeted performance for the Strategy Map objectives.
4. *How do we fund our initiatives?* Executing strategy requires that the portfolio of initiatives be executed simultaneously in a coordinated manner. This requires explicit funding for the portfolio of initiatives.
5. *Who will lead the execution of strategy (create theme teams)?* Companies are introducing a new accountability structure for executing strategy through strategic themes. Theme owners and teams provide accountability for and feedback on the execution of the strategy within each theme.

Stage 3: Align the organization with the strategy

At this stage, managers ask three key questions,

1. *How do we ensure that all organizational units are on the same page?* This is about devolving the scorecard to lower level business units.
2. *How do we align support units with business unit and corporate strategies?* This is about creating Strategy Maps and scorecards for support units such as HR and finance, as two examples.
3. *How do we motivate employees to help execute the strategy?* Essentially this is about proper communication and the linking of personal objectives and (more common in the commercial sector) incentive compensation to the scorecard.

Stage 4: Plan operations

Companies need to align process improvement activities with strategic priorities. At this stage managers focus on two key questions.

1. *What business process improvements are most critical for executing the strategy?* Companies must focus on Six Sigma, reengineering and other efforts on improving performance to a strategic objective. Moreover, they should create customized dashboards consisting of key indicators for local process performance.
2. *How do we link strategy with operating plans and budgets?* The process improvement plans and the high level strategic measures and targets on the Balanced Scorecard must be converted into an operating plan for the year.

Stage 5: Monitor and learn

This is where the organization monitors the execution of its strategic and operating plans and learns from experience. To do this they hold two meetings: an operational review meeting and a strategy review meeting, which answer two questions.

1. *Are our operations under control (operational review meeting)?* Companies hold these meetings to review short-term performance and respond to recently identified problems that need immediate attention.
2. *Are we executing our strategy well (strategy review meeting)?* These meetings review the progress of the strategy, identify problems and order remedial action.

Step 6: Test and adapt the strategy

This is where organizations question whether their fundamental strategic assumptions remain valid. Managers ask one question:

1. *Is our strategy working (hold a strategy testing and adapting meeting)?* Periodically, the senior team meets to question and challenge the strategy and, if necessary, to adapt it.

THE VALUE CREATION MAP

One of the variations to the classic Balanced Scorecard we consider in this book is The Value Creation Map. First introduced within Bernard Marr's best-selling book *Strategic Performance Management: Leveraging and Managing Your Intangible Value Drivers*,[12] the Value Creation Map concept evolved from analyzing and learning from the work of many people in the area of strategic mapping.

Although brought to wide attentions through the work of Kaplan and Norton, the work in mapping strategy was actually first developed in the military hundreds of years ago. It was then brought into the business context by researchers at Massachusetts Institute of Technology in the 1950s. Another influence on the development of the Value Creation Map has been work done by academics mapping the interrelationships between components of intellectual capital in order to get a better handle on the real drivers of performance and value in an organization.

Value Creation Map explained

In essence, the Value Creation Map allows an organization to create the linkages between the organizations value proposition (why it exists), its core competencies, and the underlying performance drivers and their interdependencies. This allows organizations, in a simple step-by-step process, to design a performance management framework that clarifies the relationship between resources (tangible and intangible), capabilities, and core competencies in value creation. With the Value Creation Map as the central steer, the framework is supported by strategic initiatives, key performance questions (KPQs), Key Performance Indicators (KPIs) and, in a complete framework, a value creation narrative.

Audit Scotland case example

Although we describe strategy mapping and KPQs/KPIs in subsequent chapters, as an introduction to the Value Creation Map and supporting framework, consider the strategic performance management framework in place at Audit Scotland.[13]

Headquartered in Edinburgh, Audit Scotland exists to provide the Scottish Auditor General and the Accounts Commission with the services that they need to check that public money is spent properly, efficiently and effectively. With about 300 full-time equivalent employees and an operating budget of £27.5 million, the organization arranges the audits of about 200 public accounts, such as the Scottish Government, 32 councils and 44 joint boards and committees (including police and fire and rescue services). Importantly, Audit Scotland is independent of the bodies that it audits.

Having amassed a wealth of useful data and information regarding stakeholder priorities over the coming years (the organization completed dialogs with stakeholders to identify key outcomes that mirror the work of the City of Christchurch). Audit Scotland faced the not uncommon challenge of distilling this down into something that was focused and manageable.

"The more data and information that was generated from surveys, discussions and other formats, the more challenging it became to identify and focus on the critical few things that will really make a difference to our performance," comments Diane McGiffen, Director of Corporate Services, who was responsible for introducing the map into Audit Scotland.

To achieve this distillation, Audit Scotland engaged the services of the Advanced Performance Institute (API). During the winter of 2008, API worked with Audit Scotland to create a corporate strategy map (shown in Figure 2.12) which identified the key strategic objectives and supporting activities that would be required to deliver to its vision that: "On behalf of the Auditor General and the Accounts Commission,

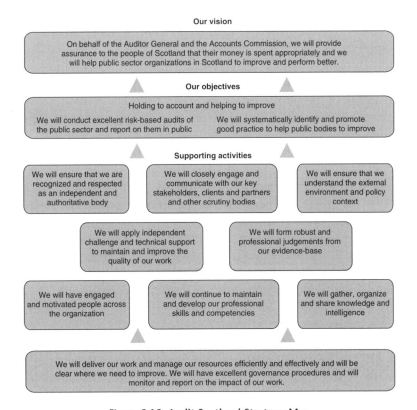

Figure 2.12 **Audit Scotland Strategy Map**

we will provide assurance to the people of Scotland that their money is spent appropriately and we will help public sector organizations in Scotland to improve and perform better."

Each objective and supporting activity serves as a doorway to a host of performance management and measurement focal points – primarily captured through KPQs and KPIs – that work together to provide an overall picture of how well Audit Scotland is performing and, ultimately, to steer the organization toward the delivery of its vision and priorities.

Although KPIs are commonly used within organizations, KPQs are substantially less so. Described in more detail in Chapter 5, a KPQ focuses on and highlights what the organization needs to know in terms of executing existing strategic objectives. KPQs enable a full and focused discussion on how well the organization is delivering to these objectives and serve as an important bridge between organizational goals and KPIs. Indeed KPQs are used to provide a performance context to KPIs and help to more effectively prioritize the indicators chosen.

We will now explore how the objectives on the map, KPQs and KPIs work together within Audit Scotland's strategy management framework.

Audit Scotland's Strategy Map includes just two core activities (called objectives in their case), these being: "we will conduct excellent risk based audits of the public sector and report them in public," and "we will systematically identify and promote good practice to help public bodies to improve."

Although both objectives are equally important, a key message that emerged from extensive stakeholder consultation that informed the map, KPIs, etc was that they were looking to Audit Scotland to do more to help them to improve performance (or becoming more effective). The KPQs to support the "improve" objective include: "to what extent has our work led to improvement" and "to what extent are we identifying and actively promoting good practice (or better ways of doing things) to help public bodies improve." Such questions ensure that KPIs chosen lead to the description of outcome – as opposed to an output.

KPIs for these KPQs include "impact reports," "client feedback," "number of presentation at meetings, events and conferences which include best practice guidance," and "performance audit reports with good practice recommendations." How Audit Scotland achieves its objectives is largely through the delivery of enabling objectives (called supporting activities in their case). In creating the map, the senior team strived to ensure that there was a balance of activities focused on significantly improving stakeholder-facing, internal process and staff performance.

For a stakeholder-facing improvement, as an example, consider the activity: "We will closely engage and communicate with our key stakeholders, clients and partners, and other scrutiny bodies." Audit Scotland recognizes that it is only through close engagement and communication that it can effectively identify appropriate topics for its audit work. Closely engaging and partnering with other scrutiny bodies and improvement agencies also helps to avoid duplication of effort and maximizes Audit Scotland's contribution to the improvement of public services.

To support the improvement objective it is also recognized that it must clearly communicate its findings and recommendations to ensure that its messages are heard and its recommendations are followed up. KPQs used for this activity are "to what extent are we keeping our stakeholders informed about our programs of work and their role/implications" and "how well do we engage the people we work with." KPIs include "positive stakeholder feedback" (engagement levels, clarity about and acceptance of roles), "website statistics" (downloads, click throughs) and the "number of shared risk assessment frameworks in local government."

We will return to Audit Scotland's scorecarding work in later chapters. One element that Audit Scotland was still developing at the time of preparing this book was a value narrative, which is an optional element of the Value Creation Map and framework.

Value narrative

In essence, a value narrative provides the contextual description of the strategy that is visualized on the map. Even though a picture can say a thousand words, sometimes we need words to provide additional context and to clarify the map. Moreover, there are good people-focused reasons for using both a map and a narrative. People who are left-brain focused, respond better to words than pictures; conversely those that are right-brain focused, respond better to pictures and diagrams than to words. The lack of a narrative device has often been a criticism leveled at the "classic" Balanced Scorecard.

Belfast City Council value narrative

As an example of a value narrative, consider this one that was created by Belfast City Council, an early pioneer in working with a Value Creation

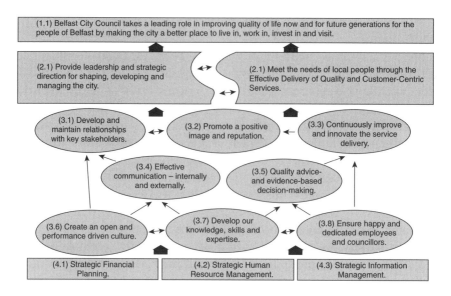

Figure 2.13 **BCC Strategy Map**

Map.[14] With facilitation from API, the council created the narrative to support its original Value Creation Map (shown in Figure 2.13).

"The main purpose of Belfast City Council is to help improve quality of life for the people of Belfast now and in the future by making the city a better place to live in, work in, invest in and to visit. To do this we must be good at two things. The first is to provide strategic leadership and direction and work with others to shape, develop and manage a shared city. We will also continue to meet the needs of local people by providing a wide range of quality and accessible services. As a Council we have identified a number of key areas we will focus on to achieve our goals.

"We have a wide range of key stakeholders including European, central and local government, the voluntary and private sector, public agencies, citizens, funding bodies, neighborhoods, media, politicians, academia and professional bodies. We recognize the need to work well with all of these stakeholders if we are to improve the co-ordination of service planning and delivery and assist with the implementation of the Review of Public Administration (RPA). To do this we will build public confidence by promoting a more positive image of the Council among the media and by supporting Councillors in their work to represent the organization and the City. This will require improving officer/ Councillor relationships to build trust, and facilitating more two way dialogue among employees and stakeholders. We will be clear about what our priorities are and will effectively communicate and listen in an open and transparent way.

"To achieve these improvements we will create an open, performance driven culture built on trust, where performance is discussed openly and used to help the organization learn and improve. Everyone will know what we want to achieve and how they contribute to this, in an environment where performance counts, is valued and is at the heart of everyone's job.

"We will also identify the skills and expertise necessary to be a successful organization and Councillors and employees will work together to develop skills and improve how knowledge is shared across the organization. BCC will be a place where people are happy and motivated to do a good job. All decision-makers will have access to the right information and expertise to allow them to make informed decisions. This will involve improving our structures to ensure all decisions are transparent, made at the right level and are acted on quickly.

All parts of the Council will work to bring about innovative improvements in service delivery for the benefit of our customers. To do this we will re-align resources, make better use of technology, bring about more joined-up working and encourage and reward innovation and improvement at all levels."

CONCLUSION

In this chapter we have explained that public sector organizations must first and foremost become focused on understanding their strategic goals before they identify performance metrics. We have stressed that organizations must first identify the "outcomes" that they must attain before looking at the "outputs" that they produce.

We have also described the two key Balanced Scorecard frameworks that we will mainly focus on within the rest of the book the "classic" Balanced Scorecard and the Value Creation Map and framework. Usage of these frameworks will be fully explicated in the case studies that we use within this book.

Given the nature of the funding and economic realities that public sector organizations will face over the coming years, much attention will be paid to ensuring that in delivering to its strategy, much focus will be on efficiency gains, as we have noted. A prime approach in delivering the step-change efficiency gains will be the deployment of Lean methodologies, which we consider in the next chapter.

3

USING LEAN THINKING TO IMPROVE STRATEGIC PERFORMANCE

The most dangerous kind of waste is the waste we do not recognize.
Shigeo Shingo (pioneer in Lean thinking) 1909–90

INTRODUCTION: THE "LEAN" ATHLETE

Consider this sporting analogy. To perform at an optimal level, an athlete must be lean. If he or she is carrying unnecessary fat then he or she will be sluggish: this will have a detrimental impact on their performance. At the same time the athlete must not be *too* thin as this will make them weaker and less energetic than is required, which will also significantly impair performance. A world-class athlete strives to have *exactly* the right amount of body fat required to deliver optimal performance and so increase the likelihood of them beating the competition.

But as well as the appropriate body fat, a world-class athlete has the optimal amount of muscle required to succeed in their chosen discipline: not too much and not too little – and in all the right places.

The public sector: A sluggish athlete

Unfortunately, few public sector organizations can be favorably compared with a world-class athlete. Although there are exceptions (and we can point to many of our case study organizations as being such) most public sector bodies carry too much fat, and indeed many can fairly be described as obese. Furthermore, most do not have organizational muscles of the appropriate size or in the right places – that is being worked in the areas that deliver the most value to stakeholders. From the perspective of the efficiency/effectiveness balance that we stress throughout this book, a "Lean" public sector organization has the right body-fat percentage (which powers the efficiency performance dimension) and appropriately defined muscles (the driver of the effectiveness side of the high performance equation).

Lean explained

In this chapter we provide an overview of how Lean thinking and methodologies can support a Balanced Scorecard system in the optimizing of the performance of public sector bodies (in Chapter 6 we provide greater granularity and detail as to how Lean – as we shall call the approach – should be used to inform the selection of the initiatives that are used to drive the organization toward ultimate strategic success). But first a brief description.

In essence "Lean" refers to a way of working that through systematic approaches identifies and eliminates waste from a process. In the simplest terms it means delivering the same, or more often than not enhanced, value to the customer with reduced effort and resources. Put another way, Lean can be viewed as a commonsensical approach to ensuring that resources are spent on value creation.

Lean enterprise institute definition

The US-headquartered The Lean Enterprise Institute states that: "A Lean organization understands customer value and focuses its key processes to continuously increase it. The ultimate goal is to provide perfect value to the customer through a perfect value creation process that has zero waste... to accomplish this, Lean thinking changes the focus of management from optimizing separate technologies, assets, and vertical departments to optimizing the flow of products and services through entire value streams that flow horizontally across technologies, assets, and departments to customers."[1]

Lean: A collection of methodologies and approaches

It is important to stress that Lean is *not* a single approach or methodology. Rather, Lean can be understood as an umbrella term that encompasses a broad grouping of interventions deployed for waste elimination and process improvement purposes. Approaches such as "value stream mapping," which analyze the flow of materials and information currently required to bring a product or service to a consumer; "kaizen," a philosophy or practice focusing on continuous improvement in manufacturing activities or business activities in general; "poke-yoke" (error, or mistake-proofing) and the Toyota Production System (that works systemically to eliminate waste, make to use and crucially has the people who know the work solve the problems).

Perhaps the most popular of Lean approaches in recent year has been Six Sigma (which we describe in detail below), which, as part of a wider process improvement methodology has a goal of reducing error rates to 3.4 per million opportunities.

THE BALANCED SCORECARD, LEAN AND TQM

In considering how the Balanced Scorecard and Lean principles work together to deliver strategic success and efficiency and effectiveness gains, it is worth pointing out that both the scorecard and Lean share a common heritage: Total Quality Management (TQM). Six Sigma, Kaizen, etc are basically TQM approaches. As we cited in the previous chapter, the genesis of the term Balanced Scorecard can be found in a corporate "quality" scorecard that was in place within Analog Devices in the 1980s. This scorecard included performance measures relating to customer delivery times, quality and cycle times for manufacturing processes, and effectiveness of new product development, as well as financial measures. The "scorecard," was therefore a balance of financial and non-financial metrics – and was a core element of Analog Devices' TQM program.

TQM: A brief history

As a quick explanation, the TQM philosophy gained hold in Japan after the Second World War, when the ideas of the US-born Dr W. Edwards Deming (1900–1993) and the Hungarian-born American citizen Dr Josef Juran (who died in early 2008 aged 103) were deployed to rebuild the industrial foundations of the shattered Japan.

Dr Deming is certainly worth exploring in any discussion that includes Balanced Scorecards (and indeed Lean). As part of his philosophy of management Deming articulated 14 principles that organizations should take heed of when seeking superior performance (see Sidebar 1). In the underlying philosophy, the following examples of principles show a strong resemblance to the goals of the Balanced Scorecard.

Constancy of Purpose

Constancy of Purpose is essentially about allocating resources to provide for long-term needs rather than short-term profitability. It is about balancing the long-term with the short-term. The Balanced Scorecard has a similar long-term/short-term approach. Moreover consider this against the core focus of the Balanced Scorecard to allocating resources to strategically critical, and longer-term, initiatives or action programs.

Improve every process

The principle "improve every process" sets out to improve constantly and forever every process for planning, production and service. Improving process performance is a critical focus of the Balanced Scorecard – and is a central tenet of the Lean methodologies.

Institute leadership

Institute leadership is essentially about ensuring that leaders are focused not on controlling people but on helping to get the best from them. As Mobilize Change through Executive Leadership is principle one of the five principles of the strategy-focused organization as described by Kaplan and Norton (see Chapter 2). It is leadership that drives the scorecarding process. Without leaders putting in place the processes that help to get the best out of people and to get them focused on the strategy, the scorecard will fail.

Drive out fear

Dr Deming stipulated that fear should be driven out of the workplace. He encouraged two-way communication and other means to drive out fear from the organization so that everybody may work effectively and more productively for the company. The authors of this book have long noted that cultural barriers, most notably the fear of measurement, often represent significant obstacles to a scorecard implementation program. Driving out fear and thus creating a culture and environment where employees are focused on continuous improvement rather than being afraid of punishment, is crucial to a Balanced Scorecard implementation effort.

Break down barriers

The principle "Break-down Barriers" is primarily about getting people to work in cross-functional teams to improve performance, rather than taking a siloed approach to organizational management. The Balanced Scorecard methodologies recognize that an organization should be aligned, or synergized, working "as one" and focused on the same strategic goals. In short, all functions and departments should be aligned behind the strategy of the organization. Cross-functional working is also critically important when implementing Lean, as highlighted by the Lean Enterprise Institute's definition above.

ALIGNING LEAN TO STRATEGIC GOALS THROUGH THE BALANCED SCORECARD

Throughout this book we strongly recommend that public sector organizations deploy both a Balanced Scorecard system and Lean in the implementation of strategy and the realization of efficiency and effectiveness gains. However, this does not imply equality. Rather Lean must be deployed in support of the strategic objectives that appear on a Balanced Scorecard Strategy Map (the creation of which we describe within the next chapter). Or perhaps more accurately, Lean must be deployed as a tool to help implement the strategy – which is described within a Strategy Map. Therefore build the Strategy Map *before* thinking about Lean projects and interventions.

Simply put, when organizations identify the strategic priorities that become the objectives within the Strategy Map, they can check that the aligned strategic processes are Lean, and if not launch the appropriate "Lean" initiatives. In their book: *The Execution Premium: Linking Strategy to Operations for Competitive Advantage,*[2] Drs Kaplan and Norton outline the importance of starting with the strategy. "Quality and process improvement projects [which we can call Lean] will generate the highest payoffs when they are selected based on criteria linked to the company's strategic objectives... In general a company is better off when more of its processes are done better, faster and cheaper. But a collection of better, faster, cheaper local processes does not make a strategy. Companies should emphasize improving those processes that contribute the most to the success of the company's strategy."

Kaplan and Norton rightly point out that most of the objectives that will be supported by Lean will be found in a Strategy Map's process perspective within a "classic" Balanced Scorecard or alternatively within the "core activity" component of an API Strategy Map. This is appropriate as the internal process/core activity section represents the area of a Strategy Map "where work gets done," that is, where the process improvement takes place that deliver value to the customer, shareholder or stakeholder.

Lean and the execution premium

In *The Execution Premium,* Kaplan and Norton explain how process improvements and Lean approaches such as Six Sigma should be considered within Step 4 "Plan operations" of their six steps "execution premium" model to align operational performance with strategy management. Shown in Figure 2.12 and explained fully within Chapter 2 these steps are: 1 Develop the Strategy; 2 Translate the Strategy; 3 Align the Organization; 4 Plan Operations; 5 Monitor and Learn; 6 Test and Adapt.[3]

In describing the key elements of Step 4 "plan operations" Kaplan and Norton stated that as well as aligning the process activities with strategic priorities, organizations must also ensure that funding for resources to operate the business is consistent with the strategic goals of the enterprise. During the operational planning process, managers must address several key questions including: "which business process improvements are most critical for executing the strategy?" Kaplan and Norton write: "The objectives in a Strategy Map's process perspective represent how strategy gets executed. The map's strategic themes [for more on strategic theming see Chapter 3 in this book] originate in the key processes defined on the map. For example, a strategic theme to 'grow though innovation' requires outstanding performance from the new product development process: a theme to create 'heightened loyalty with targeted customers' requires greatly improved customer management processes. Some process improvements are designed to deliver the financial perspective's cost reduction and productivity objectives, whereas others focus on excelling at regulatory and social objectives. Companies need to focus their TQM, Six Sigma, and reengineering programs on enhancing the performance of those processes identified as critical for delivering the desired improvements in the strategy's customer and financial objectives."

Now Kaplan and Norton's language, and indeed most of that pertaining to "Lean" speaks to a manufacturing, or at least profit-based organization. This is not surprising. TQM (the parent of Lean) was first developed as a methodology (or collection of methodologies) for use within the Japanese manufacturing sector, and then was transferred for use within Western manufacturers such as Xerox. Of the various Lean approaches the Toyota Production System is clearly manufacturing based (although its usage has broadened somewhat since, for instance a version is used within the finance function of the giant aluminum producer Alcoa).[4] Six Sigma originated in Motorola in the 1980s and was further developed by organizations such as General Electric. Even the word "Lean" originated in the term "Lean manufacturing" or "Lean production." This hardly points to a rich history of Lean usage in the public sector.

LEAN AND THE PUBLIC SECTOR

Indeed in looking at the case organizations within this book, there is little strategic usage of Lean methodologies. By some distance the most advanced in the usage of TQM principles (and some Lean derivatives) is Christchurch City Council New Zealand, which deploys a national version of the US Malcolm Baldrige Award alongside the Balanced Scorecard (for an overview of Baldrige see Chapter 2). Christchurch City Council is a recipient of the country's Performance Excellence Study Award, which is given to organizations that demonstrate excellence to the Malcolm Baldrige criteria.[5] While preparing this book the Ministry of Works (MoW), Bahrain changed the title of its Strategic Planning Section (which is essentially the Ministry's Office of Strategy Management – see Chapter 9) to Strategic Planning and Quality Management Section, so to signal the importance of the section's role in driving TQM and Lean principles ministry-wide. In accordance with the advice in this book, within the MoW, TQM and Lean are deployed in support of strategic objectives, and understood as such. The most important, and overarching, performance framework in the MoW is the Balanced Scorecard.[6]

Amongst our other case studies, the Information Management Services (IMS) department of the UK's Her Majesty's Revenue & Customs (HMRC) was in the process of introducing Lean methodologies across the department.

Types of waste in the public sector

What public sector organizations such as the IMS Department of HMRC are beginning to realize is that Lean is basically about driving waste from activities and processes and that waste is as evident within a not-for-profit setting as a for-profit setting. The UK's Office of Government Commerce (an independent office of Her Majesty's Treasury, established to help Government deliver best value from its spending) classified "service" waste in a public sector setting as:[7]

1. Process waste
2. Information waste
3. Work waste
4. Human energy waste

1.   Process waste

This was broken down into the following components:

Strategic waste: effort wasted as a result of processes that are not focused on customer or stakeholder value

Unbalanced flow waste: this is the resource we commit to material that pile up between workstations

Standardization waste: the effort required to correct the consequences of optional methods applied by individual employees

Reliability waste: correction of unpredictable process outcomes due to initially unknown causes

Checking waste: the effort spent in inspection and rework

Boundary waste: correction of errors/re-keying that occurs when work moves from one area to another.

2.   Information waste

Translation waste: the effort required to change data or formats between process steps

Missing information waste: effort driven by the absence of key information

Irrelevant information waste: the cost of having to sort through or deal with irrelevant material

Inaccurate information waste: effort driven by dealing with inaccurate information.

3.   Work waste

Processing waste: inefficient work as a result of inadequate training, missing information

Motion waste: movement that does not add value

Waiting waste: people waiting for information, a meeting, a signature or approval.

4.   Human energy waste

Lack of clear focus waste: not consistently aligned and energized to address critical issues

Ineffective structural waste: waiting for approval, action, etc

Lack of ownership waste: no clear ownership of the issues

Ineffective control of quality waste: non-productive supervision and no feedback on action and outputs

Tampering waste: arbitrary changes to process without understanding the consequences

Inappropriate assignments waste: working on unnecessary or inappropriate tasks

Goal alignment waste: working at cross purposes and duplicating work.

Lean usage in the Scottish public sector: Research findings

With "waste" identified we should highlight that there is compelling research evidence that demonstrates how successfully Lean (and the removal of waste) can be implemented within a public sector setting and therefore its appropriateness for use outside of its traditional manufacturing/process homeland. A particularly powerful piece of research was conducted by faculty from the prestigious Warwick Business School, UK and published in the 2006 report "Evaluation of the Lean Approach to Business Management and its use in the Public Sector," which was undertaken on behalf of the Scottish Executive (Scotland's devolved parliament) and focused on Lean usage in the Scottish public sector.[8]

   Through extensive desk research, survey mechanisms and case interviews this in-depth study concluded that Lean was certainly effective for improving performance within a public sector setting. The research found two types of positive outcomes from Lean: tangible and intangible. Whereas the former refers to measurable outcomes, the latter refers to more qualitative outcomes.

Research findings: Tangible outcomes

The research uncovered a wide range of tangible outcomes that specific organizations reported, including:

- Improving customer waiting times to first appointment in the health sector from an average of 23 to 12 days
- Improving processing times by two thirds in one local government department
- Achieving more work in less staff time
- Bringing services up to a standard
- Improvement of customer flow time for patients by 48%
- Reduction in staffing and costs of 105 person reduction in manpower and £31m budget saving in ten months.

There was also a range of intangible outcomes in delivering benefits to the customer, the organization and the staff which can be summarized as:

- Process change to speed up the process
- Culture change to focus on customer requirements and encourage joined-up working
- Greater focus on prevention rather than correction of errors
- Support for the development of a culture of continuous improvement
- Greater understanding of the whole system and how it fits together
- Better understanding of the needs of the customer
- Improved performance measurement and use of data to manage performance
- Greater staff satisfaction and confidence in themselves and the organization.

Crucially, and in keeping with the views of this book, the research found that by aligning Lean to more strategic aims of the business more sustainable wins are made and commitment from staff to the change process is enhanced. The authors wrote:

Analysis from the research with organizations in the Scottish public sector, together with evidence from the literature, indicates that Lean is transferable to the public sector and can be used to develop more seamless processes, improve flow, reduce waste and develop an understanding of customer value. Lean is most suited to organizations with high volume, repeatable tasks that allow greater standardization and integration, supported by a less hierarchical management structure that allows empowerment and engagement of the workforce. However, to ensure greater successes, organizations require an awareness or realization of the need for improvement; the capacity within the organization to deal with change; and an organizational culture which is receptive to understanding the customer and process analysis and is able to use relevant data to drive improvement.

Importantly, the research went on to say: "For longer-term impact and sustainability, implementation of Lean should be tied to more strategic objectives. By tackling the barriers and ensuring the provision of the factors contributing to success, this research finds that

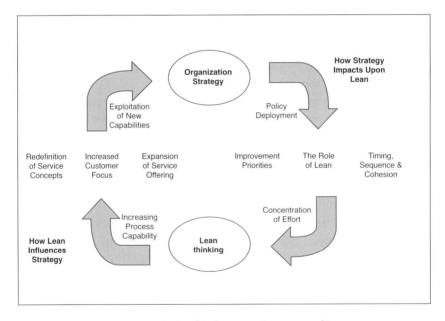

Figure 3.1 **Relationship between Strategy and Lean**

Lean is a suitable methodology for improving performance and embedding a continuous improvement culture in the public sector."

Figure 3.1 (which is taken from the cited report) clearly illustrates the advantages, benefits and outcomes of having a clear relationship between strategy and Lean. Being aligned to strategy it allows clear policy deployment and concentration of effort which in return, allow increased process capability and exploitation of new capabilities.

Six Sigma

Although, and as we have explained, Lean is not a single intervention but a collection of methodologies and approaches that are closely related in that they are focused on waste reduction and the continuous improvement of processes, we will spend some time providing a general understanding of what is likely the most popular Lean approach – Six Sigma. This metric and methodology has generated a huge consulting business, and significant numbers of online forums and books. The explosion in this "industry" does provide some concerns, which we will explain later. But first we will explain Six Sigma and in doing so will start with an image that neatly conveys the breakthrough performance promise of the approach which, as already stated, has a measure of 3.14 defects per billion of opportunities.

Soccer goalkeeper analogy

Consider a goalkeeper of a soccer team who plays 50 games in a season and who in each game faces 50 shots from the opposing team. A defect can be described as when the opposing team scores a goal. Therefore, a goalkeeper that performs to a Six Sigma standard would concede one goal once every 147 years! Just imagine such a level of performance.

As the football analogy illustrates, as a metric it represents an extremely low defect rate. Moving from the football field to an organizational setting, for a business process the "Sigma capability" is a metric that indicates how well the process is performing. Sigma capability measures the capability of the process to perform defect-free work. A defect is anything that results in customer dissatisfaction. As defects go down, the Sigma level goes up.

Sigma levels

There are other Sigma (which is a Greek word that stands for "standard deviation," and that describes how much "variation" exists in a set of data, a group of items, in processes, in transactions or outputs) scores that represent various performance levels. As shown in Figure 3.2 attaining a One Sigma level represents 691,500 errors per million opportunities (a 69.15% error rate), whereas Five Sigma equals 230 errors per million opportunities (a 0.00023% error rate).

DMAIC

As a methodology (and this is important as the approach is more than a simple metric) Six Sigma represents a set of tools that enable continuous improvement (and in many instances breakthrough performance). These tools are based on the DMAIC principles. DMAIC stands for:

- Define customer requirements (internal or external); that is their expectation of the process
- Measure the current performance; what is the frequency of defects?
- Analyze the data collected and map to determine cause of effect and opportunities for improvement; why, when and where the defects occur?
- Improve the target process by designing solutions to improve, fix or prevent problems

Sigma level	DEFECTS PER MILLION OPPORTUNITIES	% ERROR
1	691,500	69.15
2	308,500	30.85
3	66,800	6.68
4	6,200	0.62
5	230	0.00023
6	3.4	0.0000034

Figure 3.2 **Levels of Six Sigma Performance**

- Control the improvements to keep the process on the new course; how can we ensure that the process stays fixed?

Core Six Sigma assertions are that:

- Continuous efforts to achieve stable and predictable process results (and reduce process variation) are of vital importance to business success
- Manufacturing and business processes have characteristics that can be measured, analyzed, improved and controlled
- Achieving sustained quality improvement requires commitment from the entire organization, particularly from top-level management.

In addition to these accepted quality precepts, implementation of the Six Sigma methodology requires:

- A clear focus on achieving measurable and quantifiable financial returns from any Six Sigma project
- An increased emphasis on strong and passionate management leadership and support
- A special infrastructure of "Champions," "Master Black Belts," "Black Belts," and "Green Belts" to lead and implement the Six Sigma approach (see below)
- A clear commitment to making decisions on the basis of verifiable data, rather than assumptions and guesswork.

The following is a useful all-compassing description of Six Sigma:

> [Six Sigma is a] comprehensive and flexible system for achieving, sustaining and maximizing business success. Six Sigma is uniquely driven by close understanding of customer needs, disciplined use of facts, data, and statistical analysis, and diligent attention to managing, improving and reinventing business processes.[9]

Six Sigma popularity

By the end of the 1990s it was estimated that about two-thirds of the Fortune 500 organizations had begun Six Sigma initiatives with the aim of reducing costs and improving quality. In Chapter 6 we explain how to choose Six Sigma projects and how to ensure that these are part of the strategic initiatives component of a Balanced Scorecard system. Indeed as we explain in that chapter a new approach called

Balanced Six Sigma has emerged to ensure the dovetailing of the Six Sigma methodology with the Balanced Scorecard.

Building the in-house Six Sigma competencies

An often cited strength of the Six Sigma methodology (and one that has not been equally said of the Balanced Scorecard, which is partly why the OSM idea is now becoming so popular across commercial and public sector organizations) is the emphasis placed on identifying, training and developing a cadre of in-house expert practitioners. Notably there is a hierarchy or "ranking" of practitioners, each with designated roles and responsibilities.

Executive leadership

This includes the CEO and other members of top management. They are responsible for setting up a vision for Six Sigma implementation. They also empower the other role holders with the freedom and resources to explore new ideas for breakthrough improvements. As with any major change program it is recognized that achieving breakthrough performance through using the Six Sigma tools and methodology will not be achieved without active support from the very top.

Champions

These are responsible for Six Sigma implementation across the organization in an integrated manner. Crucially a Champion is chosen by the Executive Leadership team and is drawn from upper management. Champions also act as mentors to Black Belts.

The core roles of a Six Sigma Champion are to:

1. Create the vision of Six Sigma for the company
2. Define the path to implement Six Sigma across the organization
3. Develop a comprehensive training plan for implementing the breakthrough strategy
4. Carefully select high impact projects
5. Support development of "statistical thinking"
6. Ask Black Belts many questions so that they are properly focused
7. Realize the gains by supporting Six Sigma projects through allocation of resources and removal of roadblocks
8. Hold the ground by implementing Black Belt recommendations

9. Make sure that project opportunities are acted upon by the organization's leadership and the finance department
10. Recognize people for their efforts.

Master Black Belts

Identified by champions, Master Black Belts act as in-house coaches on Six Sigma. They devote 100% of their time to Six Sigma (meaning therefore that it is a full-time role). They assist the Champions and guide Black Belts and Green Belts. Apart from statistical tasks, their time is spent on ensuring consistent application of Six Sigma across various functions and departments.

The core roles of a Master Black belt are:

1. Understand the big picture
2. Partner with the Champions
3. Develop and deliver training to various levels of the organization
4. Assist in the identification of projects
5. Coach and support Black Belts in project work
6. Participate in project reviews to offer technical expertise
7. Help train and certify Black Belts
8. Take on leadership of major programs
9. Facilitate the sharing of best practices across the corporation

Black Belts

Black Belts operate under Master Black Belts to apply Six Sigma methodology to specific projects. They also devote 100% of their time to Six Sigma. They primarily focus on Six Sigma project execution, whereas Champions and Master Black Belts focus on identifying projects/functions for Six Sigma.

The core roles of a Black Belt are:

1. Act as breakthrough strategy experts and be breakthrough strategy enthusiasts
2. Stimulate champion thinking
3. Identify the barriers
4. Lead and direct teams in project execution
5. Report progress to appropriate leadership levels
6. Solicit help from Champions when needed
7. Influence without direct authority
8. Determine the most effective tools to apply

9. Prepare a detailed project assessment during the measurement phase
10. Get input from knowledgeable operators, first-line supervisors and team leaders
11. Teach and coach Breakthrough Strategy methods and tools
12. Manage project risk
13. Ensure that the results are sustained.

Green Belts

Green Belts are employees who take up Six Sigma implementation along with their other job responsibilities. They operate under the guidance of Black Belts.

Roles of Green Belt:

– A Green Belt is an employee who has done the Six Sigma DMAIC training and does at least one project within one year
– A Green Belt is not full time as he or she is responsible for doing a Six Sigma project while performing their regular duties.

Six Sigma challenges

Although we might applaud the fact that there has been a concerted attempt to ensure that there is a large body of available expertise in Six Sigma, there are concerns. The fostering of a cottage industry of Six Sigma training and certification has led to many critics arguing that the methodology has been oversold, with many consulting firms entering the market even though they only posses a rudimentary understanding of the tools and techniques involved. That said, the same holds true for the Balanced Scorecard and every other popular management tool. The authors of this book are constantly alarmed at the shocking advice that is given through online forums and other vehicles by "so-called" Balanced Scorecard experts. Too much of the "scorecard advice" is at best of questionable value and at worse downright dangerous.

Another criticism of Six Sigma (and indeed Lean deployment more broadly) is that the projects are typically implemented bottom-up. As a result organizations spend a lot of effort on Lean projects that look at tiny areas of their business. This way they pick the lowest hanging fruits but often miss the big opportunities: this is why approaches such as Balanced Six Sigma have some value as they force the Six

Sigma teams to choose strategically relevant projects and not just those that deliver some financial gains.

It is telling to note that some of the organizations that have become poster-boys for Six Sigma have indeed secured mouth-watering cost savings from their efforts, have simultaneously been very poor performers on the stock market and have been recognized for their strategic failures. The argument has been that these organizations have been exclusively focused on using Six Sigma to identify cost saving opportunities rather than as a tool to continuously improve performance against a strategic goal: this is *not* how to get the best from Six Sigma or other Lean projects. And even though public sector bodies are under pressure to deliver efficiency gains (which will likely be understood in cost terms) we would caution against deploying Six Sigma or other Lean approaches simply as a cost cutting tool. This will not deliver long-term success, might lead to the undermining of strategically critical processes and, crucially, will likely lead to a cultural backlash from employees worried about the safety of their jobs (we discuss the cultural implications of implementing Lean, and indeed a Balanced Scorecard, in Chapter 9).

It is telling that the research into the use of Lean in public sector bodies within Scotland concluded that "successful Lean implementations tended to view cost reduction as a secondary rather than a primary objective," and that "Headcount reduction was not seen as a primary Lean objective."[10]

CONCLUSION

We have explained in this chapter that the implementation of Lean must be in support of clear strategic goals. Once these goals are articulated and agreed by the senior team, then the principles of Lean thinking can be applied to ensure the processes linked to these high-level priorities are delivered in the most effective and efficient manner. The strategic goals are best described through a Balanced Scorecard Strategy Map.

In the next chapter we will provide step-by-step guidance for creating a Balanced Scorecard Strategy Map, while in Chapter 5 we provide equally clear guidelines for designing key performance questions (KPQs) and key performance indicators (KPIs). In Chapter 6 we consider how to identify strategic initiatives that support the strategic objectives that appear on the map. Lean thinking must be fully integrated into this complete process.

SIDEBAR 1

Slightly edited version of Dr. W. Edwards Deming's 14 Principles of Good Management[11]

1. **Constancy of purpose**
   Create constancy of purpose for continual improvement of products and service to society, allocating resources to provide for long range needs rather than only short-term profitability, with a plan to become competitive, to stay in business, and to provide jobs.

2. **The new philosophy**
   Adopt the new philosophy... We can no longer live with commonly accepted levels of delays, mistakes, defective materials, and defective workmanship.

3. **Cease dependence on mass inspection**
   Eliminate the need for mass inspection as the way of life to achieve quality by building quality into the product in the first place.

4. **End lowest tender contracts**
   End the practice of awarding business solely on the basis of price tag. Instead require meaningful measures of quality along with price... The aim is to minimize total cost, not merely initial cost, by minimizing variation.

5. **Improve every process**
   Improve constantly and forever every process for planning, production, and service. Search continually for problems in order to improve every activity in the company, to improve quality and productivity, and thus to constantly decrease costs. Institute innovation and constant improvement of product, service, and process.

---

6. Institute training on the job

Institute modern methods of training on the job for all, including management, to make better use of every employee. New skills are required to keep up with changes in materials, methods, product and service design, machinery, techniques, and service.

7. Institute leadership

Adopt and institute leadership aimed at helping people do a better job. The responsibility of managers and supervisors must be changed from sheer numbers to quality... Management must ensure that immediate action is taken on reports of inherited defects, maintenance requirements, poor tools, fuzzy operational definitions, and all conditions detrimental to quality.

8. Drive out fear

Encourage effective two way communication and other means to drive out fear throughout the organization so that everybody may work effectively and more productively for the company.

9. Break down barriers

Break down barriers between departments and staff areas. People in different areas... must work in teams to tackle problems that may be encountered with products or services.

10. Eliminate exhortations

Eliminate the use of slogans, posters and exhortations for the work force, demanding Zero Defects and new levels of productivity without providing methods. Such exhortations only create adversarial relationships.

11. Eliminate arbitrary numerical targets

Eliminate work standards that prescribe quotas for the work force and numerical goals for people in management. Substitute aids and helpful leadership in order to achieve continual improvement of quality and productivity.

12. **Permit pride of workmanship**

    Remove the barriers that rob hourly workers and people in management, of their right to pride of workmanship.

13. **Encourage education**

    Institute a vigorous program of education, and encourage self improvement for everyone. What an organization needs is not just good people; it needs people that are improving with education. Advances in competitive position will have their roots in knowledge.

14. **Top management commitment and action**

    Clearly define top management's permanent commitment to ever improving quality and productivity, and their obligation to implement all of these principles... Create a structure in top management that will push every day on the preceding 13 Points, and take action in order to accomplish the transformation. Support is not enough: action is required!

4

DESIGNING STRATEGY MAPS TO AGREE
STRATEGIC PRIORITIES

Somewhere there is a map of how it can be done.
**Ben Stein (born 1944), a US actor, writer, and commentator
on political and economic issues**

INTRODUCTION

Within the opening chapter we explained that the pressure on public
sector organizations to be efficient is much more than a short-term
phenomenon. The reverberations from the economic tsunami that
was the credit crunch will continue to hurt public sector purses for
many years into the future. Moreover, dwindling incomes from major
demographic shifts such as an aging population will also have a long-
lasting and negative impact on levels of available money. And as we
have also stressed, the general public (the consumers of public sector
products) are demanding that the quality – or effectiveness – of the
services that they receive improves, even though money is tight.

Delivering to this joint efficiency/effectiveness agenda, and particularly understanding how spending increases/decreases impacts the
efficiency/effectiveness balance has become a significant, and complex
challenge for public sector leaders.

THE BENEFITS OF A STRATEGY MAP

Based on research and client assignments, it is our observation that
the most powerful tool for successfully meeting this challenge is the
creation of a Strategy Map. This enables a one-page description of the
core capabilities and their relationships that the organization must
master if it is to deliver its strategic goals.

Strategy mapping: The most important step in Scorecard creation

As we explained in Chapter 2, within the "classic," Balanced Scorecard methodology as evolved by Harvard Business Professor Dr Robert Kaplan and consultant Dr David Norton, the idea of a Strategy Map emerged several years after the original concept of the Balanced Scorecard as a balanced measurement system. Despite being an "after-thought," strategy mapping (the process of creating the map) was soon recognized as the most important task in building a Balanced Scorecard system. Get the map right, it transpired, and it becomes much simpler to select meaningful measures, targets and initiatives.

The same logic applies to working with the Value Creation Map. It is by getting the map right that it becomes possible to select mission-critical key performance questions (KPQs) and key performance indicators (KPIs) as well as supporting action programs and the shaping of a meaningful value narrative. Get the map wrong and everything else will be wrong, thus wasting much organizational time, energy and resources.

ADVANCED PERFORMANCE INSTITUTE GLOBAL RESEARCH FINDINGS

The importance of creating a Strategy Map was clearly illustrated in the 2008 Advanced Performance Institute (API) research study *Strategic Performance Management in Government and Public Sector Organizations*.[1] The research found that of the ten principles of good performance management for Government and Public Sector organizations (see Chapter 1), none was more critical than "create clarity and agreement about the strategic aims." The most powerful way to achieve this, the study noted, is through the senior team working together to create a Strategy Map – or a highly visible plan – that depicts the strategy, with all of its components on a single piece of paper. These immediately provide focus and direction, showing at a glance what the intended outcomes are, as well as the core activities and underpinning enablers that will lead to their achievement.

Evidence shows that those organizations that visually map their strategy into meaningful cause-and-effect maps tend to have a significantly better understanding of strategy, are able to extract more value from their performance management system, and more importantly perform better. Note too that research with 157 companies conducted by the US-based Wharton School found that only 23% of companies consistently built, analyzed, and tested causal models. However, the survey also found that those organizations which used Strategy Maps had a 2.95% higher Return on assets and 5.14% higher Return on Equity than companies that didn't use cause-and-effect models.[2]

Cause-and-effect maps not being used

Therefore, it is significantly worrisome to find that according to the API study (which was the largest research program of its type thus far conducted), just 10% of public sector organizations were found to create strategic cause-and-effect maps to visualize the links between different perspectives and only 4% show the cause-and-effect linkages between their different strategic elements.

This leaves an overwhelming 86% that do not draw on this powerful technique. Even if maps are not used explicitly, business plans should contain clear cause-and-effect linkages that show how tomorrow's outcomes will be impacted upon by today's outputs, processes and inputs. Using a Strategy Map in conjunction with a more conventional business plan can help to check the assumptions made in the plan and the map itself is a more understandable way to communicate the strategy.

STRATEGIC COMMUNICATION

Indeed its value as a strategic communication tool is one of the most widely reported benefits gleaned from creating a Strategy Map. This has certainly been true of the API clients that have created a Strategy Map and that are cases studies within this book.

International Baccalaureate case example 1

Consider the case of the education provider, the International Baccalaureate (IB) organization. Although not a public sector organization, being a non-profit entity that has charitable status, operationally and strategically it has much more in common with those from the public than commercial sectors and so we have included it within this book as the case provides excellent best practice learnings. Andrea Smith, IB's Head of Strategy comments that before introducing the map, their strategic plan was not being communicated that well either inside or outside the organization. "There wasn't clarity around what our strategic plan was or what we were trying to achieve. People could understand the mission [which we speak to later in this chapter] but the next level down wasn't particularly clear," she says, adding that it was also difficult to accurately gauge how well the organization was performing against the strategy.

Since introducing the Strategy Map in early 2009, Smith points to the following, amongst other benefits. "Without question the main benefit so far is that it has got everyone thinking about and talking about the IB strategy," she says. "It has given us something useful to work with and has provided a framework through which we can reflect on the strategy and make sure that people in the organization understand what we are trying to achieve."[3] IB's Strategy map is shown in Figure 4.1.

Audit Scotland case example 1

Note too the importance of communication amongst the benefits of using the Value Creation Map listed by Dianne McGiffen, Director of

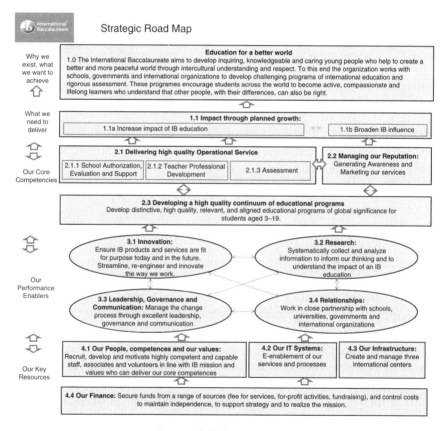

Figure 4.1 **IB Strategy Map**

Corporate Services at Audit Scotland, which put in place the map and accompanying scorecard in late 2008 and early 2009. However, in this example the benefits are not just about what the organization is trying to do, but what it actually achieves.

"From the beginning we knew that from an internal perspective we wanted to change the way we did the corporate plan and make it simpler, more focused and relevant," McGiffen says. "From an external perspective we also knew that as an organization we wanted to introduce new ways of doing things to help stakeholders grapple with increasing complexity, a changing business environment and a worsening economic climate."

"The Strategy Map is helping us to meet our external and internal goals," she continues, but adds the important point that, "But in the final analysis, it is perhaps most important that the map has better positioned Audit Scotland to be able to demonstrate to stakeholders and clients that we are doing what we promised that we would do." And for Audit Scotland she says, "doing what we promised that we would do," is delivering to a balanced efficiency/effectiveness performance agenda.[4] Audit Scotland's Strategy Map is shown in Figure 2.1.

CREATING A STRATEGY MAP: PUBLIC SECTOR DIFFERENCE FROM COMMERCIAL SECTOR

We will now turn our attention to explaining how to build a Strategy Map. Importantly, we will show that although creating a Strategy Map for a public sector organization essentially follows the same logic and process as for a commercial operation, there are differences. Most notably is the position of the "financial" perspective, which is invariably at the top of a private sector map, but rarely the case in a public sector setting. Moreover, in map creation, the public sector leaders are forced to consider the needs of a broad range of customers or stakeholders that have an equal claim for attention (and that often leads to confusion as to what the term "stakeholder" means) whereas commercial organizations have, as a prime directive, the meeting of "shareholder" needs. Figure 4.1 shows the Strategy Map for the International Baccalaureate organization which follows the Value Creation Map convention. Figure 4.2 shows the map of The Ministry of Works, Bahrain, which is architected according to the "classic" Kaplan/ Norton Balanced Scorecard. Both maps show the cause-and-effect relationships that deliver the ultimate realization of the vision or mission.

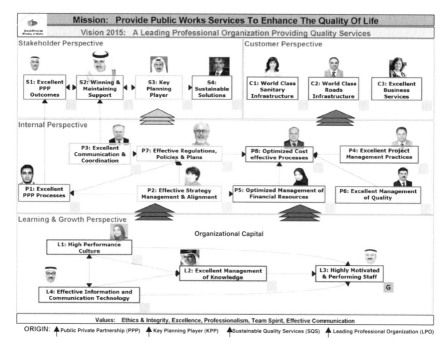

Figure 4.2 **Ministry of Works Strategy Map**

The importance of vision and mission statements

And in creating a Strategy Map, we must begin with statements of strategic intent – essentially the vision and mission statements, as it is these that capture the ultimate goals of the organization. Indeed we would argue that vision and mission statements are much more important, and useful, within a public sector organization than in a commercial sector. In the latter case vision statements, for example, are typically industry generic and uninspiring – such as being the No 1 supplier to our customers. However, in the public sector the statements of strategic intent more profoundly describe why the organization exists.

INTERNATIONAL BACCALAUREATE CASE EXAMPLE 2

For instance, consider the IB vision, which is to "create a better and more peaceful world through education," and the mission is "The International Baccalaureate aims to develop a growing number of inquiring, knowledgeable and caring young people who help to create a better and more peaceful world through intercultural understanding and respect." The delivering of this vision and mission is a primary reason why the bulk of IB's about 500 staff joined the organization. "The mission is critical to the organization and it was important that everything on the Strategy Map supported that," says Smith.

North West Collaborative Commercial Agency case example 1

Consider too the mission of the North West Collaborative Commercial Agency (NWCCA), which has also introduced a Value Creation Map to help it better steer its strategy of procuring products and services for National Health trusts in the North West of England. "We support the delivery of world-class health and the highest quality health care to the people of the North West by obtaining better quality and better value for money products and services through world-class procurement and commercial services." As with the Audit Scotland mission that was described in Chapter 2, this captures both efficiency (better value) and effectiveness (better quality) performance dimensions.[5]

Distilling the vision/mission statement

When there is a well-formulated vision and/or mission, it becomes possible to further distil this into key deliverables. For instance, the NWCCA's mission breaks down into the three deliverables of "we generate service quality and process improvements," "we generate value and efficiency savings for our members," "we generate income and

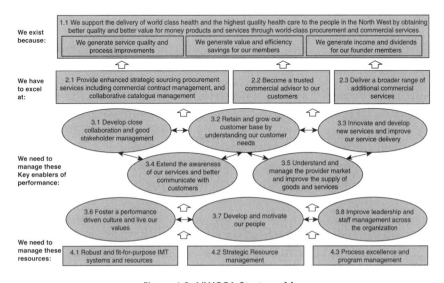

Figure 4.3 **NWCCA Strategy Map**

dividends for our founder members." As we can see, there is a further explication and description of the efficiency and effectiveness components of NWCCA's mission. This is further decomposed in the following "perspectives," of "what we have to excel at," "we need to manage these key enablers of performance," and "we need to manage these resources," as is shown in the NWCCA Strategy Map in Figure 4.3.

Avoiding the term "Balanced Scorecard"

In creating a Balanced Scorecard we also suggest to clients at the outset that they consider *not* using the term Balanced Scorecard. From our observations, many people might feel uncomfortable with the term (especially the measurement and control undertones) and actively resist its implementation. IB's Smith says that they decided to call it something that resonated with the business and that would not be viewed as a program that was separate from the everyday working of the organization, "We certainly did not want people talking about 'this thing' called the Balanced Scorecard," she says. IB simply called their first scorecard "the Roadmap." As other examples NWCCA uses the term "performance framework."

As a further example consider Christchurch City Council, which calls its scorecard a "Plan on a Page." Manager, Planning and Performance, Peter Ryan explains why. "The problem is that the term Balanced Scorecard conjures up an image of compliance and of a report card. It doesn't do justice to the aim of the methodology."[6] Which he says is primarily about large-scale strategic change.

SENIOR MANAGEMENT INTERVIEWS

For the actual building of the map, the first step is normally focused on the program facilitator (typically an external expert) conducting one-to-one interviews with the senior team, and for a public sector organization this will usually also include members of the external supervisory board. This was the case when API facilitated the design of the Strategy Map at Audit Scotland, where one-to-one interviews were completed with each member of the executive management team and the assistant directors as well as the organization's chair John Baillie and another board member.

A core benefit of one-to-one interviews is that it enables the external facilitator to gain a clear picture as to how individual senior managers view the drivers of organizational strategic success. Any differences are then debated within the workshops conducted to create the Strategy Map, with the ultimate goal of reaching consensual agreement as to the critical few drivers of success.

IB's Smith adds that individual interviews (API interviewed each member of the senior management team individually as well as members of the Board of Governors) helped the external facilitator gain a clear understanding of how each senior manager viewed the strategy and what they felt to be the opportunities for improvement. There was also another benefit, as Smith explains. "As [API] presented a consolidated view of the senior managers' views and not their individual responses, the leaders felt more comfortable in giving full and frank feedback, which strengthened the work," she says.

SENIOR MANAGEMENT WORKSHOPS

Following the senior management interviews it is then usual that the external facilitator will draw up a draft Strategy Map that is debated, amended, clarified and agreed within workshops that involve the senior team. And it is critical that the senior team go through this process of debating and agreeing the Strategy Map.

Importance of senior management involvement

Perhaps the biggest mistake that organizations make with a Balanced Scorecard is that the senior management team devolves responsibility for deciding on the content of the Strategy Map to a lower-level team. It follows that if the senior team is responsible for strategy, then it should be responsible for fashioning the enterprise-level Strategy Map. Consequently, ownership has to be by those at the top.

One reason why the senior team should be fully involved in creating the Strategy Map is that the process can be as useful to the organization as the end product. Getting the top team focused on the same high-level performance objectives/enablers as shown on a Strategy Map is extremely useful in getting each senior manager to visualize how the work of their own function relates to the work of others. Put another way it helps leaders, who are otherwise department-focused in their day-to-day work, to see the bigger picture and their responsibility for strategy formulation as part of the senior executive team. Moreover, through the process of creating the Strategy Map the senior team reaches consensus as to what the critical few drivers of success for the enterprise are.

The Royal Canadian Mounted Police (RCMP) was one organization that found that building the scorecard engendered great teamwork at the top. "One of the greatest benefits of the scorecard process is that you witness your executive managers coming together as a team and agreeing on what's important, why it matters and how to make it work," says deputy commissioner Eva Kmiecic.[7]

Challenging strategic assumptions

While stressing that "senior management buy-in is a must," IB's Smith makes the useful observation that the team must be prepared to question the current strategy and priorities and that the external facilitator must ensure this questioning process takes place. "Creating the map provides an ideal opportunity to clarify and agree on what's important to the organization," she says. "And this opportunity should not be wasted." Indeed as a result of building its Strategy Map, the senior team of IB revisited and rearticulated their strategic priorities.

Belfast City Council case example

In creating its Value Creation Map (which is shown in Figure 2.13) Belfast City Council ensured that it involved all elected members and

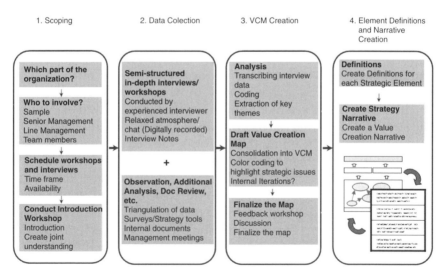

Figure 4.4 **Four Implementation Steps at Belfast City Council**

senior officers. This was important for gaining strategic consensus with a diverse political environment where there are six political parties represented in the council but where not one has overall control. There were four key steps in creating Belfast City Council's Value Creation Map. Shown diagrammatically in Figure 4.4, these were:

1. Scoping – firstly, the project was scoped and planned. As part of this it was decided who to involve in the strategy development process. In order to get a broad and balanced view across the council it was decided to involve all chief officers, heads of services, and elected members from all parties.
2. Data Collection – an experienced external interviewer conducted individual in-depth and semi-structured interviews with all chief officers, heads of services and elected members. In addition, observation data and document reviews (e.g. business plans, strategy reports, etc.) were collected and used to triangulate the interview data.
3. Value Creation Map (VCM) Creation – the interview data was transcribed and coded in order to extract themes, constructs and insights to design a draft VCM. A feedback workshop was used to present the draft Value Creation Map to senior officers and elected members. Feedback was collected during the workshop which led to minor amendments of the map. Further feedback was collected in the weeks following the workshop which led to the final version of the Value Creation Map. In a subsequent meeting the new strategy captured in the Value Creation Map was agreed on by both officers and members. For the first time the council now had an agreed and clearly defined strategy outlining its value proposition, core competencies and enablers of future performance.
4. Element Definitions and Narrative Creation – once the Value Creation Map had been created additional information was required for each of the elements on the map as to what they really meant. For that purpose a one or two paragraph definition was created for each element to provide further detail (Belfast City Council's value narrative is shown in Chapter 2). This was achieved in a series of meetings and workshops. A smaller project team was used to take this part forward and draft the definitions in close collaboration with the relevant senior officers. Feedback loops were used to ensure chief officers and members were informed about the progress and were able to provide feedback and suggestions.[8]

LOWER LEVEL MAP CIRCULATION

We would advise that once created the map should be circulated to additional staff members in order to further test the validity of the map and to begin the process of securing buy-in to the scorecard concept. At Audit Scotland, for example, the draft Strategy Map was circulated organization-wide for in-house consultation. Wide-ranging staff engagement was seen as crucial for securing buy-in to the Strategy Map concept. "Through focus groups and discussions with small groups of staff we gained feedback on what they thought of the map, what they thought were its strengths and weaknesses and where they saw areas for improvement," recalls McGiffen. "This showed us how well the management team's views were aligned with those of their colleagues and the staff feedback was used to inform the final map."

According to McGiffen, that staff found it easy to understand and talk about its contents, highlights a core strength of the map – clarity. "Within the group discussions it became evident that staff could see how it all fits together, what Audit Scotland is trying to achieve, how that will be achieved and what they must do in their own jobs to make it happen." This, she adds, was largely due to the map's simplicity and accessibility.

North West Collaborative Commercial Agency case example 2

Being an organization of just 48 people, NWCCA was able not just to circulate its map for comment but also to more fully involve all staff members in the map's creation. The process began with one-to-one interviews with the senior team, which Michelle McCusker, NWCCA's Manager, Business Performance explains were extremely useful. "The interviews provided an invaluable and balanced view as to what people within the agency believe to be our strengths and weaknesses and how they see the organization developing, going forward," she says.

This was followed by interviews at lower levels. However the interview process changed in scope and focus. At the senior manager/director level, focused one-to-one interviews were held to consider the entire strategy and to gauge each manager's take on why the organization exists, the priority areas in which it must excel and the underpinning enablers of performance. This was followed by facilitated focus group sessions for functional groups such as finance, operations, IT and marketing as examples. These sessions focused on what the functional areas must do to support the strategy as well as securing their views on mission critical strategic goals, performance enablers, etc. A further interview phase involved selected external stakeholders as well as non-executive board members, where attention was placed onto overall objectives and outcome targets and not on the internal drivers of performance.

All of the data from the three interview streams was pooled together in the creation of the performance framework's Strategy Map. Once a draft map was designed all participants were invited to feed-back workshops to finalize the map. Those staff members that couldn't attend the workshops were invited to provide written feedback via e-mail. That said the composition of the final map was the decision of the executive leadership team, which is right and proper as it is they who have ultimate responsibility for delivering the organizational strategy.

Ministry of Works, Bahrain case example 1

The Ministry of Works, Bahrain (MoW) provides another interesting take on creating the Strategy Map. Explained fully in the API case study: *Creating and Implementing a Balanced Scorecard: The Case of the Ministry of Works, Bahrain,*[9] a facilitated process of strategic theming has played a central role in Strategy Map and accompanying scorecard creation.

The MoW has identified four strategic themes that together are helping the ministry move toward a national Bahrain vision to 2030, which commits the country to massively improved standards of living, radically improved Government, widespread privatization, better education and health services and an enhanced quality of life. The four MoW themes are:

1. *Public-private partnership:* The best harnessing of private sector forces and public private partnership.
2. *A key planning player*: Ensuring effective collaboration and coordination among Government agencies in order to fully contribute towards effective National strategic and structural planning. This includes ensuring effective policy planning/making and regulatory enforcement.
3. *Quality services:* Ensuring the better management of services, projects and quality in order to deliver more and better services that are competitive, fair, customer focused, sustainable and cost effective.

4. *A leading professional organization*: Being able to attract and retain professionals and high quality competencies, and ensuring a high performance staff and organization.

During late 2006 and 2007 an external facilitator worked with the most senior 200 people (of 1600 employees) within the MoW to build and implement the Balanced Scorecard. This involved a mix of standard Balanced Scorecard strategy mapping and scorecard building techniques that focused on the five phases of creating Strategy-Focused Organization as described by scorecard co-creators Drs Robert Kaplan and David Norton: Mobilize, Translate, Align, Motivate and Govern (see Figure 2.10 in Chapter 2) interweaved with the Strategy Aligned Management (SAM) approach, (essentially a modified form of scorecard design and implementation defined by Bill Barberg of the US-based consultancy Insightformation and others). Such has been the success of the scorecarding effort that Dr Norton has publicly stated that the MoW's approach to the Balanced Scorecards is "world class" and "as good as any we've seen."[10]

The process began with strategy management and Balanced Scorecard awareness workshops and training. The strategy was revisited and out of this came a revised mission statement to "provide public works services to enhance the quality of life," a vision to be "a leading organization providing quality services," and values: "ethics and integrity, excellence, professionalism, team spirit and effective communication."

Next, cross-functional teams of managers were organized into four teams that would build sections of the Strategy Map according to the strategic themes ("theme teams" an idea that came out of the SAM methodology).

A workshop was then held to integrate the themes within a draft Strategy Map. Following further refinements the corporate level map was approved.

In line with reports from other organizations stated earlier Raja Al Zayani, Head of the Strategic Planning Section (essentially the organization's Office of Strategy Management, see Chapter 9) stressed the value of taking the time to ensure that consensus was reached as to the key corporate scorecard objectives. "This was quite challenging as people had different views of strategic priorities."

As cited, the four strategic themes guide the Strategy Map composition. Although strategic theming of objectives is commonplace today and normally recommended when creating a Strategy Map, the approach taken by the MoW was new and innovative. Whereas within a "classic" Scorecard system themes are typically articulated as a collection of objectives from the internal process and learning and growth perspectives that together deliver customer and financial outcomes (such as operational excellence, for instance) the MoW opted to describe its themes though horizontal and vertical dimensions.

The learning and growth perspective serves as the horizontal "leading professional organization" theme. The other three themes are described vertically, cutting through process, customer and stakeholder perspectives. In essence, the horizontal theme powers the delivery of the vertical themes. "It is the active participation of all employees that makes strategy happen," says Raja.

The public private partnership – PPP theme was described through three objectives from "effective PPP strategy" through to "improved PPP outcomes"; the key planning player theme was captured in three objectives from "improved communication and coordination processes," through to "a key planning player" objective; while the quality of service theme was described through five objectives from "full utilization of financial resources," through to "enhanced/expanded service delivery."

But note that these themes are viewed holistically and not as narrow, siloed efforts. For instance, through a causal relationship "improved communication and coordination processes," a key planning player objective, impacts the public private partnership and quality of service themes as well as its own.

Creating theme teams, which are led by a theme owner, is a useful way to broaden buy-in and ownership of a map. Most themes cross business units and support units. Given that getting things done across units etc requires strong leadership and mandate, it is usual that themes owners are drawn from the executive team. At the MoW level these owners are senior political figures within the ministry and not MoW employees.

Each theme owner should lead a theme team, which is a collection of people drawn from multiple business and support units. Their job is primarily to link strategic objectives within their team to operational tasks.

But ownership and accountability does not stop at the level of themes. Members of the executive team have ownership of corporate level objectives (and so must work closely with the Theme Team owners). Indeed His Excellency (HE) Fahmi Bin Ali Al-Jowder, the Minister for Works, owns the "win and maintain stakeholder support" objective. This was a purposeful ploy to ensure congruence of vision between politicians and staff. There are also owners for each objective at sector and directorate levels. "In all we have designated owners who are held accountable for all of the about 170 objective that appear within our suite of scorecards," comments Raja.

Each objective owner has their own team, members of which are often assigned ownership for measures and initiatives. Therefore every single theme, objective, measure and initiative within the MOW suite of scorecards has a designated owner.

THE VITAL FEW STRATEGIC OBJECTIVES

Note that the MoW corporate Strategy Map contains just 19 objectives. Note too that the other Strategy Maps published within this and the previous chapters are also notable in that they comprise a small number of strategic objectives/enablers. NWCCA has 17, International Baccalaureate has 16, Belfast City Council has 13 and Audit Scotland has just 11.

Keeping the number of strategic objectives/enablers to the critical few is important. However, given that public sector organizations must deliver to a wide range of stakeholder outcomes, there's a tendency to choose too many objectives – 40, 50 or even 60+ is not uncommon. The result is an organization map that describes everything the company does or is more reflective of a detailed operational map, rather than a Strategy Map that homes in on the critical few objectives that will successfully deliver the strategy. When there are too many objectives the scorecard becomes unmanageable and the program eventually dies, or if is kept alive it becomes a lower priority because people find it too exhausting to manage on an ongoing basis.

"RELEGATING" THE FINANCE PERSPECTIVE

What is also clear from these Strategy Maps is that none has "finance" as the top perspective, as was first described in a "classic," commercially oriented Balanced Scorecard. Within these and other public sector Strategy Maps, the finance perspective typically appears in as either the "second," perspective, as is the case at Brisbane City Council (Figure 2.8) or as the bottom perspective, as is the case at IB. Sometimes the finance perspective is subsumed into another perspective, such as within the "organization," (essentially internal process) perspective as another early scorecard adopter Subordinate Courts, Singapore, which only used three perspectives: stakeholder, organization and people.[11]

Sometimes the finance perspective is depicted on the left of or right of Strategy Map that then comprises the classic three perspectives of customer, internal process and learning and growth. By doing so, the public sector organization is signaling the message that although a financial outcome is not the ultimate aim, delivering to goals is dependent on how the organization manages and deploys its financial resources.

Defining stakeholder

Fairly commonly in a "classic" Kaplan/Norton public sector Strategy Map, we find that finance is subsumed into a broader "stakeholder" perspective, as is the case at the MoW. However, the use of the term "Stakeholder," can lead to some definitional challenges, as it is not uncommon that public sector leaders believe, wrongly, that a stakeholder is anyone they "do something for." For ease of differing, we like to think in terms of "output" and "input" stakeholders by using an apple tree analogy. The "output" stakeholders (and who are those that we should more accurately describe as customers) are those that want to eat our apples (that is we deliver a service that they want, which is often the central Government – as those who provide the money for the service and so are interested in the outcome and the general public, who consume the outcome). An input stakeholder is a body that helps the organization to create the environment in which the apple tree grows – such as suppliers, partners and employees.

Patricia Bush, is a public sector specializing senior consultant with the US-headquartered The Palladium Group (that was founded by Dr David Norton) and is one of the elite group of public sector scorecard experts that we interviewed for this book. She provides this useful stakeholder/customer differentiator, based on case experience. "We are helping the US Federal Bureau of Investigation (FBI), build and implement a Balanced Scorecard," she says. "In doing so, we state that the stakeholder might be the congress or President while the customers are those bodies that they work for: the law enforcement agencies." Put another way, she says "The stakeholder pays for the service whereas the customer receives the benefit. Indeed, the stakeholder might receive the benefit from the customer."

Of course this description gets a little bit confusing when we consider that, through the taxation system, those that pay for the service (the stakeholder) may well receive the bulk of their money from those that receive the services (the customer). That said, for practical purposes it is still a useful way to make a distinction between a stakeholder and a customer.

WHO DELIVERS WHAT ON A STRATEGY

Although the senior team must own the Strategy Map and therefore the identified themes/objectives, from a "Lean" viewpoint (see the previous chapter for a description of Lean and how it fits in with a Balanced Scorecard implementation) public sector organization would benefit from thinking carefully about what has to be delivered "in-house," and whether "more value for less money," can be gained through taking a more partnership approach to the delivery of elements of the strategy. In many cases strategic partnerships with other organizations can improve both efficiency and effectiveness. Here public sector organizations concentrate on the things they are actually really good at (their core competencies) and leave it to other experts who can deliver parts of the services in a better manner and be more cost effective – because it is their area of special expertise. The API white paper, "New Directions for Government: Five Principles for Sustainable Recovery," which we describe fully in the concluding chapter, explains that to properly contend with today's economic realities, public sector organizations will need to look closely at how they can forge win-win partnerships with other bodies.[12]

CASCADING THE STRATEGY MAP

One of the strengths of a Strategy Map and indeed the wider scorecard system is that an enterprise- or corporate-level map can be devolved deep inside the organization. A real benefit of doing so is that it makes strategy real to people. If, for example, a Strategy Map and scorecard are designed for a large Government ministry the goals and KPIs might be too abstract, or bland to be of practical value at the deepest levels of the organization.

But one key observation is *don't* cascade for the sake of it. Too often, organizations create a suite of Strategy Maps and scorecards from the top-to-bottom of the enterprise, without carefully considering the value of doing so. A general rule is that if the organization is not complex then perhaps one map will suffice (although some KPIs and targets will change at lower levels). However an organization of 100 people with five units of 20 focusing on different goals will probably require five maps.

Audit Scotland case example 2

Our case organization Audit Scotland has an interesting application of the Strategy Map concept, as McGiffen explains. "Our Strategy Map identifies the key support activities where we need to focus attention and commit resources," she says. "What we are doing now is creating strategy maps for specific areas where we want to prioritize major performance improvements, such as information and knowledge management and learning."

She continues: "Our stakeholders are increasingly looking to Audit Scotland to provide sophisticated and advanced knowledge sharing and collaborative capabilities. However, our technologies and methodologies don't enable us to do what we need to do to meet stakeholder requirements. We have started to invest in this area and a Strategy Map should prove a powerful mechanism for prioritizing our investments against identified stakeholder needs." Environmental performance is another area for which a dedicated Strategy Map will be created.

Belfast City Council case example 2

At Belfast City Council, it was realized that many of the strategies and actions in the corporate map would have to be implemented and measured at a Service level. At the same time the corporate map would not represent *all* of the strategies and work of individual Services which is why the process was cascaded throughout the organization.

Each Service had to design their own value creation map to:

- Clarify what the Service is about – i.e. ask *"What is our purpose?"*
- Establish what it is they need to do well to achieve this – i.e. ask *"What are our core competencies?"*
- Agree the enablers – i.e. ask *"What are our value drivers?"*

The cascading process was seen as an opportunity to streamline the entire planning process in the organization. Services were able to use the corporate Value Creation Map as guidance in order to ensure that their planning was aligned with the corporate objectives. The mapping process allowed every service to make their strategy explicit and easy to communicate which also encouraged Services to integrate their strategy with operations at Unit and Departmental level. In Belfast City Council the Value Creation Map process has now replaced the previous corporate planning process.

Initially, two cascades were conducted for the Parks Section and the Information Systems Belfast (ISB).

These maps were designed using the same approach as that used for the creation of the corporate map: senior officers and members were interviewed, the data was analyzed and a draft map was created, the map was refined in a feedback workshop and a final map was created. Once the map was complete, project teams within the two services took on the coordination role of defining the elements, key performance questions, and key performance indicators.

For the remaining 24 Service cascades, a more time and resource efficient way of cascading was developed. Belfast City Council created a workbook "How to create your Service level Value Creation Map" which outlined and explained the necessary steps involved in designing local value creation maps, KPQs and KPIs. This workbook explained the aims of the entire initiative and outlined the process step-by-step using

Figure 4.5 **BCC Workbook**

examples and illustrations from both the corporate and the two Service level implementation (see Figure 4.5). The workbook was widely distributed inside the organization and outlined the following six steps of the cascading process: Establish your team, collate and analyze all relevant information, agree your initial Value Creation Map, define your strategic elements, develop and expand your performance indicators, and agree your ongoing review and reporting mechanisms.

Each Service was asked to establish a team to take on the responsibility of coordinating and facilitating the cascade within their Service. This team was then asked to collate the necessary and relevant information about the current strategy such as the business plan and other strategy related documents.

A workshop was arranged for each Service to facilitate the design of their Value Creation Map. The Service level cascade team together with the head of Service decided who else from their Service they wanted to invite to the cascade workshop. The workshops were attended by groups of between five and 20 people from each Service.

Externally facilitated by API, the aim was to complete the key elements of the Value Creation Map using the existing maps as guiding examples. Once the maps were created, the internal Service level cascade team took on the role of moving the cascade forward and the responsibility of coordinating and facilitating the creation of definitions, key performance questions, key performance indicators as well as future reporting and review processes. However, this team was not left without support to do this. A member of the corporate Core Improvement Team was assigned to each Service in order to provide support. This also allowed continuous communication and reviews to take place and ensured that everyone was learning from each other. Most importantly, it ensured that the planning process was coordinated centrally in order to achieve alignment between corporate and Service level strategies, as well as alignment across the different services.

Christchurch City Council case example

As a further case example, consider Christchurch City Council. It created a Strategy Map and Balanced Scorecard at the executive level and then down to the units. Each Plan on a Page houses core of "vital few," objectives (with supporting measures and targets). These align all the scorecard levels. These objectives, which Planning and

Performance Manager Peter Ryan refers to as "the spine of the organization," are:

Customer: deliver long-term plan levels of service and projects

Finance: deliver services and projects to budget

Process: "create the long-term council community plan for 2009–19," plus "instill customer-centric processes"

People: implement organizational workforce planning ("right people, right place, right time") and "increase staff engagement" (measured via international Hewitt methodology).

Figures 4.6 and 4.7 show the Plan on the Page Strategy Maps for City Environment and the Strategy and Planning Group.

What is notable about The City of Christchurch's Plans on the Page is that they do not show cause and effect linkages which we stress is critical in designing useful Strategy Maps. Ryan explains his thinking. "There is usually a many-to-many relationship in our strategies, which makes the documenting of cause and effect problematic," he says. He provides the relationship between staff engagement and service delivery as one example. "This relationship alone

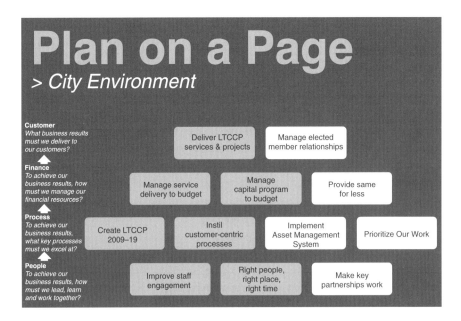

Figure 4.6 **City Environment**

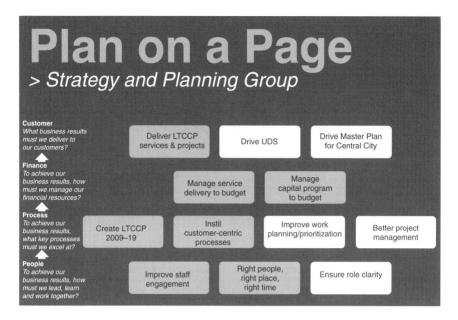

Figure 4.7 **Strategy & Planning Group**

could generate twenty cause and effect arrows on the Strategy Map, which would be confusing."

"So we test for these cause and effect relationships when building the scorecards, but we don't plaster dozens of cause and effect arrows all over them when we communicate the maps." Ryan concludes that there is a point in strategy development where a balance must be struck between the academic correctness of the game plan and the ability to communicate that plan. "Finding that point – where the strategy has integrity but is also appealing and comprehensible to staff – is what makes for a good implementation," he says.

Ministry of Works case example 2

Following the creation of the corporate map, cascaded maps and scorecards were created at sector and directorate levels (14 devolved scorecards in total) within the Ministry of Work's (MoW) Bahrain. As with the corporate Strategy Map, each devolved map had to align to four strategic themes: public/private partnership, key planning player, quality service and leading professional organization.

For instance, consider the Strategy Map for the "roads sector" (Figure 4.8). While keeping the same "leading professional organization,"

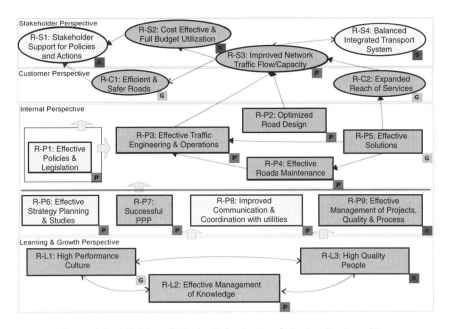

Figure 4.8   **Ministry of Works, Bahrain, Roads Sector Strategy Map**

objectives (as described in the learning and growth perspective), roads captures the "key planning player" theme through objectives such as "effective strategy planning and studies" within the internal process perspective and "balanced integrated transport system" from the stakeholder perspective. The quality service theme is captured through objectives such as "effective management of projects, quality and process" from the internal perspective and "expanded reach of services" from the customer perspective. A full scorecard of measures, targets and initiatives support the map.

As a powerful example of how the "theme" cascade extends to the support units, note the Strategy Map for the Human Resources function (Figure 4.9). Not surprisingly the bulk of its objectives relate to the "leading professional organization" theme, but also well represented are objectives that relate to the "quality of service" theme, such as "improved HR project management practices" within the learning and growth perspective and "enhance HR process excellence" within the internal perspective. Once more, the map is supported by a scorecard of measures, targets and initiatives. For example, "better management of people" an objective from the internal process perspective is supported by a measure of "leadership and management style" and an initiative to implement an employee satisfaction survey.

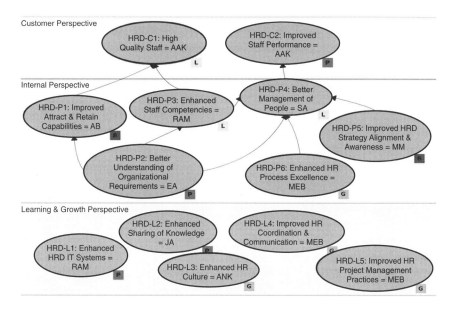

Figure 4.9   **Ministry of Works, Bahrain, HR Strategy Map**

3-D STRATEGY MAPS

The US-based consultant Bill Barberg played an important early role in the MoW scorecard program and as cited the scorecarding approach drew heavily on his methodology. He was also one of the scorecard thought leaders who we interviewed as a part of the research for this book. He provides this innovative technique for cascading. "Here is where we emphasize a concept of 2-D and 3-D cause and effect logic. 2-D cause and effect are the traditional relationships that can show up on a classic Strategy Map, which is 2-dimensional. The logic typically flows up and is between objectives for that particular organizational unit. The 3-D cause and effect logic is about cascading, and the mental picture is to have stacked Strategy Maps or scorecards and in some cases, the cause and effect logic is through the 3rd dimension, linking between maps or scorecards. So, by the usage of software we encourage people to think in terms of both the 3-D cause and effect (supporting the objectives on higher-level scorecards) and the 2-D cause and effect (the logic of drivers within their own organizational unit)."

Heat maps

At whatever level the Strategy Map is built, a technique that we encourage for the identification of improvement opportunities is a heat map

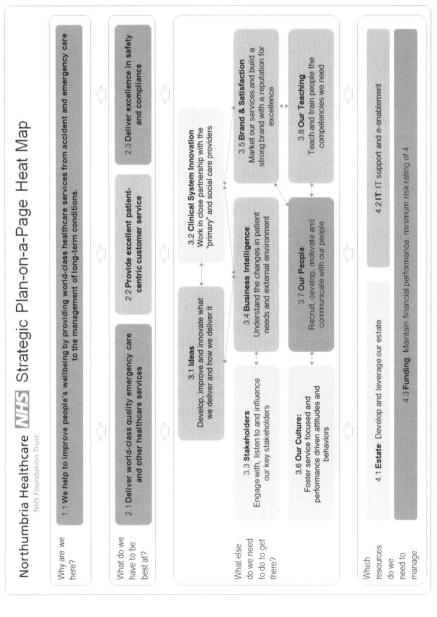

Figure 4.10 **Northumbria Healthcare Heat Map**

(an example of which is shown in Figure 4.10). A heat map is a color coded version of a strategy map that highlights current performance levels. The typical colors that we recommend are:

- Blue: Better than expected
- Green: Everything good
- Yellow: Some issues
- Amber: Bigger issues
- Red: Not good at all.

Although it is through assessment to key performance indicators that performance colors are assigned on an ongoing basis, NWCCA is one example of an organization that created its first heat map from the initial interviews used to create the map. "The feedback provided excellent insights into what was working well and what wasn't," explains McCusker. "It meant we were quickly able to use the Strategy Map as a performance management tool and to prioritize improvement efforts."

And using a heat map as the basis for prioritization is an important observation. The purpose of color-coding is *not* to turn everything green, but rather to provide prioritization at the strategic level, which requires a balance between green, amber, yellow and red.

CONCLUSION

In this chapter we have explained that creating a Strategy Map – through strategy mapping – is the most important step in a Balanced Scorecard creation process. Get the map right and it becomes a much simpler task to identify the KPIs, initiatives etc, which will transform the organization.

We also explained that building Strategy Maps is still uncommon in public sector organizations, although our plentiful case examples show best practice.

Moreover, we explained that although creating a Strategy Map for a public sector organization follows the same logic as for a commercial enterprise, there are differences: most notably that in the former, the financial perspective is typically relegated in hierarchical order. We also showed a Strategy Map can be properly devolved to deeper levels of the enterprise.

With the map in place the next step is to create the KPQs, KPI and targets that populate the Balanced Scorecard, and this is the focus of the next chapter.

5

AGREEING HIGH LEVEL STRATEGIC OUTCOME TARGETS AND KEY PERFORMANCE INDICATORS

The greater danger for most of us lies not in setting our aim too high and falling short; but in setting our aim too low, and achieving our mark.

Michelangelo, Italian sculptor, painter, architect and poet (1475–1564)

INTRODUCTION

Let's be very clear before we start this chapter that this is not a book about performance measurement. We focus on driving performance improvements using tools like the Balanced Scorecard and Lean, which are both not measurement systems. That said it is our observation that many managers – and unfortunately significant numbers of management consultants – wrongly believe that this is precisely what a Balanced Scorecard is. To an extent this is understandable, as the earliest generation of the Balanced Scorecard, as described by Harvard Business School Professor Dr Robert Kaplan and consultant Dr David Norton, the originators of the "classic" scorecard system, was essentially a "balanced measurement system," that was architected to overcome the problem of organizations being singularly reliant on financial metrics as a performance steer (see Chapter 2).

Furthermore, the term Balanced Scorecard itself strongly suggests a "measurement," focus. As Peter Ryan, Planning and Performance Manager at Christchurch City Council said in the previous chapter: "The problem is that the term Balanced Scorecard conjures up an image of compliance and of a report card. It doesn't do justice to the aim of the methodology," which he says is primarily about large-scale strategic change.

Although we strongly endorse the point that the Balanced Scorecard is not a measurement system metrics, it is of course, an essential part of the framework, as we will explain in this chapter. But within a scorecard context we will pay less attention to the process of measure selection, building and management and the required data collection component than can be acquired elsewhere. Those readers that require a fuller explication of how to build and deploy measures, or Key Performance Indicators (KPIs) within a public sector setting are directed to Bernard Marr's book: "Managing and Delivering Performance: How Government, Public Sector and Not-for-profit Organizations can Measure and Manage What Really Matters."[1]

AN INCREASED MEASUREMENT FOCUS

As the leaders of public sector organizations come under severe pressure to cut costs and drive significant efficiency gains, it can be expected that many will become even more measurement-focused and rush to identify and implement a suite of "cost-cutting," metrics.

Although understandable, this will likely lead the organization into a performance sub-optimizing cul-de-sac. The actions put in place to deliver to the metrics might cut costs, but at what cost to service delivery and to the long-term stakeholder relationships (especially with the consumers of public sector services who will not countenance any degradation of services). To understand the broader "costs," efficiency saving metrics must be understood within a wider strategic performance management framework, such as the Balanced Scorecard.

CREATING THE STRATEGY MAP FIRST

It is crucial to point out that KPIs must only be chosen after the Strategy Map (see Chapter 4) has been created. KPIs must fully support and be aligned to the critical few objectives/enablers that the senior team has identified as the drivers of strategic success. As Ryan (who while with Brisbane City Council, Australia[2] led the scorecard implementation that resulted in the organization becoming the first public sector body in the southern hemisphere to be inaugurated into The Palladium Group's Balanced Scorecard Hall of Fame – which is reserved for those who achieve breakthrough performance using the scorecard[3]) says, "Once a sound Strategy Map is built and tested, selecting measures is relatively easy. The need for each measure should have been defined precisely, which makes its identification and characteristics straightforward." Each of the best practice case studies that appear in this book started with the Strategy Map and *then* identified the supporting KPIs and targets (we consider targets later in this chapter). Unfortunately, such organizations are very much in the minority.

COLLECTING MEANINGFUL AND RELEVANT INDICATORS

The Advanced Performance Institute's (API) global survey of over 1100 public sector organizations that led to the white paper "Strategic Performance Management in Government and Public Sector Organizations,"[4] found that "collect meaningful and relevant performance indicators," was one of the ten principles of good performance management (see Chapter 1) as exhibited by those public sector bodies that demonstrated superior performance. But worryingly, the research study reported that only 15% of respondents felt that all of their indicators were linked to the strategy of the organization. Even fewer (6%) believed that all of their performance indicators were meaningful and relevant. Moreover, a staggering 92% reported that many of the indicators were neither meaningful nor relevant.

Externally imposed indicators

Part of the problem, the research finds, is due to the large number of externally imposed indicators placed on public sector organizations by the central Government and other regulatory bodies. Many public sector organizations seem to make the assumption that these are the only indicators they need to collect. As a consequence, they are relying on third parties to tell them how to measure the organization for success.

Unfortunately, many externally imposed measures and targets are *output*-focused, and collected for comparative purposes, to benchmark results with other government and public sector organizations. They provide little insight about the unique strategic objectives of individual organizations and they don't help to measure their unique enablers.

KEY PERFORMANCE QUESTIONS

As cited, KPIs must follow Strategic Maps in the scorecard creation process. In creating a "classic" Balanced Scorecard, KPI selection comes *directly* after map formulation. However, one innovation that many scorecard users have found helpful is the formulation of so-called Key Performance Questions (KPQs).[5] KPQs are a concept developed by Bernard Marr and which has been used extensively by many of our case study organizations.

Key Performance Questions described

To explain, a KPQ is a management question that captures exactly what managers want to know when it comes to reviewing each of their strategic objectives. The rationale for KPQs is that they focus our attention on what actually needs to be discussed when we review performance and most importantly they provide guidance for collecting meaningful and relevant performance indicators. Far too often organizations jump straight to designing indicators before being clear about what they want to know. By first designing KPQs organizational leaders are able to ask themselves: "What is the best data and management information we need to collect to help us answer our key performance questions?" Starting with KPQs ensures that, by default, all subsequently designed performance indicators are relevant. In addition, KPQs put performance data into context and therefore facilitates communication, guides discussion and directs decision-making.

Google case example

If we might be momentarily permitted to interject a short case illustration form the commercial sector, an example of how powerful KPQs can be in strategic performance management comes from Google – one of today's most successful and admired companies. Google Chief Executive Officer (CEO) Eric Schmidt says:

> We run the company by questions, not by answers. So in the strategy process we've so far formulated 30 questions that we have to answer [...] You ask it as a question, rather than a pithy answer, and that stimulates conversation. Out of the conversation comes innovation. Innovation is not something that I just wake up one

day and say "I want to innovate." I think you get a better innovative culture if you ask it as a question.[6]

Audit Scotland case example

Switching our attention back to the public sector, consider Audit Scotland, which has used KPQs to form the bridge between strategic objectives and enablers (as described on its Strategy Map – see Figure 2.12) and KPIs as well as prioritizing and providing performance context to the indicators chosen.

Diane McGiffen, Audit Scotland's Director, Corporate Services, describes how KPQs work alongside KPIs: "People in most organizations, and we are no exception, have quite rightly developed strong disciplines in KPIs as a way to monitor and improve performance," she says. "KPQs do not replace KPIs but are an enhancement. KPQs help us to capture a much richer set of information than can be gained solely from performance data."

Today, KPQs are used to discuss performance at many organizational levels within Audit Scotland. They are used within the senior management team and initially through dedicated coffee mornings in which members of the senior team use KPQs to discuss performance with a wide selection of staff. McGiffen makes the interesting observation that in general she finds that people prefer working with KPQs than KPIs. "Employees see KPQs as more real and meaningful as they enable a focused and rich discussion, which is much more difficult with drier indicators."[7]

MAPS, KPQs and KPIs

We will now provide illustrations of how the objectives on the Strategy Map, KPQs and KPIs work together within Audit Scotland's Balanced Scorecard framework to provide this richer view of performance.

Audit Scotland's Strategy Map includes just two core activities (called objectives in their case), one of which is "we will systematically identify and promote good practice to help public bodies to improve." The KPQs to support the objective include: "to what extent has our work led to improvement," and "to what extent are we identifying and actively promoting good practice (or better ways of doing things) to help public bodies improve."

Note that the KPQs focus on both "lagging," (that is how we have performed) and "leading," (how we will improve performance) dimensions, thus enabling a fuller overview of past, present and likely future performance (which has always been a core promise of the Balanced Scorecard).

KPIs for these KPQs include "client feedback," "number of presentation at meetings, events and conferences which include best practice guidance," and "performance audit reports with good practice recommendations."

How Audit Scotland achieves its objectives is largely through the delivery of enabling objectives (called supporting activities in their case), one of which is: "We will closely engage and communicate with our key stakeholders, clients and partners, and other scrutiny bodies."

KPQs used for this activity are "to what extent are we keeping our stakeholders informed about our programs of work and their role/ implications," and "how well do we engage the people we work with." KPIs include "positive stakeholder feedback," (engagement levels, clarity about and acceptance of roles), "website statistics" (downloads, click throughs), and the "number of shared risk assessment frameworks in local government."

Another supporting activity within Audit Scotland is: "We will deliver our work and manage our resources efficiently and effectively and will be clear where we need to improve. We will have excellent governance procedures and will monitor and report on the impact of our work."

The KPQs for this activity include "to what extent have we effectively and efficiently managed our resources to deliver our outputs," and "how effective are our internal governance arrangements for delivering to our objectives." KPIs include: "percentage of audit reports delivered on-time and to budget," "reducing our carbon footprint by one per cent," "percentage of invoices paid within 30 days" and "internal best value reports published."

As a final example of supporting activities, consider: "We will maintain and develop our professional skills and competencies." The KPQs for this activity include "to what extent are our employees engaged and motivated" and "to what extent do we have strong and effective leadership in the organization." KPIs include "staff survey results," "staff focus group feedback." and "360 degree feedback (through which employees are appraised by a range of people, including their managers, colleagues and direct reports."

Scottish Intellectual Assets Centre case example

As another best practice case example of using KPQs (and staying in Scotland) consider The Scottish Intellectual Assets Centre, the operational arm of Scottish Intellectual Asset Management Limited. The center is a public sector organization developed as a joint subsidiary of the two development agencies of Scotland, Scottish Enterprise and Highlands and Islands Enterprise. The center is based in Glasgow and is sponsored by the Scottish Government and part-financed by the European Union.[8]

The Intellectual Assets (IA) Centre is another of our case examples (see also the North West Commercial Collaborative Agency) that has created a Strategy Map and accompanying KPQs and KPI, even though it is a small organization. The IA Centre is a highly professional team of just ten people when the map etc were first created in late 2006/early 2007, whose responsibilities reflect the company's commitment to the highest standards of efficiency, business effectiveness and their key strategic role in Scotland's economic future (therefore, once more stressing the efficiency/effectiveness balance that we stress throughout this book).

The Strategy Map for the IA Centre is shown in Figure 5.1. The top level (1) describes the key stakeholder proposition; level 2 describes the core competencies; and level 3 the key enablers or value drivers.

A project team was set up within the IA Centre to take the design of KPQs forward. In close communication with both staff and managers, a set of KPQs was drafted. Once the questions were finalized, the

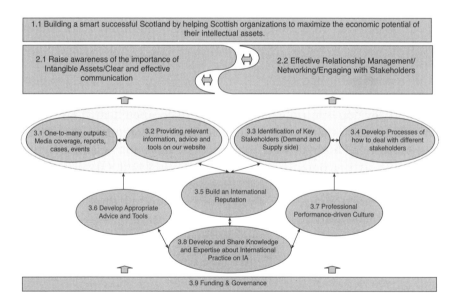

Figure 5.1 **IA Centre Strategy Map**

TABLE 5.1 **KPQ and KPI examples from the Scottish Intellectual Assets Centre**

Core competence	Key Performance Questions	Key Performance Indicators
Raise awareness of the importance of core competences/clear and effective communication	Is there an increasing awareness of the value of IA?	Annual customer satisfaction survey
	Has the typical representative of corporate Scotland a degree of familiarity with IA and interested/motivated to take it further?	Baseline study output Customer survey and follow up questionnaire
	Is the effective Intellectual Asset Management by Scottish organizations improving/increasing?	Outputs of external projects evaluation Number of business accessing further IA support Number of intermediaries developing their IA services to clients
Key Enabler/Value Driver		
Build an international reputation	What has been the increase in our profile?	Survey results (international portal)
	Has our national reputation been enhanced (as a center of excellence)?	Result of baseline study Testimonials
	Have we enhanced our reputation internationally?	International requests for comments, articles, advice, presentations, meetings, etc.
Develop and share knowledge and expertise about international practice on IA	Are we learning and increasing our knowledge?	Conference attendance, papers and articles, study visits, research conducted Number of studies undertaken Number of case studies developed Employee survey
	Are we sharing knowledge/experience?	Increase in records held centrally Access to records – file server log

same team facilitated the design of performance indicators to help answer the Key Performance Questions. Note that the team found the discipline of designing KPQs to be instrumental in designing meaningful performance indicators as the process forced a reflection on how to collect data with real information value instead of just counting anything that is easy to measure.

Table 5.1 provides examples of KPQs and KPIs that support several of the IA Centre's Value Creation Map elements: the core competence "raise awareness of the importance of core competences/ clear and effective communication," and the key enablers/value drivers "build an international reputation," and "develop and share knowledge and expertise about international practice on IA."

International Baccalaureate case example

As a final case example of using KPQs, consider the International Baccalaureate (IB) organization.[9] Each "bubble" within the Strategy Map (see Figure 4.1) is supported by KPQs and KPIs.

"The process of thinking about and designing key performance questions has proven extremely useful," comments IB's Head of Strategy, Andrea Smith, "We already had a set of KPIs in place, but when we looked at them through the lens of the KPQs we found that they weren't that useful," she says. "They were much more operational that strategic and it became evident that we didn't have any KPIs that were really tracking the long-term health of the organization," she says, adding that, "The senior team is really focused on our strategic priorities and in understanding what it is that we are trying to do. That is why it is important to get the questions right and to make sure that KPQs and KPIs work together in delivering to the map."

Examples of IB KPQs are provided by the "teacher development," core competence. For this, IB has identified four KPQs, including: "to what extent are we offering the teacher development people want," which in turn is supported by KPIs such as "teacher feedback," and "school feedback" (impact of IB performance on school training). Another "teacher development," KPQ is "To what extent are we training more teachers," which is supported by the KPIs "number of teachers trained to teach IB courses," and "number of teachers trained per authorized program."

Switching attention to IB's key performance enablers, "research" is supported by three KPQs, such as "to what extent do we understand the impact of an IB education" and "to what extent are we collecting evidence to inform our product development," both of which are supported by KPIs that focus on research findings.

Finally, consider IB's "our key resources" perspective. "Our people and our values," is supported by KPQs such as "to what extent are we keeping and managing our talent," which has the supporting KPI of "staff turnover/experience profile," while the KPQ: "To what extent do we have the diverse workforce that we need," has the supporting KPI "diversity profiles."

A 10-STEP GUIDE TO CREATING KPQS

The following is a powerful ten-step guide for creating KPQs, which has been used successfully by many of our case study organizations.

1. Design between one and three KPQs for each strategic objective on the Strategy Map
2. Ensure KPQs are performance related
3. Engage people in the creation of your KPQs
4. Create short and clear KPQs
5. KPQs should be open questions
6. KPQs should focus on the present and future
7. Refine and improve your KPQs as you use them
8. Use your KPQs to design relevant and meaningful performance indicators
9. Use KPQs to refine and challenge existing performance indicators
10. Use KPQs to report, communicate and review performance.

We will now discuss each of these ten steps in a little more detail and provide more practical advice for creating good KPQs.

1. Design between one and three KPQs for each strategic objective on your Strategic Map

Key questions should be based on what matters in your organization – your strategy. Once you have clarified your strategic objectives and captured them within a Strategy Map you can start designing KPQs.

We would recommend that you design between one and three KPQs for each strategic objective or strategic element on your Strategy Map. As with the logic that it is better to restrict a Strategy

Map to a critical few objectives (so to enhance focus and clarity as to what's really important) the fewer KPQs you have the better – and for the same reasons of focus and clarity.

2. Ensure KPQs are performance related

A KPQ has to be about performance. The aim is to design questions you need to regularly revisit and answer in order to better manage your organization. Performance related questions are those that enable an understanding of how well you are implementing your strategic objectives and to what extent you are meeting your objectives and targets.

3. Engage people in the creation of your KPQs

KPQs should not be designed in the boardroom alone. Designing KPQs is a great opportunity to engage everyone in the organization as well as some external stakeholders. Try to involve people in the process and ask them what question they would see as most relevant. Once you have designed a list of KPQs take this back to the subject matter experts or different parts within and outside the organization to collect feedback.

4. Create short and clear KPQs

A good KPQ is relatively short, clear, and unambiguous. It should only contain one question. We often produce a string of questions which makes it much harder to guide meaningful and focused data collection. The language should be clear and not contain any jargon or abbreviations that external people might not understand. Likewise, try to stay away from management buzz words and ensure that the question is easy to understand and use language that people in your organization are comfortable with, understand and use.

5. KPQs should be open questions

Questions can be divided into two types: closed questions and open questions. Closed questions such as "have we met our budget?" can be answered by a simple "yes" or "no," without any further discussion or expansion on the issue. However, if we ask an open question such as "how well are we managing our budget?" the question triggers a wider search for answers and seeks more than a "yes" or "no" response. Open questions make us reflect, they engage our brains to a much greater extent, and they invite explanations and ignite discussion and dialogue. Whenever possible, KPQs should be phrased as open questions.

6. KPQs should focus on the present and future

Questions should be phrased in a way that addresses the present or future: "To what extent are we increasing our market share?" instead of questions that point to the past, e.g. "Has our market share increased?" By focusing on the future we open up a dialogue that allows us to "do" something about the future. We then look at data in a different light and try to understand what the data and management information means for the future. This helps with the interpretation of the data and ensures we collect data that helps to inform our decision-making and performance improvement.

7. Refine and improve your KPQs as you use them

Once KPQs have been created it is worth waiting to see what answers come back – i.e. how well the KPQs help people to make better informed decisions. Once they are in use it is possible to refine them to improve the focus even more. This is a natural process of learning and refinement and organizations should expect some significant change in the first 12 months of using KPQs. Experience has shown that after about 12 months the changes are less frequent and the KPQs become much better.

8. Use your KPQs to design relevant and meaningful performance indicators

Once you have designed a set of good KPQs linked to your strategic objectives and following the above guidelines, you can use them to guide the design of meaningful and relevant performance indicators.

9. Use KPQs to refine and challenge existing performance indicators

KPQs can be used to challenge and refine any existing performance indicators. Linking them to your KPIs can allow you to put them into context and justify their relevance.

10. Use KPQs to report, communicate and review performance

KPQs can also be used to improve the reporting, communication and review of performance information. In performance reporting and communications, organizations should always put the KPQs with the performance data that is being presented. This way the person who looks at the data understands the purpose of why this data is being collected and is able to put it into context. Furthermore, it allows senior managers to reflect on the answers.

KEY PERFORMANCE INDICATORS

As cited, the best indicators are those that help to answer an organization's most important unanswered questions. API has created a performance indicator design template (Figure 5.2) that, amongst other things, ensures that the KPQ link is in place. Note too that at the

Strategic Objective	
Key Performance Question (KPQ): What Question do you want to have an answer to? What are our information needs?	
Who is asking this question? Who is the information customer?	
What will they do with the information? Why are they asking?	
Performance indicator basics:	
KPI ID	
KPI Name	
KPI Owner	
How will the data be collected	
What is the data collection method?	
What is the source of the data?	
What is the formula/scale/ assessment method?	
How often, when and for how long do we collect the data?	
Who collects the data?	
Target	
What is the target or performance threshold(s)?	
Good measures tests	
How well is the indicator measuring performance?	
What are the costs for collecting the data? Justified?	
What dysfunctional behavior could this indicator trigger?	
Reporting	
Describe the audience, frequency, channel and formats for reporting	

Figure 5.2 **KPI Design Template**

top of the template is "Strategic element being assessed," which further ensures that the KPI is strategically relevant.

Strategic and operational measures

It is also important to stress that strategic measures are different from those required to monitor operational performance. While with operational measures, it is desirable to get closer and closer to "real time" measurement, for strategic measurement that is not even what you're striving for. You don't monitor strategic measures day by day, and certainly not hour by hour. (Having said that, the strategic measures may identify some operational measures that need to be more frequently monitored, but they are different from the strategic measures.) Since the strategic measures are more about monitoring progress toward achieving your new and different envisioned destination (as opposed to just doing things better), they don't change that often.

The value of strategic measures is often how they serve as a catalyst for people to understand to where the organization is trying to go and to motivate the work on the journey. Mark Friedman, the creator of Results-Based Accountability, refers to "headline measures" that might show up on the headlines in a newspaper to show dramatic progress. High level strategic measures often fit that description.[10]

In making the final selection of metrics, there might be a requirement to select several in order to illuminate the subject from different angles. Taking the Brisbane City Council Strategy Map (see Figure 2.8) as an example, satisfied customers should, at first glance, be easily dealt with by an overall measure of customer satisfaction. However, other measures were also used – satisfaction with service responsiveness, satisfaction with employees' skills and knowledge, call center transaction times, segmentation and so on. "Using this mix of outcomes and outputs means any lapse in overall satisfaction can be immediately subjected to root cause analysis," explains Peter Ryan.

Extracting insights from metrics

This is an important observation. The purpose of using metrics is to trigger performance improvement. Indeed the API report "Strategic Performance Management in Public Sector and Government

Organizations,"[11] found that one of the ten principles of good performance management was "use indicators to extract relevant insights."

Once organizations have collected meaningful data, they must analyze it before they can work out what it means – e.g. how they may need to change things in order to improve against key strategic goals.

"Performance Management analytics," provide tools and techniques enabling organizations to convert their performance data into *relevant* information and knowledge. Without it, the whole Performance Management exercise is of little or no value to the organization.

Yet many organizations seem to spend the majority of their time and effort on *collecting and reporting* data and not enough time on *extracting valuable and actionable insights* from it. More than half of the respondents to the API global research program (59%) believe that their organization does not have sufficient capabilities to comprehensively analyze performance data; while as many as 87% feel that their analysis capabilities need to be improved. The difference between good and bad information is determined by how well it supports critical decision-making.

Moreover, the research found that the majority of organizations feel that their performance data does not support effective decision-making. Either the data is too operational or the analysis is not being taken to a strategic level, with the largest proportion (36%) disagreeing with the statement "Our performance indicators help us to make better strategic decisions", and a further 3% strongly disagreeing.[12]

Reviewing metrics

Another of the ten principles of good performance management was to "keep the strategic objectives and performance indicators fresh and up-to-date." Simply put, as the organization's strategy and goals are developed and refined, so too must the performance management strategy be flexible. It is of concern that more than one-third of respondents disagree or strongly disagree with the statement "our performance indicators are regularly reviewed and renewed." Just 5% strongly agree with the statement (Figure 5.3).

One key influence to the lack of review is that too many public sector organizations work with a huge amount of metrics. Indeed, 68% of research respondents feel that they have too many indicators.

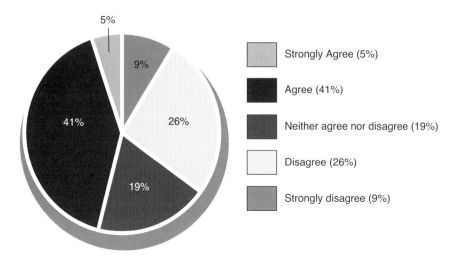

Figure 5.3 **Performance Indicators are Regularly Reviewed**

It's all very well to keep adding new indicators, but if the organization doesn't delete the outdated measures, reporting becomes confused and so overwhelming that decision-makers can't see the woods for the trees.

Quantitative and qualitative indicators

But even when organizations limit the number of KPIs, there's still a predilection for choosing quantitative metrics rather than those that are more qualitative in nature; the former being hard, or objective performance measures with the latter being softer, or subjective. This is not surprising as quantitative data is easier to collect and to translate into meaningful metrics.

Moreover, most of the metrics collected to deliver to external reporting requirements are quantitative, which they must be for benchmarking purposes and the collation of league tables (as is common in education and health, as two examples).

But the fact is that both quantitative and qualitative measures are required in order to get a full picture of organizational performance. A good way to explain this is to use the analogy of a torch. You enter the room – that is so dark that absolutely nothing is visible – and shine the torch into one small area. This provides one view of the room but the information captured would only provide a very narrow understanding of the room. The only way to get the "full picture," is to shine the torch into as many parts of the room as possible and to then analyze, and so make sense of, all of the differing perspectives, insights and observations that the multiple spotlighting provides.

It is typically a good idea to start with a "qualitative," assessment of performance, as this can be a powerful way to highlight issues that are important to stakeholders (focus groups of key stakeholders or simply observing "customer" behavior are two powerful mechanisms for collecting qualitative data). Quantitative metrics (through which the data is collected by using surveys, etc) are then powerful to test ideas and confirm the thoughts that emerge from the qualitative assessment. If the proposition is then proven valid, it will be sensible to use the qualitative approach by which a select few interviews are undertaken to better understand the improvements required and then design the appropriate action plan to make the changes (which we discuss in detail within the next chapter).

Good practice tips for using KPIs

The following provides some extra good practice tips using KPIs.

Common definitions

To be useful for aggregation, comparison and best-practice sharing, measures should be commonly defined organization-wide. Typically this is an early and difficult challenge as it is not unusual to find that performance is measured in many different ways across the enterprise.

The danger of repackaging

It is also important that organizations choose strategic metrics that truly do support strategic objectives and are not a simple repackaging of measures that are already in existence. Indeed it is not surprising for up to 50% of preferred measures to be unavailable on launching the scorecard. Organizations then have to either create the measure from scratch or if data sourcing would prove too time-consuming or expensive opt for proxy measures (a close assimilation).

Ownership

As with strategic objectives, ownership and accountability should be assigned to metrics. Objective and measure ownership is crucial for the operationalizing of the strategy. One of our case study organizations, the Ministry of Works, Bahrain, for instance has owners for more that 170 objectives and supporting metrics and initiatives.

Actionable

Metrics should be actionable. Measures that are nice to know but do not trigger step-change performance improvement typically have no place on a Balanced Scorecard. For instance if an organization has an objective to retain talent and has clearly defined what constitutes talent and has an agreed common enterprise-wide metric, and the measures shows that strategically critical employees are walking out the door, then this should trigger an intervention. Simply put, we have a strategic objective, the measure indicates we are failing to meet that goal and so we do something about it. This represents the most basic, and oldest, premise of the Balanced Scorecard – turning strategy into action.

SETTING TARGETS

Once KPIs are agreed, then targets are assigned for each metric. This is usually a more difficult task for public sector organizations than for their commercial counterparts. Whereas for the latter the choosing of targets can usually be considered in the context of ultimate delivery of shareholder value, for the public sector group there is a host of stakeholders to consider as well as the managing of externally imposed targets.

Moreover, target setting is a challenge for a public sector organization because their performance to targets is typically closely scrutinized by both central Government and national and/or local media. As a result many public sector leaders are reluctant to set challenging or "stretch" targets because of the negative consequences of failure (even if the actual performance is better than the previous year).

Targets for external and internal consumption

Given such scrutiny, we would suggest that targets are set for external consumption and others, more stretching, for internal usage. Those that are external will still need to demonstrate improvement and be positively benchmarked against similar organizations, but will not represent the step-change performance improvement that is central to a successful scorecard implementation. Importantly, we would suggest that while the external targets must of course be monitored, they should typically not be designated "green" or breakthrough performance on the scorecard. They might, for instance, just represent "amber" performance.

Color coding reporting

Color-coding reporting (typically through traffic-light system) is commonly used to report performance to the scorecard. API typically suggests five colors:

- Blue: Better than expected
- Green: Everything good
- Yellow: Some issues
- Amber: Bigger issues
- Red: Not good at all.

Using a color-coding system has interesting applications when considered against performance to longer-term stretch objectives. Bill Barberg, a US-based management consultant, and one of the select few global experts that we interviewed for this books puts it this way.

"The first important thing for targets – especially in a public sector case – is to gain a common agreement on the approach or philosophy for targets and color bands," he says. "If, for example, the target is to achieve a high school graduation rate of 90% by 2020 – and let's assume for this example that the current graduation rate for that community is 65% – then the question is how will the targets and color bands be phased in over time? If 90% was considered the target for every year from 2009 to 2020 and if anything less than 82% was considered "red" then the scorecard is going to look bad for a long time – even if rates are improving nicely in 2010 and 2011. This is an extreme example, but there are many cases where the target is significantly better than current results, and there should be a well-communicated agreement that targets (and the related color bands) will be phased in over time. That means that the same performance that gets a green color in 2009 may become yellow in 2010 because it didn't increase as fast as the target. Charts showing the trend of the actual values and both past and future targets are helpful for this."

Barberg adds that the people who are involved with achieving the targets must be involved with setting them, and the discussions should be about what levels of performance would indicate that they are accomplishing the strategic objectives. "This is one reason that it is important to nail down the details of the strategic objectives before putting too much focus on the targets and initiatives," he says. "Also if the process is helping many different parts of a government entity or community work in a more aligned and coordinated manner, people can begin to envision much more aggressive targets as possible."

Barberg also makes the critical observation that it is very important to establish a clear expectation of how targets will be used. "The message must be delivered that measures are not intended to punish individuals for failing," he says. "Instead, they are ways to determine if the system and processes are achieving satisfactory improvements, and if not, what needs to be done to improve them. Otherwise, people can feel that they are putting bullets into a gun that will be pointed at their own heads."

This observation is important. Metrics should be used as mechanisms for delivering breakthrough (or at least continuous) performance improvement and for learning, and not for "naming and shaming." When the latter is the case, there will be widespread and systematic resistance to the scorecard and the program is unlikely to succeed over the longer term (we speak more about the cultural challenges of scorecard implementation in Chapter 9).

Ministry of Works, Bahrain, case study

One of case organizations, the Ministry of Works (MoW), Bahrain (which was inaugurated into the Palladium Balanced Scorecard Hall of Fame in 2009) is one organization that uses a four as opposed to the conventional three color-coded traffic lights. Red (poor per formance), yellow (less that targeted performance), green (good or targeted performance), and blue (breakthrough performance). Raja Al Zayani, the MoW's Chief of the Strategic Planning Section, states that "adding blue has allowed greater room for differentiation in reporting."

Note that for the reporting of performance to objectives, the status of the four lights is clearly understood as *not* being according to the traffic light metaphor, which is reserved instead for the reporting of initiatives. Raja explains. "The MoW defines objective performance status reporting as a *backward* looking indicator that is based on historical data only, whereas Initiative reporting is in essence the 'management of expectations', and as such is a form of '*forward*' reporting," she says. "Therefore the traffic light metaphor makes sense for the latter but not the former."

Raja comments that a notable weakness of the Balanced Scorecard literature to date is a lack of a discussion of the practical requirements for clarity in the meaning of the reporting of objective and initiative performance status and the differences between the two. "We have gone to great lengths to ensure that a very clear shared understanding of the difference is established and embedded," she says.[13]

Target-setting guidance

As a general guidance to target-setting we propose the following.

1. *Targets and Performance Thresholds* identify the desired level of performance in a specified timeframe and put expected performance levels into context. A long history of research in goal setting theory and target setting practice allows us to state that targets should be (1) specific and time bound, (2) stretching and aspirational but achievable, (3) based on good information. Many studies have shown that well defined targets lead to a greater increase in performance, as opposed to generalized targets of "do your best," which tend to lead to lower performance levels. Targets can be set as absolute targets (increase by five), proportional or percentage targets (increase by 5%), relative to benchmarks (within the top three hospitals in our area or top quartile), or relative to costs or budgets (increase or reduce by 5% of budget). Here are a few tips for setting better targets:

   • Use existing information and review trends and history
   • Consider variations in performance, e.g. peaks, troughs and seasonal factors
   • Take account of national targets, best practice benchmarks, etc
   • Take into account the cause-and-effect relationships, e.g. don't set top level outcome targets before you have set appropriate targets for the enablers and inputs
   • Take into account time lags (consider the time lags between the objectives on the Strategy Map)
   • Take into account any dependence on others such as partner bodies.

Here are some examples of good and poor targets:

Good: "We will reduce the number of missed household bin collections by 5% by next year."

"We will cut the number of unfilled places in primary schools by 10% by 31 December 2011."

"We will increase the number of visits to local libraries by 20% before the end of 2011."

Poor: "We aim to have the best bus service in the region."

"We will improve the way we handle complaints."

"We will answer 75% of all letters within five days" (a poor target if the remaining 25% take three months to answer).

CONCLUSION

This chapter has positioned performance metrics, or KPIs, in their appropriate place within a Balanced Scorecard system. We explained that, although critically important, KPIs are secondary in importance to the Strategy Map. Indeed, organizations should not even consider KPIs until the Strategy Map is agreed.

With best practice case study evidence we also explained that KPQs prove a powerful bridge between the strategic objectives that appear on the Strategy Map and KPIs. The use of KPQs helps better select and prioritize appropriate KPIs.

Furthermore, we explained the process for target selection, explaining that oftentimes this is more of a challenge for the public sector because of the level of scrutiny from various stakeholders.

In the next chapter we describe the process for choosing the strategic initiatives that are selected to drive the organization toward target achievement and ultimate delivery of the strategic objectives. Given the economic and funding challenges faced by public sector organizations, we will major on the deployment of Lean methodologies in the selection and delivery of strategic initiatives.

6

SELECTING STRATEGIC INITIATIVES

There is nothing so useless as doing efficiently that which should not be done at all.

Peter F. Drucker (writer and management consultant)
1909–2005

INTRODUCTION

The Advanced Performance Institute's (API) research report: "Strategic Performance Management in Government and Public Sector Organizations,"[1] found that "align other organizational activities with the strategic aims outlined in the performance management system," was one of the ten principles of good performance management, as exhibited by those public sector bodies that demonstrated superior performance (see Chapter 1 for an overview of the principles and findings).

The research, which was based on a survey of more than 1100 organizations from across the globe, noted that: "When organizations lose sight of what they should be managing and why, they waste a great deal of time and resources producing something which is of little value internally, while potentially de-motivating staff. With this in mind, a Strategic Performance Management system should be used to guide and align other organizational processes – such as budgeting, performance reporting, the management of projects and programs and the management of risks." The report continued to say that: "All too often, however, Government and public sector organizations are found to be running their reporting, risk management, project management and budgeting processes in parallel – as though these are completely unrelated activities."

As we can see from Figure 6.1 although 73% have aligned their performance reporting with strategic aims, less than half have aligned their budgeting and project and program management, and just 14% risk management. A primary message of this book is that everything that an organization does should be connected to the strategy and the objectives that are housed within a Balanced Scorecard Strategy Map (see Chapter 4). In other parts of the book, we explain how other organizational activities should be aligned to the strategy, such as in Chapter 7 where we explain how to make sure that financial management, especially the budgeting process, is hardwired to strategic goals. In this chapter we are concerned with the alignment of strategic initiatives, or the projects or programs that the organization launches as part of the Balanced Scorecard system. It is clear from the API research that in most public sector organizations, the process for managing initiatives is not aligned to the strategic management system, which significantly lessens the likelihood of successful strategy execution.

THE ROLE OF STRATEGIC INITIATIVES

As a quick overview of where initiatives sit within a Balanced Scorecard system viewed sequentially the Strategy Map describes the logic of the strategy, delineating the critical objectives/themes that create value (be that shareholder in a commercial setting or stakeholder for a public sector organization). The second "component" of the system identifies the appropriate metrics and targets for each

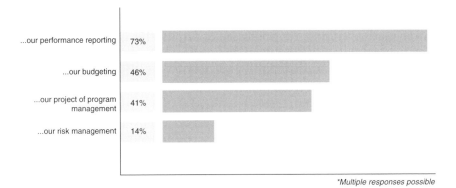

Q: Our Performance Management system is fully aligned and integrated with...

...our performance reporting 73%

...our budgeting 46%

...our project of program management 41%

...our risk management 14%

*Multiple responses possible

Figure 6.1 **Alignment with Performance Management**

113

strategic objective (see the previous chapter). The third "components" represents the action programs (initiatives and budgets) that must be launched to deliver the performance outcomes. Choosing strategic initiatives is, therefore, the final step in creating a complete Balanced Scorecard.

The importance of strategic initiatives

Although sequentially the selection of strategic initiatives is, and quite rightly, the final step in the scorecard creation process, it is certainly not the least important. Indeed, we would argue that in a hierarchy of importance it is trumped by only strategic objectives. This is because the deployment of initiatives is where "the rubber hits the road," as some would say. Put another way, it is where the real work of strategy implementation takes place. Organizations do not move forward, and certainly do not achieve breakthrough performance simply by identifying objectives (however appropriate). And measures are essentially how we track performance to those objectives.

Of course selected initiatives need to be resourced, in both human and financial terms. For public sector organizations, the appropriate allocation of resources will likely be a highly challenging and complex process for some years ahead. The increased Government debt burdens across the world, as a result of the funding required to introduce massive rescue packages and increase spending to divert nations from potentially cataclysmic economic recessions following the so-named credit crunch, will mean significant constrictions in public funding. Reduced budgets will mean less in the way of resources on which to operate.

Naturally, the easiest way to contend with budget reductions is to simply slash spending. For public sector firms if this is done it will likely lead to a reduction in service quality. But another core message of this book is that even when finances are restrained this is simply not an option. Citizens (the consumers of public sector services and products) will demand that a high level of service quality is maintained. Simply put, public sector leaders have to find ways to deliver "more with less," as we have titled this book. Delivering more value with money will require close attention be paid to the initiatives that the leaders of public sector bodies green-light: contending with reduced budgets means that public sector organizations need to be clearer than ever regarding their remits and priorities.

INITIATIVE SELECTION: THE STRATEGIC LINK

And this brings us to a discussion on initiative selection. As part of the scorecard creation process, the first important point to make is that in choosing strategic initiatives the overriding criteria is that they must link directly though to objectives on the Strategy Map. Simply, no initiative should be launched or funded unless this link is unequivocally proven. This is because the purpose of an initiative is to close an identified gap between actual and required levels of performance to achieve a strategic outcome. Indeed, if an initiative is deemed critical for the success of the organization and does not correspond to an objective, then it signals a failing of the Strategy Map.

International Baccalaureate case example

The leadership team of our case organization International Baccalaureate (IB) is fully aware that successfully delivering to the objectives on the Strategy Map (see Figure 4.1) is largely dependent on the performance improvement initiatives that are subsequently launched (and in keeping with our best practice process after the relevant KPQs and KPIs are identified). To that end, IB's Head of Strategy Andrea Smith and her performance management team liaised with the organization's project management office to ensure that projects green-lighted by the organization were fully aligned to the Strategy Map. "Projects will be agreed by the senior team based on the strategic relevance and the needs of the map," explains Smith.[2]

Ministry of Works, Bahrain case example 1

Our case organization the Ministry of Works, (MoW) Bahrain, is another that involves the project management office in ensuring initiatives are strategically relevant. Indeed the MoW considers itself a leader in integrating strategy management with performance and project management which work together to reinforce the ability to execute upon the MoW strategy. The Minister of Works His Excellency Fahmi Bin Ali Al-Jowder comments "Strategy and performance management go hand in hand, and we continue to link core business and management initiatives with operational projects and this will ensure improved performance at technical, managerial and individual levels."[3]

The close involvement of the project management office at both IB and MoW are examples of how to ensure that "project/program" component of the "align other organizational activities with the strategic aims outlined in the performance management system," good practice principle of the cited API research. Of course, it also ensures that initiatives (which are oftentimes expensive and resource hungry) are fully aligned to strategic goals.

INITIATIVE SELECTION TEMPLATES

Cutting costs by "doing nothing"

In a moment we will consider some initiative selection templates. But first we will highlight one, oftentimes under-valued, aspect of selecting initiatives as part of a properly architected Balanced Scorecard system and one that should capture the attention of senior public sector leaders that are grappling with the dilemma of how to deliver "more value with less money." The fact is that case evidence proves that the simple process of initiative selection (so the steps taken before any projects actually go live) can itself lead to significant cost savings. So money can be saved without actually "doing" anything.

To explain, when objectives are clear and limited to the select few that really drive strategic performance, a properly designed process of initiative selection will typically lead to the jettisoning of well-established, and often expensive, projects. It is not unusual that perhaps 50% or more of existing projects will be cancelled as a consequence of a properly architected Balanced Scorecard framework. Some organizations have found that simply listing all the initiatives underway enterprise-wide and killing those that might have been launched for good reasons but are no longer strategically relevant, often leads to savings that have been calculated in the millions of dollars (as was celebrated in the case at Wells Fargo Online Banking, an early scorecard pioneer).

However, cancelling high-profile projects may lead to resistance from the senior executive that sponsors the initiative. Describing through the scorecard why the initiative is no longer strategically relevant may help overcome this resistance. The scorecard should make clear what needs to be achieved to deliver to the strategy – and why. If compelling evidence is still not enough to convince the sponsoring executive to kill a project, then it is the responsibility of the CEO to order project cancellation. The political complexities in giving such an order clearly demonstrate why the CEO must not just pay lip service to the scorecard, but demonstrate support with clear action. Indeed, a couple of years ago one of the authors of this book spoke at a Balanced Scorecard conference and while there sat in dismay as he listened to a practitioner from one large commercial organization explain how the scorecarding process has identified a multi-million dollar project that was no longer strategically relevant and was top of the list for cancellation – however the program continued because the CEO "did not want to challenge the senior manager that was championing the project."

As well as projects that are no longer relevant, there's a further bunch of initiatives where several departments are tackling the same issue, and are unaware of each other's efforts. The transparency of performance and activities resulting from the scorecard creation enables managers to bring these teams together and so reduce the number of initiatives and cost burden. Later in this chapter we highlight the importance of launching strategic initiatives that cut across functions and departments.

A HIGH LEVEL GUIDE TO INITIATIVE SELECTION

As a high-level guide to strategic initiative selection, consider the three elements of: prioritization, resource allocation and accountability. Completing this simple exercise will likely deliver both efficiency and effectiveness dividends.

1. Prioritization

For each strategic objective simply order the initiatives (new and existing) in order of perceived importance. This is a relatively straightforward exercise, but one that can deliver immediate benefits as it

a)   shows just how many initiatives are underway enterprise-wide (the sheer number and aggregate cost might surprise many of the senior leaders)

b)   enables a first discussion as to "why" these projects are being dispatched (the benefits) and therefore allow senior managers to comment on how they see the programs linking (or not) to strategic goals.

Crucially, therefore, at the corporate level, the initiative prioritization process should involve the senior team and be a key part of the scorecard creation process. Note that just as at the corporate level the senior team must be responsible for selecting objectives, measures and targets, they must also do the same for initiatives: especially important because it is only at the initiative level that money is spent. This takes us to Step 2:

2. Resource allocation

Step 2 starts with creating a cost breakdown for each of the strategic objectives. As part of this it is important to map the required resources to the intended initiatives : this ensures that the resources are allocated in the right way. Organizations can use a heat map to get further guidance on resource allocation. As explained in Chapter 4, a heat map is a powerful tool for the identification of improvement opportunities (as an example of a heat map see Figure 4.11). A heat map is a color coded system that highlights current performance levels. The typical colors that we recommend are:

– Blue: Better than expected
– Green: Everything good
– Yellow: Some issues
– Amber: Bigger issues
– Red: Not good at all.

For initiative selection, the red areas might point to areas where the significant improvement of performance might require the implementation of a strategic initiative. Simply mapping ball park budgets and man-days to the initiatives will bring out potential imbalances.

Belfast City Council case example

Using a heat map for initiative prioritization has been central to the strategic improvement efforts at our case organization, Belfast City Council.[4]

Once the city council officers had defined and agreed the strategy and created the Strategy Map (see Figure 2.13) and KPQs and KPIs they realized alignment and prioritization of organizational initiatives and programs needed to take place. To help with/enable this process a heat map was created. In order to facilitate the process all existing corporate initiatives, projects and programs were identified and mapped onto the Strategy Map. This was a powerful process as it provided insights such as:

- Some elements of the new strategy had few or no initiatives, projects or program linked to them – indicating that new initiatives would be needed in order to deliver on the strategy.
- Some projects couldn't be mapped against any of the strategic elements on the Strategy Map, indicating that such projects would not contribute directly to the implementation of the new strategy. The implication of a mismatch between strategy and projects can be twofold – either the strategy has to be revised because important elements of the organizations are missing, or – which is more likely – a serious discussion needs to take place about the reasons for doing these projects.
- The balance of projects/initiatives was wrong. A few of the strategic elements had the majority of the projects linked to them, whereas others – often the red or amber ones – had few projects, initiatives or programs linked to them. This triggered a discussion about readjusting the balance.

With Belfast City Council, this process of identifying, mapping and prioritizing initiatives, projects and programs became the basis for their business planning going forward.

Figure 6.2 shows a template, originated by the consultancy Palladium, that shows how to map initiatives against strategic objectives on the Strategy Map. It shows where objectives have no initiatives and others than have more than one initiative. The most powerful initiatives are those that impact more than one objective and will typically receive preference over others.

3. Accountability

Public sector organizations have a reputation of initiating major initiatives with little or no accountability. Some high profile examples include the Big Dig in Boston, USA (a highway project that was estimated in 1985 at $2.8 billion but actually cost a staggering $22 billion.[5]

As an example of good project management consider the Metro in Delhi (the vision is to cover the whole of Delhi with a Metro network by and be to world-class standards in regard to safety, reliability, punctuality, comfort and customer satisfaction). This project made its project manager Elattuvalapil Sreedharan (now its CEO) a famous

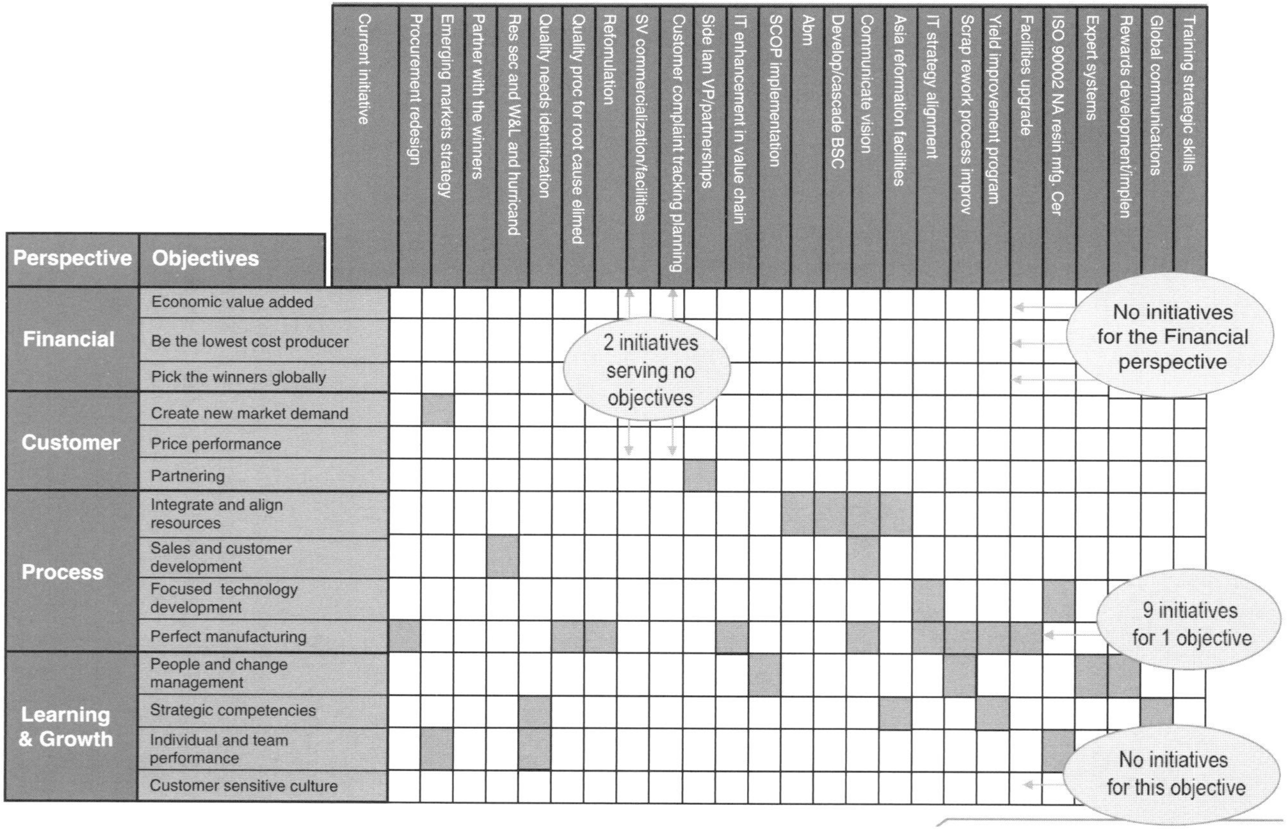

Figure 6.2 Palladium Template for Initiative Selection

Initiatives (rows):
- Training strategic skills
- Global communications
- Rewards development/implen
- Expert systems
- ISO 90002 NA resin mfg. Cer
- Facilities upgrade
- Yield improvement program
- Scrap rework process improv
- IT strategy alignment
- Asia reformation facilities
- Communicate vision
- Develop/cascade BSC
- Abm
- SCOP implementation
- IT enhancement in value chain
- Side lam VP/partnerships
- Customer complaint tracking planning
- SV commercialization/facilities
- Refomulation
- Quality proc for root cause elimed
- Quality needs identification
- Res sec and W&L and hurricand
- Partner with the winners
- Emerging markets strategy
- Procurement redesign

Current initiative

Perspective / Objectives (columns):

Perspective	Objectives
Financial	Economic value added
	Be the lowest cost producer
	Pick the winners globally
Customer	Create new market demand
	Price performance
	Partnering
Process	Integrate and align resources
	Sales and customer development
	Focused technology development
	Perfect manufacturing
Learning & Growth	People and change management
	Strategic competencies
	Individual and team performance
	Customer sensitive culture

Callouts:
- No initiatives for the Financial perspective
- 9 initiatives for 1 objective
- No initiatives for this objective
- 2 initiatives serving no objectives

120

and highly celebrated person in India – he was actually voted "Indian of the Year."

Just as it's critically important that accountability is assigned to each objective on the Strategy Map and to each KPI, it's equally vital that one person is assigned responsibility and accountability for each strategic initiative.

Ministry of Works, Bahrain case example 2

Our case organization the MoW is one firm that ensures that owner-ship is assigned to each strategic initiative, thus ensuring that defined accountabilities are in place.[6] Indeed ever single strategic theme, objective, KPI and initiatives within the MoW's suite of 15 Balanced Scorecards has a designated owner.

The MoW's initiative selection process

The initiative selection process within the MoW begins with the generating of an inventory of all programs – present and new. These are then mapped against the strategic objectives they would support so to determine their strength of alignment. The initiatives are then scored against importance and difficulty dimensions. Criteria include resource impact, predicted risk and project benefits (see Figure 6.3). A first filter assesses initiatives based on their importance and a second filter assesses initiatives based on their balance between their benefits and their difficulty (costs, risks, complexity). The final list of initiatives is then prioritized using an automated score as a base for a final judgment-based prioritization. Those selected initiative appear on the relevant scorecard and are tracked and reported on accordingly.

MoW initiative examples

As an example of how initiatives support objectives and metrics within the MoW's corporate Strategy Map, consider "effective management of knowledge," a strategic objective within the learning and growth perspective and part of the "leading professional organization," theme. Metrics include "comprehensiveness of knowledge management practices and policies," which is supported by strategic initiatives such as "implementation of the strategic information system plan," and "initiate knowledge management practices."

Initiative Name		Initiative ID	
Initiative Description			

Supported Objective ID	Driving Theme	
Supported Objective ID	Theme Owner	
Supported Objective ID	Proposed Initiative Owner	

Strategic Importance		Difficulty	
Alignment		Risk/Capability/Readiness	
Payoffs/Benefits		Cost/Complexity	

Strategic Dependencies Initiative ID	D1	D2	D3	D4	D4

Major Milestones	FY 2007				FY 2008				FY 2009				FY 2009			
	Q1	Q2	Q3	Q4	Q1	Q2	Q3	Q4	Q1	Q2	Q3	Q4	Q1	Q2	Q3	Q4
1																
2																
3																
4																
5																
6																
7																
8																
9																
10																

Resource Requirements	FY 2007	FY 2008	FY 2009	FY 2010	Total
People					
$					
Other					

Figure 6.3 **Initiative Selection Template**

As a further example from the "quality of services" theme, "improved management of quality," is an objective within the internal process perspective. Metrics include "continual quality management (QM) practices," and is supported by initiatives to achieve QM certification and implement Total Quality Management programs. The MoW corporate Strategy Map is shown in Figure 4.2.

The difference between objectives and initiatives: The MoW experience

A final observation about the MoW's approach to identifying and deploying strategic initiatives is that the organization has taken the time to fully understand the difference between a strategic objective and a strategic initiative and ensure this informs the relevant objective/ initiative description and selection process.

Understanding the difference is something of an ongoing challenge within the scorecard community as oftentimes strategy maps are actually a collection of initiatives, not objectives. This confusion led to the MoW's first attempt at using a Balanced Scorecard to be less successful that it should have been, as Raja Al Zayani, Chief of the Strategic Planning Section explains. "As a result, the reporting of performance often became more about measuring progress against an initiative rather than performance to strategic objectives." This led to some initial resistance to the scorecard effort in the early days.

Today, however, the MoW clearly differentiates between objectives and initiatives. The MoW defines an objective as a desired state – indeed it might represent an as yet unrealized position. And it can be argued that a strategic objective *should be* something that has yet to be realized, and therefore represents breakthrough performance. Keep in mind that the Balanced Scorecard is a framework for step-change, not incremental improvement.

As examples from the MoW's corporate map, objectives are "world-class roads infrastructure," and "effective strategy management and alignment." So these are in essence destinations. They are what the MoW *intends* to achieve.

Where "doing" words (or work) come into play is typically at the initiative level. So initiatives within the MoW include "initiate knowledge management practices," as already cited. As another example "implement an employee satisfaction survey" is an initiative to support an objective focused on "excellent management of people." In short, an objective describes "what" an organization wants to achieve, whereas an initiative describes "how" the objective will be achieved.

As we explain more fully in Chapter 8, the MoW uses a four-color code for reporting performance to objectives (with blue – or breakthrough performance being added to the more conventional green, yellow and red) and the traditional three color code for reporting initiatives, believing that reporting to objectives is backward looking whereas reporting to initiatives is forward looking. As much as anything this shows that the MoW recognizes that it is through initiatives that the real work of strategy implementation takes place.

As further examples of initiative selection processes, consider the following that have been deployed by public sector organizations at various times over the past decade or so and been observed by the authors of this book. Indeed within the public sector there are many approaches to initiative selection, and many that have been proven useful over time.

State of Washington, USA, Department of Revenue case example

In identifying initiatives, the Department of Revenue within the State of Washington, USA, put in place a three-tiered hierarchical system for initiative prioritization, and therefore for resource allocation to initiatives.[7] The three tiers are:

Tier 1: Essential – initiatives with the organization's highest level of commitment, which are certain of funding.
Tier 2: Important – those that are very important, but must be considered against others if funds are limited.
Tier 3: Beneficial – initiatives that are only pursued if they do not infringe upon higher level priorities.

Within the Department of Revenue, initiative identification begins with brainstorming in each of its divisions, after which the executive coordinating team, comprising divisional heads, selects initiative candidates. Team members individually sort these candidates into the three-tier order with the final priorities being agreed to by consensus within the group.

As a result, the organization has created a common understanding of resource priorities amongst the senior team. If budgets need to be scaled back during the year for any reason, it is clear which initiatives will be affected first.

An example of a Tier 1 initiative that ran from 2003–2009 is e-government, which connects to the department's strategy for delivering enhanced service through the Internet and other electronic means.

As a final example, an employee survey found concerns around morale, trust and respect. The initiatives to improve performance in these areas were prioritized and became one of the top three initiatives in the Tier 1 level of the strategic business plan.

Hertfordshire Fire and Rescue Service UK, case example

As part of its Balanced Scorecard effort, The UK-based Hertfordshire Fire and Rescue (F&R) Service shaped what it called a "both feet" model.[8]

Through this, managers have to make a robust business case for funding. The model has to provide an impact analysis for any proposed initiative. This has to cover the following criteria:

B – Business objectives.
O – Opportunities for work/life balance.
T – Training.
H – Health and safety.
F – Finance and resources (people and property).
E – Equalities.
E – Environment.
T – Technology.

"In making a proposal based on the 'both feet' model, managers have to show how the initiative will positively impact at least one of our critical success factors," explained then Deputy Chief Jim Wallace, "If they can't do this then the proposal will not even be considered."

Scottish Enterprise case example

A different twist on the initiative funding process is provided by the development agency Scottish Enterprise. The organization separated out initiative funding from the annual budgeting process (we discuss how Scottish Enterprise revamped its budgeting process to more strategic in nature and in support of a Balanced Scorecard in Chapter 8).[9]

Director of Network Performance and Learning Julian Taylor provided the background: "It became clear that there was often a real challenge in launching longer-term strategic initiatives that had to be re-budgeted for 12-month cycles. The Balanced Scorecard approach encourages clear thinking and a commitment to strategy execution on a continual basis: an annual planning process is simply too rigid."

As a consequence, the process for initiative funding takes place away from the annual budgeting cycle. Essentially, teams are assured that resources will be made available for their projects so long as they fulfill two very strict criteria:

(a) Every project must be rigorously appraised. It must demonstrate how it is the optimal way of achieving a particular strategic objective. (These objectives are set out in longer-term plans and agreed on a rolling basis). This need to be undertaken for every project, but with a strong degree of proportionality – so that large projects with higher levels of risk require more thorough approval than smaller ones.

(b) Every project robustly forecasts – and regularly re-forecasts – both inputs and outputs to give the whole organization a line of sight on future requirements. Project managers are encouraged to manage their projects within their own natural "lifecycles," rather than the artificial lifecycle of a financial year. This allows a strategic "steering" of resource requirements, rather than hoping that the "once and for all," annual allocation is right.

"It's a continuous journey in refining resource allocation, of honing the utilizing of resources based on strategic intent," Taylor says. "In doing so, critical longer-term strategic initiatives are protected from the potential guillotine of the annual budget – where shorter term financial considerations take precedence."

StratEx – An overview

This "protecting" of funding points to the recently launched concept of Strategy Expenditure (StratEx). We consider StratEx in the next chapter where we explain how to align financial management processes with strategic management processes. It is closely linked to this chapter as through StratEx a pot of money is set aside specifically for the funding of strategic initiatives (and so avoids the annual budget guillotine). StratEx is particularly useful in the funding of cross-functional or cross-organizational initiatives that might fall outside the conventional departmentally focused budgeting process.

SELECTING CROSS-CUTTING INITIATIVES

While it is true that the real work of strategy implementation takes place through the strategic initiatives that are selected and funded, it is equally true that it is typically the case that the projects that drive the most powerful, or breakthrough performance improvements, are those that span functions – or impact end-to-end processes. Bill Barberg of the US-based consultancy Insightformation, and one of the select few global thought leaders that we interviewed while researching this book suggests that Theme Teams should play a central role in selecting cross-cutting initiatives.

As an explanation, a Theme Team is set up to manage a specific theme within a scorecard, such as within the MoW, which had four teams in place to manage the themes of: "public/private partnership," "key planning payer, "quality services," and "leading professional organization."

"Theme Teams are best suited to help evaluate the different suggestions and provide guidance on how to prioritize the resources," he comments. "Theme Teams should be cross-functional, so their discussion on which options to advocate is not based on the selfish interests or biases of any one department."

Barberg also makes the useful recommendation that Theme Teams look for opportunities to "trade up" from less valuable efforts to ones that are determined to be more strategically valuable; rather than seeking funding for functional or unit-specific projects that might lead to incremental improvements only that they identify intervention that will dramatically improve performance to a theme – that will invariably be cross-organizational in nature.

"This mindset should – hopefully – allow people to feel less need to defend their functional programs and resources," he says. "Achieving the strategy is going to take more resources than the public organizations have, so when Theme Teams are taking a cross-organizational view of performance they get a better sense of what needs to be done to create value."

But note that there is always a danger that although cross-functional, Theme Teams might fall into the trap of replacing a narrow "functional" view of performance with a "theme view." This might also lead to requests for funding that fail to optimize overall organizational performance.

Clearly this narrow viewpoint must be avoided. At the MoW for example, great care has been taken to view themes holistically. For instance, through a causal relationship "improved communication and coordination processes, a key planning player objective, impacts the public private partnership and quality of service themes as well as its own." This cross-theme impact of objectives ensures that Theme Teams take a broader view of performance.

APPLYING LEAN THINKING TO INITIATIVE SELECTION AND IMPLEMENTATION

Within Chapter 2, we provided a definition of "a Lean organization" from the US-headquartered The Lean Enterprise Institute. In this chapter, that considers the selecting of strategic initiatives it is worth repeating. "A Lean organization understands customer value and focuses its key processes to continuously increase it. The ultimate goal is to provide perfect value to the customer through a perfect value creation process that has zero waste... to accomplish this, Lean thinking changes the focus of management from optimizing separate technologies, assets, and vertical departments to optimizing the flow of products and services through entire value streams that flow horizontally across technologies, assets, and departments to customers."[10]

As we can see, according to this definition "Lean" is about optimizing processes, wherever they are found in the organization – and they will typically be cross-functional. Cross-functional teams should be also used to identify how Lean can support the implementation of strategy, and should report to a Theme Owner, where used.

The first question to be asked when choosing a Lean project as with any initiative is "how will this help my organization to implement its strategy." The Lean selection process should be according to the type of criteria that we have already listed: if it does not impact one (and preferably more) strategy objectives then serious questions should be asked about the value of the project and whether resources should be allocated elsewhere.

Balanced Six Sigma

With reference to the Lean intervention Six Sigma, the emergence of the concept of Balanced Six Sigma has recently evolved to ensure that Lean projects are indeed strategically relevant. As we also explained in Chapter 2, Balanced Six Sigma melds together the principles of The Balanced Scorecard with Six Sigma, thereby pulling together a proven strategic management framework (the scorecard) and a popular and proven process improvement methodology (Six Sigma).

Dovetailing Six Sigma with the scorecard we can think of each of the perspectives on a "classic" Balanced Scorecard system as representing a voice:

– Voice of the business (financial perspective)
– Voice of the customer (customer perspective)
– Voice of the process (internal process perspective)

– Voice of employees/associates/stakeholders (learning and growth perspective)

Six Sigma interventions represent the "voice of the process" (the internal process perspective).

In choosing the Six Sigma initiatives that support the "voice of the process," organizations should listen carefully to the voice of the customer, and voice of the business. Most initiative candidates will be found in these two voices.

Voice of the customer

Many projects are initiated as a response to a particular customer requirement or complaint. Indeed when considering project candidates those where the "voice of the customer" is loudest should take precedence over any other.

Voice of the business

Projects or initiatives that are initiated from within the business tend to start from either a need to improve efficiency, reduce cost or ultimately to respond to a historical customer requirement or problem (so more of an effectiveness question).

Where both of these two voices meet is through the link to the direct outputs of the process. The outputs of any process are produced to satisfy a requirement. If the output is to an external customer then it should satisfy the Voice of the Customer. If the output is to an internal customer, then it should satisfy the Voice of the Business.

In selecting the Six Sigma candidates the teams can make use of an organization's traffic light system of green (ahead of target), yellow (on target) and red (below target) to determine the performance of a strategic objective. A red rating will alert the Six Sigma team to performance areas that might require immediate attention. As cited earlier a Heat Map can be particularly useful for this purpose.

The Six Sigma team can then design initiatives to improve these poor performing areas, which will then be considered and implemented as part of a typical Balanced Scorecard initiative prioritization process.

Being the "voice of the process" sends a powerful message as to just how important Six Sigma can be in enabling the organization to deliver to its strategic goals that are housed within the internal process perspective.

As an example of how a Six Sigma intervention might support an internal process objective within a Balanced Six Sigma project, consider the example form an Airline shown in Figure 6.4. Although not a public sector illustration, it is still useful for showing the simplicity by which Six Sigma interventions can be deployed as part of a Balanced Scorecard system.[11]

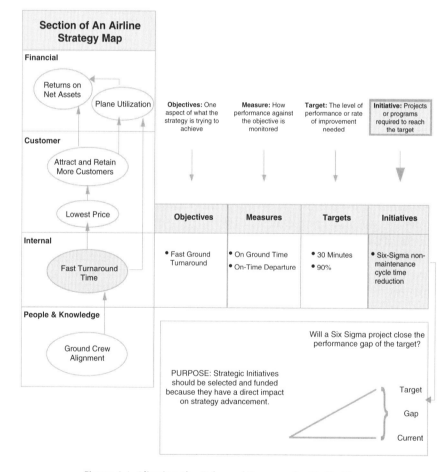

Figure 6.4 **Aligning the Balanced Scorecard with Six Sigma**

Hereford Hospitals NHS Trust case example

As a public sector example of how Lean thinking can be deployed, consider the UK-based Hereford Hospitals NHS Trust, which deployed a simple Lean-based service improvement program to improve the pathology process. In doing so, they impacted big-hitting NHS objectives around cost saving and reducing patient waiting times, as just two examples.

As background to the project note that fully 70% of clinical decisions in hospitals depend on pathology (the study and diagnosis of disease through examination of organs, tissues, bodily fluids, and whole bodies). Pathology plays a crucial role in maintaining the flow of patients and information throughout the hospital and reducing the length of stay. A report produced in 2006 stated that there was significant scope for improvement in turnaround times in pathology. Improving turnaround times, the report noted, would significantly increase throughout, improve efficiency and ultimately improve patient experience.[12]

As described in an NHS Institute for Innovation and Improvement paper, Hereford Hospitals NHS Trust responded to this challenge by launching a performance improvement program with the following objectives:[13]

– to improve turnaround times for all specimens for inpatients, outpatients and GPs
– to improve morale and use staff more effectively
– to improve quality, reduce waste and lower costs
– smooth the arrival of demand
– to make best use of the resources available

The Hereford Hospitals NHS Trust service improvement team believed that reducing turnaround times would improve flow, reduce waste and free up beds in the hospital, allow clinical decisions to be made quicker and enable staff to spend more time on direct patient care. Importantly, it was also believed that doing so would save many thousands of pounds.

To kick start the program, more than 40 staff in pathology participated in a short and focused one hour training session on improvement principles to improve the flow of work and eliminate waste. Staff were given the opportunity to complete waste identification forms. These were used to help identify issues that staff felt were important and needed improving.

In total nine days were spent actively improving pathology (typically, two days a week). To understand how work gets done, the process was observed from the request being made, to the results becoming available. The approach was to walk the entire process, identify each process step and the problems associated with those steps.

The program identified the following process problems, amongst others:

– GP, inpatient and outpatient test results were all being delayed
– Layout of department not based on the sequence of the flow of the work
– Demand varied significantly by hour, with a disproportionate amount of GP specimens arriving late in the afternoon
– Specimen reception was unmanned
– Specimens typically waited 30 minutes before they were processed
– Courier routes were not planned to stagger the arrival times of specimens
– Specimens were put into buckets – it was difficult to see which specimens arrived first
– There was unnecessary duplication of activities and a lot of wasted movement, time spent searching for equipment and staff.

Some of the improvements introduced were remarkably simple, but impactful nonetheless. For example the specimen reception was manned, which led to improved flows and with urgent work (such as for Accident and Emergency and the Intensive Care Unit) being processed immediately rather than being stuck in a queue. Also labeling, centrifuges and booking were relocated in specimen reception and synchronized. This led to many improvements such as duplicate steps removed at labeling (double handling); centrifuge optimized to improve flow at busy times; rework reduced at scanning stage; fewer staff required at labeling and booking in; quieter working area; less interruptions; more productive staff; faster turnaround times; minimized staff movement.

Table 6.1 shows some of the results to metrics pre and post change. As we can see, a remarkably simple process improvement program led to quite dramatic results – from both effectiveness and efficiency viewpoints.

The Hereford Hospitals example shows how launching a simple, and relatively "cheap" Lean program can deliver quantifiable benefits within

TABLE 6.1   Savings achieved by applying Lean principles to the pathology process of Herford Hospitals NHS Trust

Metric	Before Change	After change	Improvement	Saving £££ a year
Turnaround time (from receipt to results available)	62 minutes – up to two hours	38 minutes	40% reduction	2 beds a day £365,000 A&E targets met
Time for specimens to be picked up	13 minutes – up to 50 minutes	1–4 minutes	93% reduction	£10,000 Fewer staff needed
Double handling (labeling)	40 minutes per day	0 minutes	Eliminated	At least £3000
Time all work complete	17.30	16.45	Staff finish earlier	More time to improve quality
Centrifuge productivity (per hour – peak demand)	80 per hour (based on 4 mins spinning time)	202 per hour (based on 8 mins spinning	252% increase	Less waste £5000

areas that cause continued pain and anxiety within the NHS – patient waiting times, etc. The same logic applies across other areas of the public sector.

CONCLUSION

This chapter concludes the section of the book that describes how to build a Balanced Scorecard system – from designing the Strategy Map, through KPQs, KPIs, target setting and selecting initiatives. But there is more to succeeding with a strategic performance management framework than its design. We must consider ensuring that other management processes are fully aligned with the framework. We begin our exploration of how to do this in the next chapter by explaining how to align financial management processes with the strategic management process. As a follow on from this chapter, it explains how to ensure, through the deployment of StratEx, or similar approach, that funding is made available for the deployment of the identified strategic initiatives.

7

ALIGNING FINANCIAL MANAGEMENT
WITH STRATEGIC GOALS

*The budget evolved from a management tool into an obstacle to
management.*

Charles Edwards

INTRODUCTION: THE STORY OF NORTH EAST
LINCOLNSHIRE COUNCIL

Let's take a look at the UK's North East Lincolnshire Council – a public
sector organization that ended up in a severe financial crisis which led
to the council being rated "the worst council in England" by the UK's
Audit Commission. As background, the Audit Commission discovered
that the council was planning to spend more money than it actually
had, even when taking into account its general fund reserves. To address
the budgetary problems, the council was forced to make significant job
cuts which led to, amongst other negative outcomes, a loss of organizational memory and a fear amongst staff that services would further
deteriorate, which they did.

NE Lincolnshire Council has successfully used the principles of performance management and measurement to turn the organization around.
Amongst other disciplines, these have included better articulating
strategic aims and priorities through a framework it calls a "plan on a
page" building a "performance culture" and introducing sound financial management that is supported by robust and reliable performance
data. For more information see the API case study entitled "Using
Performance Management to Transform a Failing Organization".[1]

In the context of this work, NE Lincolnshire Council provides useful
lessons – and warnings. As public sector organizations across the globe
awaken to the fact that financial resources are dwindling and will be
restricted for many years, they are being forced to consider how they
can continue to deliver the high level of quality of services demanded

by both Central Government and the general public alike. Put another way, they must find ways to ensure that they provide the effectiveness benefits that are demanded of them, while also delivering what will become non-negotiable efficiency gains. An inability to do so, might easily lead to a similar financial and performance crisis as experienced by NE Lincolnshire Council and the resulting deterioration in services, job cuts and a collapse in morale. For many, returning from this poor position might be a long and painful journey.

THE BALANCED SCORECARD: THE FINANCIAL PERSPECTIVE

So how can public sector organizations ensure that they avoid any potential financial and performance crises? As we stress throughout this book, usage of the Balanced Scorecard is probably the most useful framework available to besieged managers today for steering their organizations through tomorrow's stormy waters and for maintaining the efficiency/effectiveness balance.

It is, of course, normal that financial objectives, measures and targets appear within a Balanced Scorecard system; although (and as we explained in Chapter 4) for a public sector organization the financial element typically does not serve as the "top," or most important perspective, as would be the case in a profit-oriented commercial enterprise.

Christchurch City Council case example 1

As an example from our case study organizations, Christchurch City Council has the financial perspective second to customer and has the objectives "manage service delivery to budget," "manage capital program to budget," and "ensure sustainable financial health," (see Figure 7.1). This is a well-balanced financial collection as it has operational, capital and sustainability dimensions.

Audit Scotland case example

At Audit Scotland, financial performance is captured within the "supporting activity" of "we will deliver our work efficiently and effectively and will be clear where we need to improve. We will have excellent governance procedures and will monitor and report on the impact of our work." (see Figure 2.12) This is supported by Key Performance

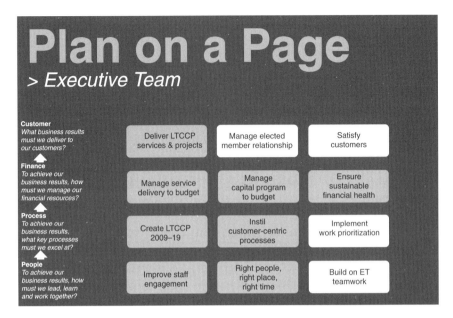

Plan on a Page
> Executive Team

Customer *What business results must we deliver to our customers?*	Deliver LTCCP services & projects	Manage elected member relationship	Satisfy customers
Finance *To achieve our business results, how must we manage our financial resources?*	Manage service delivery to budget	Manage capital program to budget	Ensure sustainable financial health
Process *To achieve our business results, what key processes must we excel at?*	Create LTCCP 2009–19	Instil customer-centric processes	Implement work prioritization
People *To achieve our business results, how must we lead, learn and work together?*	Improve staff engagement	Right people, right place, right time	Build on ET teamwork

Figure 7.1   Christchurch City Council's Executive Team's Strategy Map

Questions (KPQs) such as "to what extent have we effectively and efficiently managed our resources to deliver our outputs?" and Key Performance Indicators (KPIs) such as "percentage of audit reports delivered on time and to budget," "examples of our efficiency improvements," and "costs in line with budgets and best practice."

The Audit Scotland objectives, KPIs, etc are interesting as they speak directly to the effectiveness/efficiency balance that is at the core of today's public sector performance management challenge. Moreover, the "finance" perspective sits at the base of Audit Scotland's Strategy Map, thus signaling that in a public sector setting finance is the enabler of all subsequent and causal improvements. Finance also sits at the base of the Strategy Maps at our case study organizations Belfast City Council and International Baccalaureate, as two further examples.

Efficiency cause and effect

But although the finance perspective might be relegated in importance within a Balanced Scorecard system, in today's economic climate, performance to its objectives will certainly be closely scrutinized, and probably much more so than has historically been the norm.

Peter Ryan, Manager, Performance and Planning at Christchurch City Council, and one of the select few "thought leaders" we interviewed for this book makes this observation about the usefulness of a Strategy Map in showing how efficiently resources are being deployed and allocated and their relationship with the more effectiveness-oriented outcomes.

"It is not unusual for customer outcomes to be captured within the "top" perspective of a public sector Balanced Scorecard," he says. "This is appropriate as customer, or stakeholder, outcomes are typically more important in a public sector company than for a for-profit organization." But he continues that unless care is taken, being overly "customer-focused," can cause problems. "Using the traffic-light analogy, it is quite possible to be in the position where all of the customer objectives are green," he says. "But the fact is that funding the initiatives that led to the 'green' color might have been financially crippling to the organization, which will turn the financial objectives 'red.' So paying close attention to the causality within the Strategy Map is critical."

Of course, the converse of this example is that the Strategy Map will show how severe cuts in financial resources impacts customer/ stakeholder outcomes.

As much an anything Peter Ryan's comments signal the absolute importance of creating a Strategy Map, and why throughout this book we continually reinforce the message that it should sit at the center of an integrated performance management system. A Strategy Map quickly alerts management to serious performance issues and so enables early corrective action.

THE BUDGET

The purpose of placing both financial and non-financial objectives onto a Strategy Map is to understand the performance dynamic that delivers to the strategy and allocate and reallocate financial and other resources accordingly. But although simple and intuitive, efficaciously managing this dynamic going forward, and perhaps more tellingly making the required funding allocations to deliver to longer-term strategic goals has (in both public sector and commercial settings) been continually hampered by the existence of that other, and long-established performance management system – the annual budget.

Aligning the budget with strategy

Anyone who has observed the Balanced Scorecard since its inception in 1992 would have become painfully aware of the difficulties that most organizations have in hardwiring the budgeting process to strategic management. On one level the difficulty is understandable. Whereas the Balanced Scorecard takes a longer-term view of performance by looking at strategic goals which, in a public sector setting might be up to ten years into the future, the typical horizon of the budget is just 12 months. Not surprisingly, when financial resources are tight, short-term budgetary requirements normally trump longer-term strategic requirements.

Indeed Harvard Business School Professor Robert Kaplan, the co-creator, along with management consultant Dr David Norton of the "classic," Balanced Scorecard framework has stated that, "One aspect of the Strategy-Focused Organization that has lagged is the integration with the budgeting system. It is less developed than the objective setting, or the links to incentive systems, human resource systems, or communication systems." He added that, "I think, however, that if we don't establish the link with budgeting, then the scorecard initiatives might whither."[2]

Aligning budgets with strategy is a sub-component of Principle 4 "Make Strategy a Continual Process" of Kaplan and Norton's five principles of the Strategy-Focused Organization, which we describe in full within Chapter 2. And in recent times, Kaplan and Norton have paid attention to ensuring that the annual budget and funding of longer-term strategic goals can happily co-exist, and have developed the concept of Strategic Expenditure (StratEx), which we describe later in this chapter.

Abandoning the budget

But there are those that argue that such strategic goals/budget co-existence is inappropriate in today's complex and fast-changing world and call loudly for the total elimination of the budgeting process. This has been the constant message of the Beyond Budgeting Roundtable (BBRT), which was launched in the late 1990s as a forum to identify and share alternative approaches to financial management within the organization.[3] The sidebar provides an overview of BBRT's core principles of financial management.

Purolator case example

And there are many practitioners who question the continued validity of the annual budget – and not just from the private sector. In the 2009 report: "The Finance Function: Achieving Superior Performance in a

Global Economy," Sheldon Bell, Chief Financial Officer of Purolator, Canada's largest courier company and which is 90% Government owned, commented: "The budget is well past its sell by date... We have to look forward and evaluate where we are going, making corrections and filling in gaps where we need to. We also have to support the business from the perspective of understanding the results of actions that have been taken... We need to be focused on where we are going in 30 days, three months, one year and in 3–5 years," he says. "It is about understanding not only that movement is happening but how we can affect momentum."[4]

Becoming budget-free

Purolator has not abandoned the budget, but has de-emphasized it and places more emphasis on rolling forecasts (a technique we discuss later in this chapter). But there are organizations that have indeed completely removed the budget. These are found mainly in the private sector, such as Norway's StatoilHydro (which is one of the biggest organizations in the world), Sweden's Nordea Bank and the UK's Tomkins. But there are some, albeit very few, public sector examples, such as Scottish Enterprise. Later, we describe the approach that was taken by Scottish Enterprise (which included the Balanced Scorecard as the performance management centerpiece) but those interested in learning more about taking a "budget-free" approach to managing the organization are directed to either the BBRT site or James Creelman's work: "Reinventing Planning and Budgeting for the Adaptive Enterprise," which includes the cited case studies, as well as others.[5]

Budget research – The Hackett Group

But research shows that moving to being "budget-free" is much easier said than done, even in the commercial sector. As proof, consider the ongoing research by the USA-headquartered benchmarking specialist organization The Hackett Group. Throughout the first decade of this century it conducted research into how the planning functions of organizations (almost exclusively large, private sector firms) were reshaping planning activities (most notably the budget) to better align with fast-changing market dynamics.[6] In its 2002 survey Hackett found that 12% of survey respondents intended to abandon the budget by 2005. A follow-up survey in 2005 found that only a couple of organizations had actually made this transition. Indeed although most organizations in both the 2002 and 2005 surveys said they were going to make significant alterations to the budgeting processes over the coming years, in most cases the resulting changes were only minor. From 2002–2005 only 22% of respondents had made large-scale changes to the budgeting process, and at 27% the figure was only slightly better between 2005–2008, despite a growing library of best practice case studies and advice to draw from.

In their 2009 research Hackett explains why transforming the budgeting process is such a weighty challenge. "First, annual planning/budgeting processes are deeply rooted within organizations. Finance and operational professionals are well-trained in how to do it, having learnt how to game the system along the way. They are especially willing to endure the pain of budgeting (and rebuff efforts to alter the process) when performance to budgeted targets is tied to incentive compensation."

Of course, the incentive compensation link is rarely a barrier to change within the public sector setting. As we explain in Chapter 9, bonuses are rarely paid within public sector organizations, although there are exceptions such as Christchurch City Council.

Even so, large-scale change to the budgeting process is even less common in this sector than in a commercial setting (it is telling that as of December 2009, BBRT could not boast even one member from the public sector.)

The fact that large-scale change is not that forthcoming in the public sector is not surprising as organizations in this sector are normally given a set budget, which they must manage and account for. This clearly allows for far less financial flexibility of innovation than can be achieved in a commercial setting.

And as the pressure for efficiency gains increase, we can expect an even greater focus on how public sector bodies spend their annual financial allocation. Therefore we might not be surprised to see public sector bodies producing budget documents that are even more detailed than is presently the case (and they are already overly detailed) and that take an even more prolonged time to create. According to Hackett's research although 10% of companies are able to complete the budgeting process within 60 calendar days, almost half require between 91 and 150 days and 25% require more than 150 days.

The cost of the budget

Hackett was also able to put a cost to the length of the budget (interestingly most finance organizations are not able to put a "cost" to their budgeting process, despite their ability to put a cost to everything else).

Hackett found that for companies that complete the budget in 60 days or less, the cost of the annual planning/budgeting process is about $350,000 per $1 billion of revenues; for 91–120 days it is around $560,000 per $1 billion of revenues; and for more than 150 days, around $840,000. Although we do not have comparative figures for the public sector, we can be sure that the longer the process takes, the more expensive it will be. Public sector bodies might make efficiency gains by simplifying the budgeting process. Advice proffered through the Hackett research might be as relevant to the public sector as it is to their commercial counterparts.

Budget transformation advice

Hackett's research states that budgets in most organizations are too detailed and that the process is needlessly prolonged by multiple iterations and ends up with being a negotiated settlement about which no-one is happy. "This leads to a mindset centered on how to 'beat the budget,' rather than how to optimize performance," they say.

Hackett rightly points out that too many organizations erroneously believe that more detail enhances the likelihood of better performance. However, improving the budgeting process actually means reducing the level of detail. The number of iterations required to reach the final budget should be as low as possible.

The burden of the budget is oftentimes made worse by an outmoded top-down/bottom-up approach to the negotiation of financial targets at a high level of detail. Usually this approach is internal resource-orientated, permits incremental changes and rewards only caution and defensive behavior. An approach based on top-down target setting and bottom-up planning is much more appropriate. It is also more empowering for, although targets are set at the center, it is up to devolved management to figure how to allocate resources etc to deliver to the targets.

Linked, Light and Late

Hackett's 2009 planning research looked more broadly at planning than just the annual process. Rather, it considered strategic, mid-term and the annual process, and importantly how these three cycles should be aligned into a "single planning process." In their 2009 report "Planning for Economic Sustainability: Linking Strategy to Action,"[7] Hackett used the analogy of a triathlete. To win a triathlon the triathlete must master three disciplines; running, swimming and cycling. Similarly, with planning they must master strategic, mid-term and annual processes. Hackett proposed that a best practice approach to planning could be described as "the 3 L's." Linked, Light and Late.

"Linked. All three planning phases are seamlessly integrated. Strategic goals provide the basis for the mid-term targets, which in turn inform the budget targets at the highest level of the organization. In the annual planning/budgeting phase, top-level targets are cascaded to the rest of the organization."

"Light. The annual plan/budget received less organizational emphasis, in favor of more use of rolling forecasts."

"Late. Planning starts as late in the year as possible to increase the relevance and timeliness of the assumptions and information delivered to decision-makers."

Another Hackett research project, "Performance Metrics and Practices of World-Class Finance Organizations" (which, as with the 2009 planning study, was co-authored by James Creelman)[8] found that 45% of world-class finance organizations (Hackett has a rigorous process for defining world-class, and about 10% of their database are defined in this category) has a fully integrated strategic planning, tactical business planning and budgeting process, compared to just 24% of the peer group (those that are not world-class).

Ministry of Works, Bahrain case example 1

Let's consider some examples from our case organizations as to how strategy and the budgeting processes are linked. At the Ministry of Works, Bahrain[9] both budgets and strategic initiatives are tightly aligned to the annual strategy process. "We now provide budgets and submissions from our ministry to the Ministry of Finance with our portfolio of strategic initiatives via the Cabinet Economic Sub-committee," explains Chief of the Strategic Planning Section Raja Al Zayani. "This includes information about the strategic alignment of all initiatives based on National 2030 aspiration. [The Kingdom of Bahrain has an ambitious transformational vision to the year 2030]."

Timing of this process is crucial to ensure an effective integration of the process. For example, the 2009 budgeting process followed the annual corporate review held over January and February. These are necessarily held beforehand so that consolidated budgetary information can be obtained as an outcome of the process and to ensure that budgets are linked to strategic objectives.

Without question we would agree that the budgeting process should follow the strategic planning process. In essence, the budget should represent the first year of the strategic plan.

Christchurch City Council case example 2

Within Christchurch City Council,[10] the budgeting process fully supports the council's Long-term Council Community Plan (LTCCP). This is the council's "contract with the community," describing how it intends to deliver its community outcomes as well as other long-term goals of the council.

Reviewed every six years, the current community outcomes take the city to the year 2012 and are grouped according to the following headings: "a safe city," "a city of people who value and protect the natural environment," "a well-governed city" "a prosperous city" and "a healthy city." These outcomes are shown with supporting performance indicators in Figures 2.5 and 2.6.

The LTCCP covers a period of 10 consecutive financial years, though it is reviewed every three years; the most recent preparation being in 2008 for the 2009–2019 timeframe. This allows the council to take a long-term view while enabling it to adjust for constantly changing financial and other factors and keep its accounting and budgets up-to-date.

Peter Ryan stresses that within Christchurch City Council the strategy development and deployment process ensures close alignment between short-term operational plans and longer-term strategic objectives and outcomes for the city. How the various planning cycles within Christchurch City Council work together are shown in Figure 7.2.

Better financial reporting initiative

It is also notable that on realizing that the link between financial and strategic management was not as tight as it should be the council has launched a "better financial reporting" program that includes a revamp of budgeting and forecasting processes. The goal of the program has become an objective in the Corporate Services scorecard (corporate services include the finance function) with the title "implement generation two performance management."

Upskilling the public sector finance professionals

Indeed the City of Christchurch finance function transformation objective highlights an interesting debate – that being whether the skills sets of public sector finance professionals are appropriate for managing the various financial and performance challenges facing their organizations in the next decade of the 21st century. Our analysis finds that there might be cause for concern.

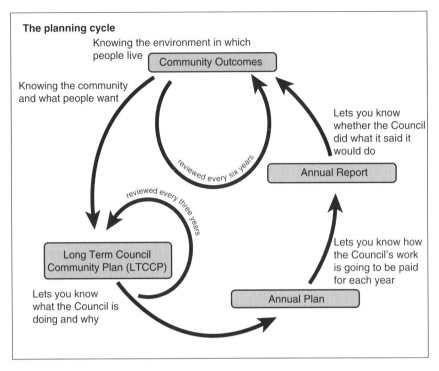

The planning cycle

Knowing the environment in which people live

Community Outcomes

Knowing the community and what people want

reviewed every six years

reviewed every three years

Lets you know whether the Council did what it said it would do

Annual Report

Long Term Council Community Plan (LTCCP)

Lets you know what the Council is doing and why

Lets you know how the Council's work is going to be paid for each year

Annual Plan

Figure 7.2 **Planning Cycles within Christchurch City Council**

Within a Christchurch City Council case study that appeared in the report: "Finance Function: Achieving Superior Performance in a Global Economy,"[11] Peter Ryan spoke of the challenges that are generally faced in getting finance professionals within the public sector to understand that value has both effectiveness (service) and efficiency (budget) dimensions. He said that although public sector finance professionals must still possess excellent financial control and cost management capabilities, a priority is an understanding of how to manage value and the role of non-financial performance indicators and outcomes.

"This may sound strange at first, but value for a Government agency is not about simply being on budget. It isn't delivering good services either. It is the relationship between those two things," he says. "They are two sides of the same coin. We use the term 'bang for buck' to simplify the concept. As a practical example, we set a level of service for the city around collecting refuse, or providing water, and we use benchmarking data to set the standard. We also cost that. Then we aim to deliver the services both to the identified standard and cost. If we succeed, that's value. But if only one half of the equation is met – we delivered to the agreed standard but blew the budget, or vice versa – that's not 'value' for the ratepayer."

Ryan adds "we have already used this bang for buck approach to value to identify services that are delivering to standard but with under-spent budgets. The resulting savings are extensive, selective, completely defensible and involve no loss of service quality. This is a stark contrast to the usual 'budget cut' model."

He goes on to make the following insightful observation, that has far-reaching implications for public sector leaders seeking to put in place the requisite disciplines, especially around finance, that ensure the effectiveness/efficiency balance is well-managed. It should also be considered by accounting bodies and educationalists.

"Accounting schools basically train students for the corporate world. They teach the mechanics of profit and loss, which is fair enough," he says. "But in not-for-profit agencies these rules only partially apply. Many Government agencies have very large budgets, but looking back on those I have worked for, the finance people they recruited had to teach themselves to manage the inflow and outflow of money when there is no profit motive. Their solutions were not always the same."

"This means the finance function in Government must teach itself how to understand how to for value (rather than how to manage for profit or to comply with budget allocation). This requires taking a strategic view of the business rather than a solely financial one. In this light our own finance managers would probably be better described as 'business managers.' They are strategic partners to the business units, not just accountants in the traditional sense."

Belfast City Council case example

Within Belfast City Council, the value creation process replaced the traditional planning processes.[12] Although not in place at the time of preparing the case study, Belfast City Council had a vision to achieve complete alignment between the value creation mapping (strategy mapping) process, the creation of the business plan, the structure of the organization and the allocation of resources and budgets. In essence therefore, the goal was for the Balanced Scorecard to sit at the center of a wider performance management system.

Scottish Enterprise case example

The central positioning of the Balanced Scorecard was certainly true at the Glasgow, headquartered Scottish Enterprise Network, which is

Scotland's main economic development agency and that is funded by the Scottish Executive (the devolved parliament of Scotland). With about 2500 employees the Network comprises Scottish Enterprise National (the coordinating body) and 12 county-based Local Enterprise Councils (LECs) that are located in the southern half of the country and cover 93% of the population (the rest of the country is covered by the Highlands and Islands Enterprise).

As explained in the report: "Reinventing Planning and Budgeting for the Adaptive Enterprise"[13] Scottish Enterprise was a pioneer in the public sector for its innovative move in replacing the annual budgeting process with a more dynamic, and adaptive approach. For the public sector, this is probably a world first.

The decision to become budget-free was not "a means," nor "an end." Julian Taylor, Director of Strategy Development and Network Performance, explained the motivation like this. "We wanted to get away from the 'rational behaviors' of the fixed annual contract."

Given that most experts would speak of the "fixed annual contract" as creating an environment conducive to dysfunctional behavior, Taylor's use of the words "rational behaviors" are carefully chosen, as he explains.

"When it comes to the budget, people might say that their behavior is dysfunctional, but the fixed annual contract expects managers to follow a specific process, without question. So if managers just do what is expected from them, and in doing so make the process work best for them, then that's entirely rational behavior. It's fully in keeping with normal human behavior."

This behavior, he continues, may – naturally – lead to a negative "gaming," culture and, particularly noticeable on public sector organizations, the ingraining of a "spend it or lose it" mentality. "This hardly optimizes the use of public resources," he rightly comments.

Scottish Enterprise first introduced the Balanced Scorecard in 2002 at both corporate and LEC levels. As a result of its deployment, the organization's leaders had become increasingly aware of the disconnect between the annual budgeting process and the successful prosecution of strategic objectives. "It became clear that there was often a real challenge in launching longer-term strategic initiatives that had to be re-budgeted for on a 12-month cycle," Taylor says. "The Balanced Scorecard approach encouraged clear thinking and a commitment to strategy execution on a continual basis: an annual planning process is simply too rigid."

In the summer of 2004, a development project was launched to design a new performance management and planning approach within Scottish Enterprise. The primary driver would be the principles of adaptive management, particularly to make resources available when needed, supported by regular rolling reviews.

The new approach to budgeting and performance management that emerged from the project was described as "a framework for managing the business," and comprised four components:

- Resource Draw Down
- Rolling Forecasts
- Quarterly reviews
- Balanced Scorecards

Although the annual budget was essentially taken out of Scottish Enterprise, it was somewhat complicated by the fact that it has to work within the confines of an annual financial allocation provided by the Scottish Executive, with no provision to "carry forward." What Scottish Enterprise did retain was the annual agreement of a three-year plan, which provides the steer for draw down and rolling forecasts.

Draw down starts from the premise that all resources belong to the entire network and should go to projects that provide the greatest impact. Therefore, when it comes to project funding (it is through projects that Scottish Enterprise delivers its services) individual business units do not receive an allocation of money, or other resource, simply as a matter of entitlement – as is the case in a traditional budget. Taylor explains that the objective is to ensure that funding priority is given to what he describes as projects that have the highest impact – or stand the greatest chance of helping teams achieve their strategic objectives.

Essentially, teams are assured that resources will be made available for their projects so long as they fulfill two very strict criteria:

1. Every project must be rigorously appraised. It must demonstrate how it is the optimal way of achieving a particular strategic objective. (These objectives are set out in longer-term plans and agreed on a rolling basis; this needs to be undertaken for every project, but with a strong degree of proportionality – so that large projects with higher levels of risk require more thorough approval than smaller ones.
2. Every project robustly forecasts – and regularly re-forecasts – both inputs and outputs to give the whole organization a line of sight on future requirements. Project managers are encouraged to manage their projects within their own natural 'life-cycles' rather than the artificial lifecycle of a financial year. This allows a strategic "steering" of resource requirements, rather than hoping that the "once and for all" annual allocation is right.

"It's a continuous journey in refining resource allocation, of honing the utilizing of resources based on strategic intent," says Taylor.

Once a quarter, the management team for the Scottish Enterprise Network – and every team within it – reviews performance over the previous four quarters and agrees to forecasts of performance over the next four to six. This provides an assessment of the external environment, how it is impacting the Network's objectives; how performance against those objectives is progressing and what that might mean for future performance. A key element of this is the ability to re-forecast financial plans and to provide an overview at an organization-wide level. This is the basis of strategic "shifts" in emphasis.

"And we ask how are we performing to our strategic goals according to the four perspectives of the Balanced Scorecard," says Taylor. "In particular, we try to use these reviews to drive performance improvement, rather than just checking to see if we will hit pre-determined output levels. This encourages us to identify and share good practice and continuously challenge how performance can be improved to meet our objectives."

Scottish Enterprises Balanced Scorecard (see Figure 7.3 for the Strategy Map as of 2005) represents its strategic plans in terms of strategic objectives grouped to the perspectives of stakeholder, customer, internal process and learning and infrastructure.

Now, of course, and in sharp contrast to private sector organizations that tread a budget free path, Scottish Enterprise *has* to abide to an annual resourcing cycle of its funders. So how does this impact the organizations resource allocation process? "With the transparency we now get from forecasting we have signals that we can respond to in Q2 to Q3 regarding required spend modifications or stimulations for the end of the year," Taylor explains.

He stresses that this knowledge does not trigger the typical response of switching projects on or off. "It's more about what can be slowed down or accelerated rather than which projects can we pull the plug on and leave stranded," he explains. "It's about seeing how everything, including money, flows through the organization. So it's about managing flows and not stocks."

ROLLING FORECAST

Most companies that become "budget-free" use rolling forecasts as a central plank of their new financial management system, such as Scottish

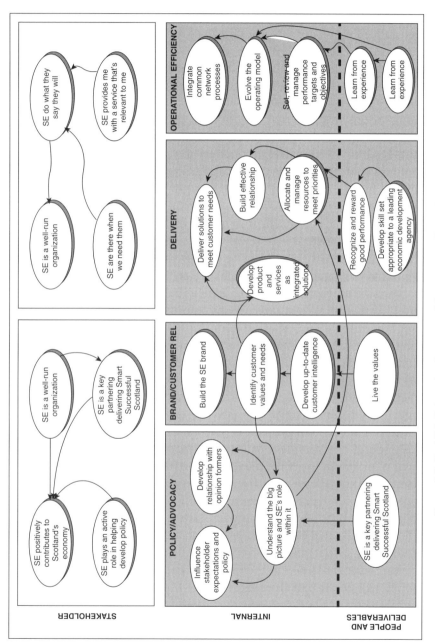

Figure 7.3 **Scottish Enterprise Corporate Management Team Strategy Map**

149

Enterprise. This has led to the belief that the implementation of a rolling forecast system requires the dismantling of the budget. This is simply not true, and most companies that use a rolling forecast maintain the annual budget. Indeed we would advocate the deployment of a rolling financial forecast alongside a de-emphases budget (that is fewer line items and a shorter timeframe for creation). The budget serves as the starting point for setting expectations for the year, but it is the rolling forecast that is used as the primary management tool.

And it should be stressed that with a rolling forecast there is always a current multi-quarter forecast available for reference. Moreover, as rolling forecasts typically look six to eight quarters ahead, there is always an available forecast to the end of the financial year so that likely performance to the annual budget can be assessed. As with the annual plan/budget, the rolling forecast should be limited to a small number of metrics. Otherwise, the organization plays down the importance of the budget only to gain an overly detailed forecast.

Moreover, a forecast should not be confused with a target. Whereas a target is what the organization would like to achieve if all goes well, a forecast is what the enterprise expects to achieve based on the best and more current information. When forecasts are honest, they serve as a powerful tool for beginning a conversation about how to close gaps to target, or whether the economic situation is such that the target cannot be reached.

In the cited Scottish Enterprise case study, Performance Manager Ed Payne provided the following useful insights: "People should forecast with as much accuracy and robustness as they can. They should genuinely try to understand the flow of resources as the play out in the natural lifecycle of a project. It really should be their best guess as to likely spend over the next four to six quarters."

"But it is important to get the message across that a forecast is just that – a best estimate. And we know that given the dynamics and unpredictability of our operations that these forecasts will change as we move forward. The whole point of implementing rolling forecasts is that we know things will change, something that can't be recognized in a conventional budget."

"So my view is that we're not replacing budgets with forecasts. We're not making forecasts targets in themselves. If people see forecasts as targets then they will do all that they can to meet those targets, which means that we'll be straight back into the dysfunctional or 'rational,' behaviors caused by the budget."

As a final point on rolling forecasts, as they almost invariably look out beyond the current financial year they provide useful insights into the continued appropriateness of mid-term operating targets, which in turn provides an early warning signal regarding the likelihood of delivering the strategic plan. In short, rolling forecasts are a powerful mechanism for aligning financial management practices with strategic goals.

STRATEGY EXPENDITURE

Although, and because of what would be quite severe political challenges, few public sector bodies would contemplate a "budget free" approach to financial management we are observing that a few organizations are beginning to create a matrix of two different budgeting processes. One is the classic departmental "big level" budgets and the other is a budget that focuses on strategic themes.

This idea has been perhaps most fully fleshed out in Kaplan and Norton's Strategic Expenditure (StratEx) concept, which they have developed essentially as a way to safeguard the investment in longer-term strategic goals against the requirement to adhere to shorter-term budgetary goals and horizons. Kaplan and Norton argue in their book *The Execution Premium*[14] that such is the importance now assigned to managing to strategic goals that organizations now require a resource pot known as StratEx in addition to the common OPEX (operating expenditure) and CAPEX (capital expenditure). A formal process to determine the level of StratEx enables companies to subject strategic initiatives to rigorous, disciplined reviews just like those conducted for CAPEX spending on tangible assets.

According to Kaplan and Norton this discretionary spending can be guided by rule of thumb – for example, and using a commercial sector example, 5% of sales. Executives use similar rules of thumb to establish funding levels for categories such as general and administrative expenses and research and development expenditures. If spending falls short of the StratEx target, then the organization might be under-funding its future growth. If spending exceeds this number, there might be a question about the adequacy of the controls.

Kaplan and Norton also recommend that StratEx should be a separate authorized line item on the company's internal budget or financial forecast. They write:

> Executing strategy requires that the portfolio of initiatives be executed simultaneously in a co-ordinated manner. This requires explicit funding for the portfolio of strategic initiatives. The traditional budgeting system focuses on the resources provided to existing organizational functions and business units, and the accountability and performance of these units. The strategic investments, for initiatives that cross functions and business units, must be removed from operational

budgets and managed separately by the executive team. The creation of a special budget category called StratEx… facilitates this process.

The Ministry of Works, Bahrain, is one of our case organizations that is planning to introduce StratEx as a funding pot.

ALIGNING PERFORMANCE MANAGEMENT SYSTEMS

The Ministry of Works, as with other companies such as Scottish Enterprise, Christchurch City Council and Belfast City Council, firmly believe that performance management should be a "joined up" exercise, that is, that all performance management systems are aligned and work in unison – and this is more than just linking budgeting and strategy, however important that is.

Advanced Performance Institute research

Research by the Advanced Performance Institute (API) into the performance management practices of more than 1100 organizations across the globe, the findings of which were first reported in the white paper: "Strategic Performance Management in Government and Public Sector Organizations,"[15] found that "align other organizational activities with the strategic aims outlined in the performance management system," was one of the ten principles of good practice as exhibited by superior performing organizations (see Chapter 1).

Simply put, when organizations lose sight of what they should be managing, and why, they waste a great deal of time and resources in producing something that is of little value internally, while potentially de-motivating staff.

Therefore, a strategic performance management system (which in best practice examples will likely have a Strategy Map and scorecard as its core element) should be used to guide and align other organizational processes – such as budgeting, performance reporting, the management of projects and programs and the management of risks. This is certainly true at our case organization The Ministry of Works, Bahrain, where a project management office is fully integrated with the Strategic Planning Section (essentially an Office of Strategy Management, see Chapter 9). Moreover, a development in late 2009 saw risk management incorporated into the responsibilities of the OSM, which is also in charge of Total Quality Management, Activity Based Costing and Evidence-Based Management, amongst other duties.

HMRC IMS case example

Information from the Balanced Scorecard and risk management are used to inform the monthly management meeting – in particular the financial conversation – at our case organization The Information Services Management (IMS) department of the UK's HM Revenues and Customs.[16]

"When we go to the board and talk about how our finances are being invested we now always take the scorecard and the risk register," explains Richard Ryder, IMS' Head, Planning and Performance. "By doing so we can clearly show how, for example, cutting back investment in one area will impact another," adding that IMS has always understood the links between planning and risk and performance management, but had never had something to hang it on. "With the Strategy Map and Balanced Scorecard, we now have," he adds. This example is powerful as it shows one of the great benefits of a scorecard system – the ability to show how, for example, making a decision that will lead to efficiency gain will impact the effectiveness of the organization. It also points to the importance of integrating various elements of performance management into a single decision-making process.

A failure to integrate

All too often, however, public sector organizations are found to be running their reporting, risk management, project management and budgeting processes in parallel – as though these are completely unrelated activities. They are certainly not unrelated, and should be brought together to deliver to the strategic goals of the enterprise.

Simply put, if the performance management process has delivered a clear strategy, it would make sense to also use this to create and manage budgets, coordinate and manage projects and programs, and to report on performance, as a number of our case organization demonstrate. It will mean that all of the performance activities of the organization are pointing in the same direction, and working together (likely under the day-to-day management of an OSM).

Furthermore, risks are basically the flipside of performance. Performance indicators allow organizations to understand whether they are delivering the designated performance levels, whereas risk indicators allow organizations to understand the risks of not being able to deliver performance. These should therefore be closely aligned. Indeed, the integration of risk management has recently become a core focus for many in the Balanced Scorecard community, in the aftermath of the credit crunch.

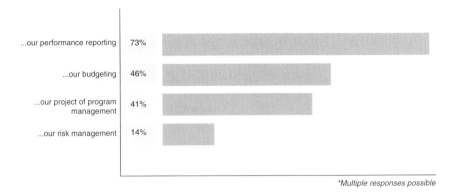

Figure 7.4 **Alignment with Performance Management**

Unfortunately, The API research shows that alignment is still a major problem in public sector and government organizations; while 73% have aligned their performance reporting with their performance management system, less than half have aligned their budgeting and project and program management. It is also extremely worrying that only 14% of organizations believe their risk management is fully aligned with their Performance Management system (see Figure 7.4). Most public sector bodies have some way to go before they can claim they have a fully integrated performance management system.

CONCLUSION

In this chapter we have explained that the funding constraints that public sector organizations will face over the coming years might lead many into a financial and performance crisis as they attempt to maintain high levels of service with dwindling incomes.

The Balanced Scorecard we explained is the ideal framework for being able to visualize the efficiency/effectiveness balances and trade-offs and allocate and reallocate resources accordingly.

We also explained that there is an increasing awareness that the annual budgeting process constrains attempts to effectively implement strategy, and we provided case examples of how public sector leaders might approach this conundrum. We also described the emergence of StratEx as a powerful tool for safeguarding longer-term investments against the annual budgeting process.

Finally we explained that performance management should be used as the central steer for aligning all organizational activities such as the budget and risk management. It is by doing so that an organization truly becomes a strategy-focused organization. Performance reporting is another of the organizational activities that should be included in an integrated performance management system. Performance reporting is the subject of the next chapter.

SIDEBAR

Beyond budgeting 12 principles

The Beyond Budgeting Roundtable has identified a set of 12 principles for going beyond budgeting. The first six principles are concerned with taking the right leadership actions to address the drivers of change, and the second six align management processes with leadership actions. The contrasts in the table (i.e. the do's and don'ts) show the differences in practice between the Beyond Budgeting and Command and Control models.

Leadership actions	
1. Customers	Focus everyone on their customers, *not on hierarchical relationships*
2. Processes	Organize as a Lean network of accountable teams, *not as centralized functions*
3. Autonomy	Give teams the freedom and capability to act, *don't micro-manage them*
4. Responsibility	Create a high responsibility culture at every level, *not just at the center*
5. Transparency	Promote open information for self-management, *don't restrict it hierarchically*
6. Governance	Adopt a few clear values, goals and boundaries, *not fixed targets*

Aligning management processes with leadership actions	
1. Goals	Set relative goals for continuous improvement, *don't negotiate fixed contracts*
2. Rewards	Reward shared success based on relative performance, *not fixed targets*
3. Planning	Make planning continuous and inclusive process, *not a top-down annual event*
4. Controls	Base controls on relative indicators and trends, *not variances against a plan*
5. Resources	Make resources available as needed, *not through annual budget allocations*
6. Coordination	Coordinate interactions dynamically, *not through annual planning cycles*

According to the BBRT these principles are closely inter-related and the actions of one have profound effects on others. Consequently, the claim that adopting a few principles whilst ignoring the others could well lead to an unsatisfactory or even a failed implementation.[17]

8

KEEPING YOUR EYES ON THE BALL: REPORTING AND REVIEWING PERFORMANCE

Our work is the presentation of our capabilities.
Edward Gibbon, English Historian, 1737–94

INTRODUCTION

Public sector organizations have many stakeholders to whom they must report performance: from central Government to regulators to local community groups. As financial resources dwindle over the upcoming years stakeholders will likely more thoroughly scrutinize such reports to ensure that money is not being wasted – and, as we have stressed throughout this book, that service standards remain intact.

This chapter does not look at the interventions and transformations that will inform such reports (and that will make up the content of a Balanced Scorecard), but rather at what we mean by reporting scorecard performance and how to construct a best practice report. This essentially breaks down into three components, each of which we explore in detail.

1. How should we capture, store, disseminate and report scorecard data and information: the software conversation
2. What does a best practice report look like: ensuring a balance of textual and numeric information
3. What are the different types of meetings that should be used to review and report on scorecard performance: and what are the different functions of each.

The Balanced Scorecard: The software conversation

Moving from simple office-type tools for capturing, storing and reporting scorecard performance to a fully automated system is not an inexpensive transition. Typical spending for a reasonable sized organization is in the region of $200,000 (and can be much more). A realistic starting price is about $30,000. So it might seem strange that in a book that continually reinforces the message that falling public sector revenues requires the significant tightening of belts that we are holding a conversation about purchasing an expensive software package to support a Balanced Scorecard implementation. But the fact is that the efficacious management of organizations today requires an appropriate IT infrastructure and the proper use of Business Intelligence tools and other performance-enhancing disciplines. When it comes to strategic performance management, it is important to use IT to make the most of the data and information available to decision-makers.

In his recent book: *The Intelligent Company: Five Steps to Success with Evidence-based Management*, Bernard Marr explained that organizations have wasted billions of dollars purchasing Business Intelligence solutions in the hope that it would solve all of their data and analytics problems.[1] In this book we can say that companies waste untold millions in software in the mistaken belief that it will instantaneously, or at a click of a button, solve all of their strategic management problems. Holding such a belief can lead to making the wrong decisions, buying inappropriate software and will result in a significant waste of time, energy and money.

Not only will it undermine the entire strategic performance management effort, but in today's financially constrained times will severely damage the credibility of the CEO and their senior team, lead to widespread negative publicity and, in many cases, the removal of members of the senior team. Public sector leaders need to think carefully about the purchase of software to support their strategy management, or Balanced Scorecard efforts.

The Balanced Scorecard is not a software solution

In an earlier chapter we stated that the Balanced Scorecard is not a measurement system, a message that is still difficult to get many leaders to accept. In this chapter we will add that neither is it a software solution (it is not a simple reporting exercise either, as we explain later). From our field observations we find it very worrisome that many organizational leaders (and this holds true for both the commercial and public sectors) can be seduced into believing that good software is *all* that they require for an efficacious performance management implementation.

Indeed, a few years ago James Creelman, one of the authors of this book, sat through a meeting with the senior team of a UK local authority, where he was told that they wanted to implement a Balanced Scorecard and were deciding on whether to finance consulting support or buy a software package (note they were not going to do both). The Finance Director strongly supported the latter approach, which won the day – even though it was clear he had little understanding of the scorecard. What he did believe, was that to successfully implement the scorecard, all that was required was the right software. The scorecard was an installation issue, not a change program.

Vendor failings

To a large extent, vendors have been responsible for creating this erroneous belief that the scorecard is an installation – or IT – issue. Selling all singing and dancing software solutions, with lots of bells and whistles, the message has been delivered strongly by many vendors (but certainly not all, we must add) that "simply press this button and all of your Balanced Scorecard – and by implication strategic management – needs are met."

Bill Barberg, a US-based management consultant puts it nicely: "So far software and the Balanced Scorecard have been conducting a dysfunctional dance. Most vendors have tried to use the Balanced Scorecard as a way of selling their product rather than understanding the process and how it works," he says. "This means that the scorecard message has got muddled. Although things are getting better, historically we have found that many management consultants have been resentful of software vendors as all they were seeing were vendors causing confusion. And oftentimes purchasing software did more harm than good."

He makes the important addition that: "The software is not the star of the show. It is more like the supporting cast that makes the star look good. The star of the show is the process for cascading and deploying strategy."

What software cannot do

Before considering in more detail the benefits of scorecard automation, let's briefly stress what software cannot do. Most importantly, perhaps, a software solution cannot remove the need for going through the process of managerial discussion and debate that is required to build the scorecard content. Put another way, software cannot create an organization's Strategy Map and Balanced Scorecard. That is exclusively the role of the senior team and is an intellectual and not an IT exercise. You cannot "plug and play," a scorecard framework. There are no scorecard templates that can be purchased fully-loaded with industry specific objectives, measures, targets and initiatives and if any are offered they should be fiercely resisted. Always keep in mind that a Strategy Map and scorecard must be unique to the organization, not generic to an industry or sector.

Similarly, the adoption of software will not by itself solve the many cultural and change management issues that are inevitably raised during a scorecard effort. Note the words of Peter Ryan, Planning and Performance Manager at the City of Christchurch, New Zealand, a case study in this book: "Rolling out the scorecard is not an IT issue or even a management issue, or even about KPIs and numbers," he says. "It's a people issue."

Other pre-purchase questions that need to be asked include "how will the solution integrate with existing IT infrastructure? How will the information be used? What sort of analytical capabilities do we need? etc. Only then should the organization look for software."

A performance enabler

Note that all of the case study organizations within this book fully understood that software was an enabler of good strategic performance management and that it might be inappropriate to rush to automate. Raja Al Zayani, Chief of the Strategic Planning Section at the Ministry of Works (MoW), Bahrain says that they waited more than a year before purchasing a software solution because they wanted to be careful that the Balanced Scorecard did not become a technology-led framework – advice we would certainly endorse.

THE BENEFITS OF AUTOMATION

That said there are myriad benefits of automation. Most notably technology can greatly support the implementation of a scorecard that is based on a well structured development program that has gone through all the key steps from Strategy Map definition to scorecard design, as was the case at the MoW.

Furthermore, one of the main benefits of automation is that it enables the scorecard and its performance to reach every member of the organization with a computer on their desks, or access to the web (solutions are all now web-enabled). Organization-wide networks give high-visibility to performance to the scorecard objectives, measures, targets and strategic initiatives. They also enable employees to provide feedback about their experience of implementing the scorecard and help to facilitate the strategic learning process.

Advanced Performance Institute findings

In the Advanced Performance Institute (API) research white paper "Strategic Performance Management in Government and Public Sector Organizations," API held the position that no organization-wide performance management system can work without the appropriate support of specialized performance software as the variables are too complex, the margin for error too risky.[2]

The paper reported the findings of a survey of over 1100 agencies across the globe. Based on this evidence API distilled ten practices of good performance management as exhibited by those organizations that demonstrated superior performance, which we describe fully within Chapter 1. One of these principles was "Use the appropriate IT infrastructure to support performance management activities." It also listed "Report and communicate performance information well," which we will consider later in this chapter.

Most organizations, the paper noted, usually begin to work with the scorecard with a paper-based system and spreadsheets alongside PowerPoint presentation tools. However they inevitably run into some common problems: for instance, they soon discover the problems encountered when compiling information from multiple spreadsheets, from many people, with lots of updates. The fact is that spreadsheets have many severe shortcomings when it comes to data analysis, communication and scalability. Spreadsheets are not an efficient way to collect or share information. There will also likely be many errors.

Moreover, data collection and performance reporting can become a major drain on resources if these tasks have to be carried out with a great deal of human intervention. Managing the scorecard soon becomes more important than using the scorecard to manage performance.

The right Performance Management software applications, the API research noted, allows companies to integrate the data and communicate performance appropriately. Furthermore software enables performance to be analyzed by everyone, and has been shown by multiple research studies to have a strong, tangible impact on organizations' delivery against strategic business goals.

Not surprisingly, the majority of spreadsheet users in the survey report being unhappy with their performance management capabilities. By contrast, users of specialized packaged applications are generally the happiest. Although over half of responding organizations still rely on spreadsheet applications (which is a somewhat worrying finding given the cited problems, and will certainly not help public sector bodies increase efficiency and effectiveness) – compared with 23% that use specialized packaged applications and 22% that use custom-built applications – the research found that users of packaged applications were significantly happier with the way their software supports performance management in their organization, followed by custom-built applications and, last of all, spreadsheets.

Figure 8.1 indicates that users of packaged applications are again significantly happier with the way their software helps to engage people in their performance management activities.

Packaged versus custom built solutions: Case study evidence

Interestingly, our two case study organizations that are the most mature in their usage of Balanced Scorecard software, the Ministry of Works, Bahrain and Christchurch City Council provide contrasting examples of purchased and custom-built packages.

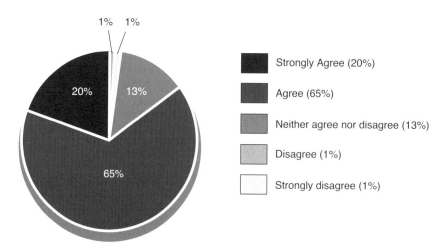

Figure 8.1 **The Software Applications We Use Help Us to Better Manage Performance**

Ministry of Works, case example 1

In 2007 the Ministry of Works (MoW) Bahrain[3] purchased the Executive Strategy Management (ESM) Balanced Scorecard software solution recently introduced by Palladium, co-founded by Dr David Norton, the co-creator with Harvard Business School Professor Robert Kaplan of the "classic" Balanced Scorecard system.

Raja Al Zayani says that the ESM solution has greatly improved the decision-making, objective performance assessment and assessment of the progress of initiatives while also taking a large documentation and reporting burden off their hands. "Previously a strategic management repository was in place using SharePoint and associated tools, but this was found to be insufficient for the growing needs and demands for strategic management information," she comments. The software solution is now used actively by over 200 people for management and reporting purposes and by more for viewing purposes. A fulltime administrator is responsible for managing the ESM solution.

Importantly, Raja stresses that the MoW will not be relying solely on the ESM solution for all its needs; that it will continue to use a diverse set of information systems and tools to support its strategy management process. "For example we expect several areas of Business Intelligence to increasingly require more sophisticated tools, especially in terms of supporting strategic hypothesizing."

Christchurch City Council case example

Christchurch City Council, New Zealand has opted for a custom-built application. Peter Ryan (who also spearheaded the introduction of a custom-built application within Brisbane City Council, which was the first public sector body in the southern hemisphere to be inducted into the Balanced Scorecard Hall of Fame[4] – which is reserved for those that demonstrate breakthrough performance against several of the principles of the strategy focused organization) explains why he has decided not to select a packaged solution. "From what I have seen, I don't believe that packaged solutions are bad solutions, but I have so far found them inappropriate for a public sector situation," he says. "I'm a local government specialist and how you get data, where it comes from and its sheer diversity, which cannot be matched by even the most complex commercial organization, makes it difficult to find an appropriate off-the-shelf solution."

Christchurch City Council[5] has created an in-house developed software system that it calls Horizon. This contains the City's comprehensive collection of metrics, targets and initiatives.

"Horizon combines the key features of an executive information system with project management and value analysis, providing a clear line of sight from strategy to operational tasks," Ryan says. Moreover, it is fully transparent and can be accessed by anyone in the organization. "Such openness helps create a performance-oriented culture as everyone can see how everyone else is performing." We should add here that such transparency and openness are key strengths of scorecard automation but can also lead to building of bulwarks of resistance, if the culture is inappropriate and built around punishing poor performance (we consider culture in the next chapter).

Horizon provides both the summary view against the Plan on a Page (as it calls its Balanced Scorecard) targets, as well as any exceptions. In the case of the "deliver levels of service" objective, as one corporate example, this means the report summary provides a single result against the target (say 83% of levels of service achieved) but it also means seeing a list of any services that are not on track, who is running them and what that officer recommends going forward. "It is summary reporting at the strategic level and exception based reporting at operational level," explains Ryan.

Figure 8.2 is a screenshot of the Horizon online front-page, which provides employees with a navigational aid for going to any of the organizational scorecards and viewing performance to any of the perspectives or indeed individual performance areas. Using City

Figure 8.2   **Screenshot of the Horizon Online Front Page**

Figure 8.3   Screenshot of Performance on Horizon System

Environment (a devolved Plan on a Page) as an illustration, Figure 8.3 provides an overview of actual performance against designated targets, with the responsible manager clearly identified.

Figure 8.4 provides information on which people are assisting with the delivery of a particular initiative. "It is not possible for the accountable manager to throw the light on the measure without looking at how the supporting initiatives are performing," explains Ryan.

The system also enables the loading and tracking of the individual's performance plan for the year and for monitoring how an individual is

<< Back					
☐ Show Comments					
Level Of Service Description	Responsible Manager	Target	Status	Updated	History
Repair time for hazardous defects	Beuzenberg, Alan	Potholes / Ice / Bleeding bitumen - 95% within: Potholes - 48 hrs. / 20 minutes / 60 minutes			🕒

Associated Tasks	Responsible Officer	Due Date	Status	Updated	History
Identify	McDonald, Peter	30-Jun-2007			🕒
Planning	McDonald, Peter	30-Jun-2007			🕒
Maintain	McDonald, Peter	30-Jun-2007			🕒
Operate	McDonald, Peter	30-Jun-2007			🕒
Monitor / Review	McDonald, Peter	30-Jun-2007			🕒

Figure 8.4   Screenshot of Initiative Responsibility on Horizon System

165

performing at any point in time. Accountability for measures and their supporting initiatives is therefore very clear and cascaded to individuals on a methodical basis.

Advising the purchase of a packaged solution

Although there are organizations, such as Christchurch City Council, that have successfully built their own Balanced Scorecard software solution, it is our observation that it is generally more cost effective, and indeed safer, to purchase a packaged application rather than to create your own. Those that succeed with a home-grown solution tend to have an extremely good understanding of strategic performance management functionality (such as Peter Ryan at Christchurch City Council who has been successfully building customized scorecard solutions since 1997, previously with the Hall of Fame winner Brisbane City Council). When this expertise is missing it is always wise to opt for a packaged solution as the risk of failure in building your own will be high – a risk that is probably not advisable in today's economic climate.

Besides the cost factors, packaged applications are usually quicker to implement with vendors offering a wide variety of ancillary services such as conversion assistance, implementation training and system integration. These packages also tend to represent the cumulative efforts of many individuals and organizations over a longer period of time, which usually results in better, more user-friendly applications than most first-time attempts to create "home grown" applications.

Guidelines for a scorecard solution

For an in-depth guidance for selecting a scorecard solution we would direct you to Bernard Marr's white paper "Selecting Balanced Scorecard Software Solutions."[6] Additionally, Bill Barberg provides these useful guidelines, based on his experience and observations.

a) The model should be built around strategic objectives, not data cubes or complex formulas or hierarchies for linking measures.
b) Strategy Maps should not be an awkward bolt on, but should be central to the application.

166

c)   The software should support the journey, starting by providing a framework by which the high-level strategic objectives can be further articulated, refined and cascaded based on cause and effect.

d)   There should be rich information collaboration capabilities (with appropriate structure) to help refine the content of various strategic objectives – especially with regard to what needs to change, ownership, etc.

e)   Content, especially objectives and initiatives, should be able to be reused. So, once an objective is defined, it may appear in many different contexts, without needing to be redefined. The same objective may be on multiple Strategy Maps, scorecards, etc.

f)   The system should not require replicating a lot of operational data that can be viewed and analyzed in either the operational systems or operational Business Intelligence systems. These types of capabilities are best "lightly integrated" rather than trying to build a big monolithic system or have too many dependencies that interfere with deployment and a focus on strategy.

g)   The software should provide a framework that helps people follow best practices without feeling that they are swimming upstream. It should provide a framework that brings the theory to life.

DIFFERENTIATING OPERATIONAL DASHBOARDS AND STRATEGIC SCORECARDS

Barberg also adds this useful advice regarding operational dashboard and strategic scorecards. "I think that greater clarity is now coming in to play that is leading to a distinction between operational dashboard and strategic scorecards," he says. "If you think about operational dashboards this is oftentimes about checking that things are going right and if not then doing something about it. It's near real time checking and operational monitoring. That is different to a strategic scorecard – which is not about detailed day-to-day activities but future oriented goals. It's about creating a map to get somewhere that you haven't been before. It's about trying to get into the heads of people and overcoming obstacles that haven't happened yet. This required different thinking re the software solution."

Indeed operational, or KPI, dashboards and strategic scorecards will have different functions in informing the various performance meetings that we outline later.

REPORTING AND COMMUNICATING PERFORMANCE INFORMATION

We will now turn our attention to the other of the ten principles of good performance management identified by the API research[7] that is relevant to this chapter: "Reporting and Communicating Performance Information Appropriately."

Reporting and communicating performance information is a vital part of any effective performance management strategy. There is simply no point having rich findings if the relevant people don't know about them so they can hone the way they go about their jobs in the future.

This means organizations must disseminate appropriately communicated performance results, and what these mean to the organization and to individual departments, teams and individuals. Staff members must be able to understand the "so what" implications for their own roles in the organization, e.g. "How does this affect me?" and "What do I/we need to do differently in the future?"

CREATING A BEST PRACTICE REPORT: ENSURING A BALANCE OF TEXTUAL AND NUMERIC INFORMATION

For this to take place, performance information must be reported and communicated appropriately. This includes both the proper use of performance meetings (which we explore later) and the construction of meaningful and accessible performance reports.

For best practice report construction, data has to be put in context and presented in a form that is accessible, such as in tables with traffic lighting, graphs or charts. When it comes to performance data, there is often little contextualization or interpretation, with the result that the key messages are unclear, often buried in data. All too often, performance data is circulated in the form of large spreadsheets, attached to e-mails or hosted on the intranet, leaving individuals to figure out the key messages.

Yet, research has shown that it is important to communicate performance data in different formats to reach different people with different preferences. Current best practice involves making extensive use of visual aids (such as Strategy Maps, graphs and charts) supported by numerical information, and using narratives and verbal communication formats to complement, contextualize and provide meaningful interpretation.

Where data and league tables are presented without context or interpretation, individuals may misunderstand the data, creating the potential for misuse. In a political context, there will always be the temptation to "spin" data for self-serving purposes, and the more contextualized the data is, the more difficult this will become. In most organizations, the primary communication format is numeric, using tables and spreadsheets complemented by graphs and charts. This is followed by pure numeric without the graphs and charts. The least common formats are narratives with supporting numeric data, and verbal communications of performance information.

We would argue that organizations should place much more emphasis on communicating performance information in words, both written and verbal, and less in numbers. After all, the underlying messages and insights the numbers generate are what really count.

Those taking part in the API facilitated survey clearly agree, since the majority claim to be unhappy with their current communication format. Over a third feel that this is not appropriate or meaningful (see Figure 8.5).

A five-step process for creating a best practice report

To make sure that reports are compelling and powerful we have put together the following five-step process. This process involves both

Q: The communication format of our current performance information is appropriate and meaningful.

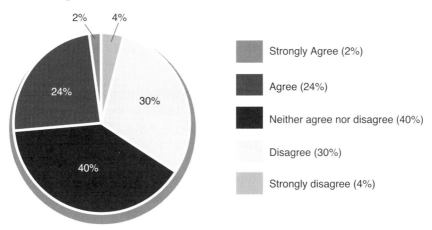

Figure 8.5 **Communication Effectiveness**

graphical and textual visual display mechanisms and, as importantly, ensures that the insights provided are strategically relevant.

1. Start with the Strategy Map
2. Frame the report with a key performance question (KPQ)
3. The KPQ should then be supported by appropriate and meaningful graphs and charts.
4. Headings should then be used to capture the salient points of the report (or the key insights)
5. Narratives should be used to better tell the story and contextualize the graphics.

Show the Strategy Map

Open the report by showing the Strategy Map: this shows how the subsequent information supports the strategic goals of the organization.

Show the Key Performance Question

For step two, show the key performance question (KPQ) that the data/information sets out to answer (we explain KPQs fully in Chapter 5). When using a KPQ it becomes immediately evident as to how the information/insights that are to be presented directly link back to a core strategic objective of the organization, as shown in the Strategy Map. As well as providing the strategic context to all that will follow it should also ensure that the report is focused squarely onto meeting a critical information need of the target audience, thus avoiding any inclination to focus on "interesting" rather that "valuable" information. If any piece of information does not directly impact that question, then it has no place in the report.

Use meaningful graphs and charts

The KPQ should then be supported by meaningful graphs and charts. Graphs are the most widely used visual display tools within organizations. Placing a graph directly after a KPQ is a great of way of quickly showing how we are progressing in answering that one focused question.

There are many different types of graphs that can be deployed to convey information. These include pictographs, tally charts, bar graphs, histograms, scatter plots, line graphs and pie charts, as some examples. Graphs provide many benefits for conveying information. They are quick and direct, highlight the most important facts, facilitate an easy understanding of the data and can be easily remembered. However, such is their pervasiveness, availability and ease in populating that it can be easy to simply create lots of graphs. The trick, of course, is knowing when and how to use graphs. Here are some more generic tips for producing useful and compelling graphs:

- Keep graphs simple and ensure that the focus is on the message the target audience requires. Too much clutter makes it difficult for the recipient to find the appropriate information.
- The eyes of the recipient of the information should be drawn to the most important piece of information – too often, everything on the page looks similar and nothing stands out.
- Try to avoid 3-dimensional graphs – they are harder to read.
- Use emphasis colors rarely and only where you want to highlight specific issues.
- Remember that people tend to relate things in different colors within different displays.
- Bear in mind that 10% of men and 1% of women are color blind. Consequently, some organizations prefer speedometer-style displays that indicate current performance in comparison to the targets' expectations.
- Don't use too many different varieties of graphs as an analysis across different graphs is difficult.
- Try to avoid any unnecessary decorations, background colors etc. The ink should only be used to show the data. Any additional and unnecessary elements are distracting and make it harder to extract the insights: if thought useful, put the additional data into an appendix.
- Graphs should not be used when the data is widely dispersed, when there is not enough data (one, two or three data points), when the data is very numerous or when the data shows little or no variations.

Use headlines

Flowing down from the graphs, a good report should then use "headlines." The headline summarizes the main finding from the data (as displayed in the graphics) and is useful in organizing textual information into a logical sequence. This technique is taken from newspapers or magazines, where the most important piece of information is captured in a "headline," which is further described and elaborated on by the following text, photographs and data.

Use performance narratives

A narrative puts context around and provides meaning to the data and provides a greater information drill than can be provided by a summary. The narrative essentially tells the performance story, so puts other data and information into the real-life organizational context. Belfast City Council is one of our case organizations that have made much use of narratives (as shown in Chapter 2).

Audit Scotland case example

Furthermore, our case organization Audit Scotland[8] was, at the time of preparing the case study, in the process of redesigning its performance reports to bring best practice to the communication and display of information. Within these reports, headlines and narratives will be used to capture the key messages, using ideas and graphic/textual formatting from magazines and newspapers. As a further communication device, Audit Scotland is planning to create an A3 summary sheet/poster each quarter to disseminate the key strategic messages.

   Audit Scotland also report performance to its Strategy Map to the senior management team and board on a quarterly basis, who particularly look to see how objectives and activities are improving and to focus on areas that are proving challenging and where corrective action might be required. More frequently, local teams use the map for performance improvement initiatives.

PERFORMANCE MEETINGS

And this brings us to a discussion on the role of meetings in analyzing information from the Balanced Scorecard. Here we are not so much looking at the Balanced Scorecard as a reporting framework. Although of course one of its core values is as a performance reporting tool, we would add that those that see it as *only* a reporting tool are missing many of its other beneficial usages that come from understanding it as a strategic management framework. Rather, we are here considering the mechanisms by which performance to the scorecard is reported.

Kaplan and Norton's three types of meetings

Within their book *The Execution Premium*: *Linking Strategy to Operations for Competitive Advantage*,[9] Drs Kaplan and Norton suggest that there are three types of meetings that are required to fully align operational and strategic activities: operational reviews, strategy reviews and a meeting for strategy testing and adapting. As shown in Table 8.1, these meetings have different information requirements, frequency, attendees, foci and goals. For example, the goal of an operational review is to respond to short-term problems and promote continuous

TABLE 8.1 **Three types of meetings as suggested by Kaplan and Norton**

	Meeting type		
	Operational review	**Strategy review**	**Strategy testing and adapting**
INFORMATION REQUIREMENTS	Dashboards for key performance indicators; weekly and monthly financial summaries	Strategy map and Balanced Scorecard reports	Strategy map, Balanced Scorecard, ABC profitability reports, analytic studies of strategic hypotheses, external and competitive analyses
FREQUENCY	Daily, twice weekly, weekly, or monthly, depending on business cycle	Monthly	Annually (perhaps quarterly for fast-moving industries)
ATTENDEES	Departmental and functional personnel; senior management for financial reviews	Senior management team, strategic theme owners, strategy management officer	Senior management team, strategic theme owners, functional and planning specialists, business unit heads
FOCUS	Identify and solve operational problems	Manage strategy implementation issues Assess progress of strategic initiatives	Test and adapt strategy based on causal analytics; Use scenario planning to evaluate tail risk events; War games to test against competitors' strategies
GOAL	Respond to short-term problems and promote continuous improvements	Fine-tune strategy; make mid-course adaptations	Improve or transform strategy

improvement; the goal of the strategic review is to fine-tune strategy and make mid-term adjustments; the goal of the strategy testing and adapting meeting is to improve or transform strategy.

Ministry of Works, Bahrain case example 2

It is interesting that Kaplan and Norton suggest that strategy review meetings are held on a monthly basis. Most organizations that hold such meetings do so on a quarterly basis. This is true of The Ministry of Works, Bahrain, where the reviews are chaired by the Minister of Works, His Excellency (HE) Fahmi Bin Ali Al-Jowder.

Starting with the three sectors (roads, sanitary and construction), a review is then held for corporate support units, services (such as HR and IT) and finance units. These reviews serve as a prelude to, and inform the corporate review.

Each review is a combined operational and strategy review. Reviewing both together on the same day is purposeful. "This ties the operational and strategic perspectives closer together to help validate the practical relationship between the strategy and operations as well as reinforce the relationship," explains Raja Al Zayani.

From being launched up until mid-2008, the first half of the event focused on the operational review with the second half dedicated to strategy. Both halves had different formats to reflect the nature of the work. For instance, the strategy review included several aspects to specifically draw upon the linkage to enhance learning. This included assessing the validity of measures in terms of actual operations.

The practical insights gleaned from this process provided MoW with significant learning and resulted in revisions to fine tune and enhance the review process and its outcomes. For example, as tying the reviews together enabled a clearer view of the strategy and operational relationship, the decision was made to pull them together into a single review. Through the new approach the strategy is the centerpiece; strategic objectives are reviewed and aspects that used to be considered operational pertaining to an objective are considered within that strategic objective discussion, either through activities managed as projects being reported as initiatives, or through activities being monitored and reported as measures.

As one outcome this has helped reduce the multitude of less significant items being reported to HE The Minister and instead to focus his rather precious time for discussing those items and issues of most significance.

Also noteworthy is that over time the strategy review has become broader than just an evaluation of implementation successes or failures. The quality of the strategy is reviewed as well as performance of strategy, with every scorecard being assessed and audited for its quality in terms of its objectives, measures, targets, initiatives, and timeliness of reporting.

Another interesting recent development within the MoW is to move away from "reporting by exception," which is commonly used in organizations. "There are some objectives and initiatives that we feel we need to discuss within our quarterly review meetings, that may be blue or green in color," says Raja Al Zayani. "While there are others that might be red that we do not feel require a performance conversation at this time." MoW uses a four-color code for reporting objectives and three color codes for reporting initiatives, believing that reporting to objectives is backward looking whereas reporting to initiatives is forward looking. Al Zayani continues: "Therefore we have introduced 'pre-qualifying' meetings within which a team of senior managers select those objectives or initiatives that will be discussed, irrespective of their status color."

Advising against combining strategic and operational reviews

The MoW has clearly succeeded in aligning strategic and operational reviews. But we would offer caution in doing so. Just as we stated earlier that custom building Balanced Scorecard software typically only succeeds within organizations that have a deep and well-entrenched understanding of strategic performance management, we would similarly suggest that aligning the strategic and operational reviews will likely only work in organizations that have a deep understanding of the different roles of both, such as is true at the MoW.

Caution against aligning strategic and operational reviews

When this is not the case there is often a lack of focus and purpose in these meetings. In those cases the discussion often fluctuates between the highest level strategic issues to the minute details of operational and project related issues. A lack of structure means that the meetings often go off course. Regularly, operational issues or "fire fighting" takes over and pushes the strategic discussion off the agenda. A lack of meeting discipline means that these meetings often start late and overrun and people tend to join or leave the meetings as they like. This means when it comes to decision-making some key decision-makers might not be there to make them.

Belfast City Council case example

As examples of other meetings that have a strategic focus, our case organization Belfast City Council[10] introduced Strategic Performance Improvement Meetings (SPIMS) to ensure performance is regularly reviewed. The aim of these meetings is not to look backwards but to learn from the performance information looking forward. The emphasis is on dialog about performance guided by the key performance questions and informed by key performance indicators. These meetings were introduced both for chief officers as well as for members and are taking place on a regular basis.

Much emphasis was placed on the fact that performance information needs to be used to inform performance improvements on an ongoing basis and that it is seen as a learning tool. There was clear awareness that with any performance management initiative there is a danger that it is seen as a reporting tool only with a focus on showing that targets were met. In such a case performance measurement is often seen as a non-value-adding administrative burden. Another danger is that it can be seen as a command-and-control tool that is used to direct subordinates and control their behavior.

Information Management Services, HM Revenues and Customs case example

As a slightly different example, the Information Management Services (IMS) department of the UK's HM Revenue and Customs[11] has set up a performance sub-committee comprising of senior members from the Business Units that meets on a monthly basis to discuss scorecard performance. Moreover, a planning and performance team (which has facilitative responsibility for the scorecard) holds monthly meetings with coordinators within the business units (who support the business unit sub-committee member in managing the scorecard) to discuss progress and share best practices.

Another meeting that has benefited from the scorecard is the monthly board meeting, and in particular the financial conversation, as Richard Ryder, IMS's Head of Planning and Performance explains. "When we go to the board and talk about how our finances are being invested we now always take the scorecard and the risk register," he explains. "By doing so we can clearly show how, for example, cutting back investment in one area will impact another," adding that IMS has always understood the links between planning and risk and performance management, but had never had something to hang it on. "With the Strategy Map and Balanced Scorecard, we now have," he adds.

Avoiding the term "review"

Both the Belfast City Council and IMS illustrations are powerful examples of how ongoing reviews can be used to ensure that strategy through the Balanced Scorecard is used for the purpose of ongoing performance improvement and therefore does not become a simple, and static reporting tool. Indeed, we would suggest avoiding the term "review" as it suggests a backward looking performance analysis, rather than something that is dynamic and forward looking, such as performance improvement meetings, for example.

Advanced Performance Institute's four performance meetings

In order to avoid the problems and confusions with performance related meetings, we suggest creating four different and distinct types of meetings to discuss performance in an organization, namely Strategy Revision Meetings, Strategic Performance Improvement Meetings, Operational Performance Improvement Meetings, and Personal Performance Improvement Meetings. These meetings are interdependent and the content and outputs influence each other. However, each of these meetings proposed here has its own clear purpose and each of them differs in terms of time horizon, frequency, outputs, focus, and supporting performance information. We will discuss each of these meetings in more detail, while a summation of the key elements are shown in Table 8.2.

Strategy revision meetings

These are meetings that are used to revise and renew the strategy. In most public sector organizations these meetings would take place on

TABLE 8.2 **Four types of meetings as suggested by the Advanced Performance Institute**

	Type of meeting			
	Strategy Revision Meeting	**Strategic Performance Review Meeting**	**Operational Performance Review Meeting**	**Personal Performance Improvement Meeting**
PURPOSE	To review and revise the strategy and to agree the content of the Balanced Scorecard	To discuss the execution of the existing strategy. To fine-tune the strategy and review and revise the existing strategy execution plans	To discuss and respond to short-term operational issues. To discuss and find solutions to "burning issues"	Forums in which employees and their line managers can discuss the strategic priorities for the next year
FREQUENCY	Annually	Monthly	Daily, twice weekly, or weekly, as required.	Annually, or twice yearly
TIME HORIZON	One to three years ahead	One to six months ahead	One week to a month	One year
INFORMATION REQUIREMENTS	Insight from various strategic analyses and performance data	Insights from various strategic analyses with performance data. Updates from strategy execution programs	Operational analytics, performance to operational targets. Operational performance feedback from various employees	Personal objectives and development plans along with departmental and enterprise Balanced Scorecards to ensure alignment between individual objectives and those of the department and enterprise
ATTENDEES	Senior team and the leader of the corporate performance management team (or Office of Strategy management) and relevant performance management analyst	Executive team together with directors and heads of departments as well as members of corporate performance management team (or Office of Strategy management) and relevant performance management analyst	Departmental managers, functional supervisors and relevant employees	Individual employee and line manager

an annual basis (it is rare that the environment is so dynamic that more frequent meetings to revise the strategy are required). The time horizon of these meetings is to look between one and three years ahead. The objective of these meetings is to agree on a new or revised Balanced Scorecard.

The meeting is the opportunity for the executive team and the directors to get together and agree on their new or revised strategy. The executive team would take the insights from various strategic analyses and performance data to firm up their strategy. It is usually recommended to also have the leader of the Corporate Performance Management team, or Office of Strategy Management, and relevant performance management analysts in the meeting. These individuals can provide answers to any data queries and analyses. Strategy revision meetings tend to be held off-site and usually last between one and two days. As with all these meetings proposed here, the emphasis is not on data presentation, but on decision-making and reaching strategic agreement.

Strategic Performance Improvement Meetings

These meetings have the purpose of discussing the execution of the existing strategy. Here, the overall strategic assumptions are not questioned, instead, the meetings take place to fine tune elements of the strategy and to revise the strategy execution plans. SPIMS (such as in place at Belfast City Council) are there to revise the operational activities of the strategic objectives on the scorecard. This would involve decisions about reallocating resources and refocusing projects. In these meetings the scorecard and in particular the key performance questions guide the agenda and performance indicators are used to guide the decision-making. The time horizon of these discussions is medium term, meaning between one and six months ahead.

Usually, these meetings would take place on a monthly basis and are attended by the executive team together with directors and heads of departments. Similarly to the strategy revision meetings, we would recommend that members of the corporate performance management or Office of Strategy Management team and relevant performance management analysts also attend the meeting to provide answers to any data queries and analyses. Strategic performance improvement meetings can also be used to model and test assumed causal relationships between different strategic objectives. SPIMS are the type of meetings that are the rarest in organizations. At the same time we believe that they are a core element of a performance driven and strategically focused organization.

Operational Performance Improvement Meetings

These are meetings to discuss and respond to short-term operational issues. Often called "performance clinics," they represent the frequent forums in which departmental managers and functional supervisors and personnel get together to talk about the "burning issues." In some organizations these meetings take place on a daily basis in others on a weekly or twice weekly basis. The discussions and decisions that take place in these meetings have a short time horizon (a week to one month). The meetings can focus on specific operational performance issues or can focus on project performance. Operational Performance Improvement Meetings are the engine rooms of an organization in which the operational decisions take place and in which any short-term operational issues are discussed and resolved.

Personal Performance Improvement Meetings

Most of the dreaded personal performance and development reviews which take place in organizations are purely administrative human resources (HR) tick-box exercises. The atmosphere is cringe worthy and the outcomes are not very constructive and tend to demotivate much more than they motivate. At most they tend to produce records of suggested training needs which are sent to the HR department and which only ever see the light of day again at the next round of meetings.

Here, we suggest a different kind of meeting: a personal Performance Improvement Meeting. They should be forums in which employees and their line managers can discuss the strategic priorities for the next year. The time horizon for these meetings tends to be between six and 12 months and they usually take place on an annual basis. More recently we have seen organizations which have successfully introduced six-monthly personal performance improvement meetings. These meetings are a great opportunity to engage everybody in the organization in a strategic discussion and ensure any personal objectives, performance plans and development plans are aligned with the overall priorities of the organization.

Indeed, we are now beginning to see advanced organizations putting the personal improvement plans (often designed as "personal Balanced

Scorecards,") online with space for managers and others to enter into a virtual dialog on performance to specified initiatives, enabling best practice sharing, managerial/co-worker coaching, tips and advice.

CONCLUSION

This chapter has explained how to ensure that performance reporting is properly architected to get the most from the Balanced Scorecard effort. This began by providing guidance on selecting a Balanced Scorecard software solution, which is required to make the most of the data and information gained as part of the scorecarding effort. We highlighted the many dangers that exist in software selection – not least in mis-understanding the role of automation, what it can do and what it can't do.

We then described how to build a best practice report and stressed that this should comprise both textual and numeric data and in-formation. Both are required to fully tell a performance story, and some people respond better to the pictures than numbers, and vice versa.

Finally we considered the different types of performance meetings that should be in place to get the best out of the scorecard effort and indeed to more firmly aligning operational activities with strategic goals and indeed individual employee performance with strategic goals.

No matter how much effort is put into building a Strategy Map and Balanced Scorecard and in automation and shaping useful reporting mechanisms, all the work will be wasted if the appropriate culture is not in place. Culture is the subject of the next chapter.

9

BUILDING A CULTURE FOCUSED ON STRATEGIC PERFORMANCE MANAGEMENT

In an organization with a strong performance culture, employees know what they are expected to accomplish and are emotionally committed to organizational success.

Howard Risher (US-based Human Resources Consultant)

INTRODUCTION

In an economic downturn, or when funding is severely restricted for any other reason, it is to be expected that there will be a negative impact on the attitudes and mindsets of the employees within the organization. People will fear many consequences, ranging from a degradation of service and the consequent rise in customer dissatisfaction to large-scale job losses and personal financial hardship. In such difficult organizational times, the internal "rumor mill," will work to full capacity and each day will likely provide new, and disturbing, stories of upcoming doom and gloom. Successfully reversing the likely collapse in motivation and reenergizing the employee-base is one of the greatest challenges of management, especially when some of the feared outcomes prove true – such as redundancies.

For leaders of public sector organizations, this management challenge will probably be front-of-mind for some time. Obviously the journey from "efficiency gains" (which we focus on throughout this book) to "redundancy" is a short one in most employees' minds as is "cost cutting" to "poorer customer service." The rumor mills within public sector organizations will be placed on a state of high readiness whenever terms such as "efficiency gains," and "cost cutting are banded about. Unfortunately, so might it be when mention is made of putting in place a strategic performance management framework to ensure (and more importantly from a "fear" perspective – to measure) that efficiency goals are delivered to and the launch of Lean or Six Sigma projects that will also look to cut costs.

The implementation of any performance measurement or improvement system always faces some (oftentimes fierce) resistance from concerned employees – who will be suspicious of the underlying motives. In an environment of significant "belt tightening," resistance to the introduction of a Balanced Scorecard should be both expected and planned for. Indeed, within the first of their series of five books on the Balanced Scorecard (see Chapter 2 for the history and chronology) scorecard co-creators Harvard Business School Professor Robert Kaplan and consultant Dr David Norton suggested that the framework might be inappropriate at a time when severe cut backs are required.[1] They have shifted their stance since, but the fact is when there is a laser-like focus on cost cutting, it can prove difficult to maintain a commitment to improving and investing in the non-financial areas relating to customers and employees, however short-sighted that might be.

And although within this book we continually reinforce the importance of maintaining an efficiency/effectiveness balance within the scorecard, making sure that both themes are equally important in financially difficult times can be a considerable challenge, and a major test of whether or not the senior team is truly supportive of the scorecard concept.

A cultural challenge

All in all, implementing the scorecard is a significant cultural challenge – employees must trust that the organization will not abuse efficiency gains and that it retains a commitment to improving performance to customer, internal process and learning and growth perspectives (to use the "classic" scorecard terminology). Only then will they be prepared to put the energy and commitment into the driving of efficiency gains and its subsequent management and measurement.

But, if we talk of a "cultural challenge," we must first explain what we mean by "culture."

Although a widely used word within an organizational setting and context it is normally poorly understood or articulated.

CULTURE DESCRIBED

In essence, an organizational culture represents the shared underlying beliefs, norms, values, assumptions and expectations, which influence the typical patterns of behavior and performance that characterize an organization.

Edgar Schein definition

In his seminal work: *Organizational Culture and Leadership*, the culture change specialist Edgar Schein wrote: "... culture [is] a pattern of basic assumptions – invented, discovered, or developed by a given group as it learns to cope with its problems of external adaptation and internal integration – that has worked well enough to be considered valid and, therefore, to be taught to new members as the correct way to perceive, think and feel in relation to those problems."[2]

The influence of culture

Culture influences the way things get done in an organization and it therefore also governs the way people react to performance indicators and use performance information. A culture, for example, that is characterized by fear will not create an organization in which employees readily embrace performance indicators or share performance information that might be construed as negative (later we explain how this leads to data manipulation and dysfunctional behavior). A culture based on trust, learning and improvement will create an organization that happily accepts performance indicators and shares information.

A winning culture described

In the report "Driving Corporate Culture for Business Success," James Creelman looked at how culture was purposefully used as a tool and intervention to win in competitive markets. He came up with the following definition of a "winning culture." "A winning culture is where there exists a visible set of performance enhancing behaviors which together form a recognizable corporate personality and healthy organizational mind."

"The organizational mind exists to deliver superior performance and as such is constantly learning about, and aligning with, changing customer and market demands."[3]

A performance-driven culture described

Another useful description of culture (and in this instance a "performance driven" culture) comes from an article written by Howard Risher, a pay-for-performance expert and published in Public Manager:[4]

> "In an organization with a strong performance culture, employees know what they are expected to accomplish and are emotionally committed to organizational success. They believe in the mission and goals and are quick to put their energy into a task without being asked or monitored. Informal conversations with coworkers frequently focus on performance problems and recent organization results. They tend to celebrate successes as a team or group. The commitment to performance is a way of life in the organization."

Culture as an organizational core capability

In their book, *The Conductive Organization*, noted thought leaders on culture and knowledge management Hubert Saint-Onge and Charles

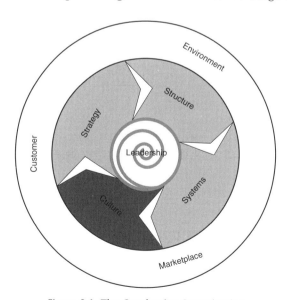

Figure 9.1 **The Conductive Organization**

Armstrong take the definition further, by going as far as to state that culture is a core organizational capability, alongside systems, strategy, structure and leadership (see Figure 9.1). They write: "Culture is a key enabler of business performance. It can make or break strategies. Employees are the ones who must implement strategies, and they will fail (or unconsciously refuse) to do so if the strategies of the corporation, no matter how sound from a business perspective, are incongruent with the organization's culture. For example, a strategy based on customer-centricity and partnerships will be difficult to implement if the culture is task-focused and based on the power of culture silos."[5]

We could add that strategies will fail if the cultural tone set by the leadership team is wrong or inconsistent. As Saint-Onge/ Armstrong stress culture, as with strategy, must be owned by the senior management team. Leaders of public sector organizations have to lead by example. As children watch their parents, employees watch their leaders. They watch the behaviors of the leaders and copy them. It's not what leaders say but what they do that's important.

EMPLOYEES IMPLEMENT STRATEGY

Let's further consider just one element of Saint-Onge/Armstrong's powerful definition: "Employees are the ones who must implement strategies." This is very important when considered within the context of the Balanced Scorecard and in getting buy-in to the scorecard. The fact is, if you haven't got employees on your side, then no matter how elegantly you formulate the Strategy Map and the accompanying Key Performance Questions (KPQs) and Key Performance Indicators (KPIs), the scorecard will fail. End of story. And clearly culture, however it is defined, is about people.

CULTURAL OBJECTIVES ON A STRATEGY MAP

Indeed scorecard users (be that the "classic" Kaplan/Norton version or the "Value Creation Map") more often than not include an objective or enabler on their Strategy Map that has something to do with culture. As examples, consider some of the Strategy Maps from our case study organizations. Belfast City Council has an enabler of "create an open and performance-driven culture," (see Figure 2.14). The Ministry of Works, Bahrain simply has an objective of "high performance culture," (see Figure 4.1). The Scottish Intellectual Assets Centre has "create a professional and performance-driven culture," (see Figure 5.1).

Even when the word "culture" is not specifically used, there are usually objectives/enablers that have a strong cultural underpinning. For instance, the International Baccalaureate (IB) organization has as a key resource "recruit, develop and motivate our staff, associates and partners in line with IB's mission and values," (see Figure 4.2). As we will explain later, values and culture are usually inextricably linked: but as with culture, values are also typically poorly understood or articulated.

The benefits of a well-defined culture: Survey results

Although we will hold up the case studies in this book as notable exceptions, too many organizations (be they from the public or commercial sectors) simply create an objective/enabler that says something about culture and deploys a metric around employee satisfaction, for instance, and believes that this is culture dealt with. And more often than not the cultural objective/enabler is handed over to Human Resources (HR) to deal with and senior management doesn't give it another thought. The folly of senior management devolving responsibility for culture was powerfully demonstrated in a cultural survey of 236 companies from across the globe commissioned to support the cited "Driving Corporate Culture for Business Success," report.[6]

Respondents were split according to how well their culture was defined ranging from those with an "extremely well defined" culture to "very poorly defined." Respondents were asked to state whether they had achieved the goals of their change progress, exceed the goals or failed to meet the goals. In companies with "extremely well defined" cultures, the results were:

Achieved its goals: 50%
Exceeded its goals: 14.28%
Failed to meet its goals: 28.57%

Whereas in companies with "very poorly defined" cultures, the results were:

Achieved its goals: 20%
Exceeded its goals: 10%
Failed to meet its goals: 60%

But consider Table 9.1, which looks at where responsibility for corporate culture lies. In extremely well defined culture it is more likely to reside at the highest level of the organization, whereas in those companies with "very poorly defined' cultures it is more likely to reside in HR. We would agree with Saint-Onge/Armstrong that culture is a core organizational capability and is therefore too important to be owned anywhere but by the executive team, as is true of the Balanced Scorecard.

TABLE 9.1   People/department responsible for corporate culture

	Overall responsibility	Extremely well defined cultures	Very poorly defined cultures
The CEO	22.55%	20%	10%
The board	18.79%	20%	0%
Senior management team	24.81%	32%	30%
HR	19.54%	12%	50%
Other	14.28%	16%	10%

Scorecard failure in implementation

Simply put, a Balanced Scorecard is a strategy management framework. And most scorecard efforts fail not because the maps and accompanying metrics, etc., are badly designed (although many are) but in implementation. And the failure in implementation is more often than not something to do with culture. Peter Ryan, Planning and Performance Manager at Christchurch City Council, and one of the select few global thought leaders we interviewed puts it this way: "The Balanced Scorecard is about strategy. And strategy is just another word for change," he says. "Rolling out the scorecard is not an IT issue or even a management issue, or about KPIs and numbers. It's a people issue." He adds that creating something that makes people want to move, rather than forcing movement on them is the greatest challenge of all. "And you must win hearts and minds, or everything dies the moment you stop putting energy in," he says. Winning "hearts and minds," is of course a cultural challenge.

OVERCOMING THE CHALLENGES OF SCORECARD IMPLEMENTATION

HMRC IMS case example 1

Although the process of putting in place the Strategy Map and scorecard within our case organization the Information Management Services (IMS) department of the UK's HM Revenue and Customs, has clearly been successful, it has not been without its challenges.[7] The structure of IMS, through which the majority of IT services are actually outsourced, led to some initial difficulties. "As we have a massive external IT contract, we do a lot of performance measurement," says Richard Ryder, IMS's Head of Planning and Performance. "But this is measuring somebody else." He goes on to say that this led to some issues around getting people inside of IMS to take accountability for their performance. "Some members of staff would say 'we can't tell you what our performance is until we speak to our supplier,' or else they would say" "we can't tell you what our performance is and we can't comment on it."

Ryder adds that much effort was expended on explaining that, even when outsourced, the IMS units were accountable for that performance. "We said that you own it, it's your performance, you outsource responsibility for it and you are accountable within the organization."

Another issue was that some staff saw IMS as simply an overhead, so couldn't figure why there was need to use a Balanced Scorecard. A further challenge was caused by the historic siloed nature of IMS's work. "Some people asked why they had to justify their work. They had trouble seeing how their work fitted in with the wider aims of IMS and indeed HMRC."

A publicity technique called "market stalls" has been used to help overcome such cultural challenges. Devised by the IMS Communication team, the planning and performance team created a "market stall" (as did the other business units) and in 2008 visited all the IMS main locations and explained their work to local staff. The planning and performance team stall included an A1 sheet with the developing

Strategy Map and scorecard. "We were able to talk people through the process and explain how the work that they did fed up into the IMS plan and then to the HMRC plan," explains Kay McNeil, Head of Performance Improvement, Finance Planning and Performance. "This sort of communication exercise had never been done before and through the map and scorecard people began to see the strategic importance of their work and the difference that they made."

The importance of getting the culture right was well understood by others of our case organizations. As well as simply articulating a cultural-focused objective or enabler most spent time to describe what they mean by "culture," and, importantly, what this meant with regard to organizational performance.

Belfast City Council case example

For example, as well as appearing on its Strategy Map, the importance of culture was highlighted within Belfast City Council's value narrative. After describing the stakeholder-facing improvements that the council aimed to deliver, the narrative said:

> To achieve these improvements we will create an open, performance driven culture built on trust, where performance is discussed openly and used to help the organization learn and improve. Everyone will know what we want to achieve and how they contribute to this, in an environment where performance counts, is valued and is at the heart of everyone's job.[8]

This description is particularly powerful as it begins to put an organization's specific meaning to "culture." For instance, it says that culture is "open and performance driven." Performance, it says is "discussed openly" and crucially is "used to help the organization learn and improve."

Let's consider the part of this description that says that culture helps the organization "learn and improve." Simply put, if an organization wishes to deliver to stretching strategic targets, it must inculcate a culture in which learning and improvement are the norm. After all, a scorecard implementation is essentially about achieving quantum, or breakthrough, performance advancements and not incremental improvements. Step-change improvement will only be achieved when the organization is geared up for learning and improvement.

ADVANCED PERFORMANCE INSTITUTE RESEARCH FINDINGS

The importance of this enabler was signaled within the Advanced Performance Institute's (API) research report: "Strategic Performance Management in Government and Public Sector Organizations."[9] Based on a survey of more than 1100 organizations from across the globe (and therefore the biggest of its type ever conducted), the research found that "create a positive culture of learning and improvement from performance information," was one of the ten principles of good performance management, as exhibited by those public sector bodies that demonstrated superior performance. More telling, alongside "create clarity about the strategy with agreements on intended outcomes, outputs and necessary enablers," this principle had the strongest impact on performance improvement. The implication is clear – gain agreement on the strategic goals and get the culture right then step-change performance improvements can be expected. Don't gain agreement on the strategy and fail to get the culture right and then improvements will likely not be forthcoming – it's that simple!

As we highlight throughout this book, there is much that is discouraging with the API survey. Therefore, we might be encouraged by the research finding that an impressive 83% of respondents reported that they placed a strong emphasis on learning from performance improvement. It would appear, therefore, that most public sector organizations are genuinely seeking to put in place a culture of learning and improvement.

However, further analysis puts a stranglehold on any cheer. Fully 68% of respondents stated that they believed that some of their performance data had been fabricated. What we can safely deduce from this finding is that most organizations were "learning," and indeed basing strategic decisions and/or improvement interventions on misleading information. As much as anything this data manipulation is a damning indictment of the cultures of most public sector organizations.

Why organizations manipulate data

But the key question is why are employees manipulating data? What can we learn about the cultural underpinnings of these organizations?

A fear of measurement

As already cited, one of the reasons for cultural resistance to a score-card implementation is a fear of measurement – or more accurately a fear of how metrics are used within the organization. And there is little doubt that in a public sector environment where "belts are being tightened" that this fear will be amplified. When the perfor-mance information that flows from KPIs is used for negative pur-poses, such as to punish or blame people (or in extreme cases to force them out of the organization) then it is to be expected that employees will do all that they can to ensure that any poor results are hidden from the view of senior managers. If the scorecard itself cannot be killed off (and in many cases it will be) then the data that informs the metrics will likely be manipulated.

Indeed, how the scorecard is used in relation to the color-based traffic light system will also go some way to deciding whether it is used to galvanize a culture of learning and improvement or is actively resisted. As Patricia Bush, Vice-President of the Palladium Group, one of the select few thought leaders we interviewed for this book com-ments: "When using a Balanced Scorecard, organizational leaders are saying that 'We're going to measure performance and hold you accountable.' This is a big change for organization and can lead to dysfunctional behavior when accountable becomes synonymous with reward and punish or name and shame and when achieving green on the traffic light system means a reward and red means punishment." She says, adding the important observation: "For the scorecard to work effectively and to be accepted within the employee-base it is absolutely critical that we change the perception that red means bad. Red might not be what you are looking for, but when such a concept persists the problem is that people can't talk about trouble or ask for help and there is an increased chance that they will change the data." She adds that overcoming the "red phobia" is a big hurdle to get over.

The problem of "red equals bad" was recognized at the Ministry of Works, Bahrain. To help overcome this, The Minister of Works, His Excellency (HE) Fahmi Bin Ali Al-Jowder, has said: "I don't care if all the objectives on the Strategy Map are red, as long as I can see stretching targets and performance improvement towards those targets." He says. "This is far more useful than a Strategy Map that is 'all green' but represents no improvement whatsoever."

HE Al-Jowder is one public sector leader who recognizes that objec-tives and their supporting metrics are about learning and improve-ment and not control. Alas, the API research discovered that he represents the exception rather than the rule. The research shed more light on why there is fear of measurement and why this might trigger the highly dysfunctional behavior of data manipulation.

Advanced Performance Institute findings

The analysis found that the majority of respondents believed that their directors and senior managers guide employees' behavior by using performance indicators to monitor the implementation of objectives (providing feedback on the achievement of set goals to control and correct unwanted variance). This practice, known as "diagnostic control," is now seen as inappropriate, because of the negative impact it has on morale and motivation. Clearly, in a culture of fear or mistrust those employees being assessed are likely to manipulate the data if they can to avoid the "wrath" of their boss.

The second most frequently used approach was using performance results to prescribe overall strategic purpose, vision and values. This is less directive and instead focuses on creating an understanding of strategic intent.

The least used approach saw directors and senior managers involve themselves regularly and personally in the decision activities (drawing attention to current strategic issues). Experts currently favor an approach that draws on a combination of the last two practices – where top management sets the direction, and then influences direction through personal interaction with people.

Another factor found to determine success is the extent to which top management focuses on controlling output, input or behavior.

Again, research has shown that controlling people's behavior in a top-down manner (where the emphasis is on compliance with articulated operating procedures) yields the least benefits. The problems here are not only the huge costs involved in surveillance and control, but the fact that this does not allow for discretion and leads to rigid and often dysfunctional behavior.

If it is the output (versus targets) that is being emphasized, this gives subordinates a bit more discretion in how they achieve the desired ends. But, while output control makes sense where there is no cause-and-effect knowledge, it can lead to an over emphasis on short-term targets (such as financial performance) to the detriment of longer-term objectives. *Input* control, on the other hand, focuses on the *contributors* to performance. This can be a highly effective approach, so long as the causal links are known – e.g. if we assign more staff to service X, customers will see a marked improvement in service. Without these causal links, there is a danger that the wrong performance drivers might be managed. As much as anything this signals the importance of a Strategy Map.

Best practice specifies that public sector and government organizations should have a clear understanding of cause-and-effect, and should then use a healthy mix of input and output controls to manage their organization.

Currently, this is not the case for the majority of public sector organizations. The API research shows that the majority of respondents feel that their directors and senior managers focus primarily on output (performance against short-term, tactical targets), followed by a focus on behavioral control, and lastly a focus on input (for example, ensuring employees have the right training, knowledge, skills, abilities and values).

In a positive learning culture, organizations proactively provide performance information and "contextualized" feedback to everyone in the organization, with a special emphasis on middle management and front-line staff. Unfortunately, the majority of those in our survey short-sightedly reserve this information for senior management and external stakeholders.

USING METRICS FOR LEARNING AND IMPROVEMENT

Belfast City Council case example 2

As a best practice example of how performance information should be used for learning and improvement purposes, we once again point to Belfast City Council.[10] From the outset the organization wanted to ensure that its Strategy Map, KPQs and KPIs were being used in the appropriate manner to inform decision-making, organizational learning and performance improvement.

Strategic Performance Improvement Meetings (SPIMs) were put in place to ensure performance is regularly reviewed. The aim of these meetings is not to look backwards but to learn from the performance information looking forward. The emphasis is on dialog about performance guided by the KPQs and informed by KPIs. These meetings were introduced both for chief officers as well as for elected members and take place on a regular basis.

Much emphasis was placed on the fact that performance information needs to be used to inform performance improvements on an ongoing basis and that it is seen as a learning tool. There was clear awareness that with any performance management initiative there is a danger that it is seen as a reporting tool only with a focus on showing that targets were met. In such a case performance measurement is often seen as a non-value-adding administrative burden. Another danger is that it can be seen as a command-and-control tool that is used to direct subordinates and control their behavior.

A large number of communication workshops and presentations were conducted to ensure that heads of services, middle managers, and front-line staff were kept informed about the process and most importantly about the aims of the strategic performance management implementation within Belfast City Council.

The effective deployment of communication mechanisms are crucial to both securing buy-in to the scorecard and for creating the cultural underpinning required to succeed with the scorecard. Communication mechanisms were used effectively by our other case organizations.

Audit Scotland case example

For example, Audit Scotland has redesigned its performance reports to bring best practice to the communication and display of information. Within these reports, headlines and narratives (essentially a performance story) will be used to capture the key messages, using ideas and graphic/textual formatting from magazines and newspapers (see the preceding chapter for more on best practice reporting). As a further communication device, Audit Scotland has created an A3 summary sheet/poster that is produced each quarter to disseminate the key strategic messages.

Moreover, to support the objective, "We will have engaged and motivated people, strong leadership and good internal communication," Audit Scotland has a KPQ of "how well are we communicating internally" and KPIs of "staff survey results," and "staff focus group feedback."

The International Baccalaureate organization has an enabler of "manage the change process through excellent leadership, governance and communication," which has a supporting KPQ "to what extent are we communicating better," and KPIs that look at staff surveys and focus groups.

CULTURE AND VALUES

As cited early in this chapter, in most organizations culture and values go hand in hand. Indeed Saint-Onge and Armstrong state that: "Culture and values are inextricably linked. Culture is a reflection of values."[11]

It is not atypical for a cultural objective/enabler to be described through a list of values. Although correct and appropriate (as most of our case organizations will testify), it is also not unusual for value statements to be hurriedly articulated, hung on a wall and forgotten about. They often are "Mother and Apple Pie" statements that no one can argue with, but have no bearing on performance.

Values become a powerful performance improvement tool when they are "lived" within the organization. Crucially, values should be seen as non-negotiable, in that employees must adhere to these values. Saint-Onge and Armstrong made the important point that the objective is not to force a complete set of values onto the individual. "We aren't suggesting that you impose on every employee the same set of individual values. All employees will have their own sets of values, prioritized as they see fit and individually configured. We suggest identifying a common set of core values on which employees can agree. The organization can then recognize and leverage them as its cultural characteristics..."

"The core set of values also allows the organization to promote diversity among individuals with confidence because it has identified the core values that employees and the organization hold in common."[12]

NWCCA case example

Such is the importance of values within our case organization, the North West Commercial Collaborative Agency (NWCCA) that a values charter is a core component of its performance framework (that also includes a Strategy Map and accompanying KPQs and KPIs). The charter lists five values (its core values) and the accompanying behaviors that employees are expected to demonstrate day-to-day in the living of these values, as shown in Table 9.2.

More than a simple list of values, NWCCA operationalizes the values through its performance framework. On the Strategy Map this

TABLE 9.2   **NWCCA's values charter**

Values	Behaviors
Customer focused in all that we do	– Committed to best in class to support healthcare delivery and improve patient outcomes – Understand, and support delivery of, customer objectives – Delivering innovative outcomes through commercial best practice – Be seen to make a difference
Integrity of thought and deed	– Loyalty – one team, one message, one common objective – Do what we say we will do – Act with trust, honesty and openness – Put the team/organizational values before our own – Collective responsibility
Aspire to excellence	– Performance/value driven – set ambitious goals – Not afraid to take positive action and managed risk – Professional role models – champion the organization – Strategically informed decision-making at all times – Encourage adoption and sharing of best practice – Active program of continuous improvement
Respect people and value their individuality	– Empower and encourage individuals knowledge, talents and experience – Support achievement of potential – Be supportive yet constructively challenging – Respect confidentiality – Be sensitive and empathetic to individual needs and feelings
Lead by example in fostering a collaborative culture	– Communicate clearly and effectively – Encourage involvement and value alternative views, discussing issues calmly – Advocate a "no blame" culture that proactively manages conflict – Be open, honest and inclusive – Learn from experience and each other – Develop relationships based on trust for long-term mutual gain

value charter is captured in the enabler "foster a performance culture and live our values." In turn this is captured through the KPQs

1. To what extent are we customer focused in all that we do?
2. To what extent is there integrity of thought and deed?
3. To what extent do we have a culture of excellence?
4. To what extent do we value people and respect their individuality?
5. To what extent are we leading by example in fostering a collaborative culture?

A mixture of customer and staff survey and focus group KPIs are used to answer these questions. Importantly, NWCCA's performance framework includes action plans, with accountabilities, that will help inculcate these values, and supporting behaviors within the organizations. Action plans include: "reinforce the cultural values of the organization as part of the induction process for all staff," "create a series of communication posters to be used to instill values and strategic aims of the organization and "share the values charter with all staff."

INCENTIVES AND REWARDS

Another intervention that can be used effectively to help stimulate a culture of learning and improvement are incentives and rewards. The old maxim "what gets measured gets done," was actually the first part of a two part statement that conclude "what gets rewarded gets done faster." (Or some such wording, as there any many variations).

INCENTIVE COMPENSATION

Incentive compensation is of course a powerful motivator and indeed a "balanced paycheck" is listed as a key contributor to the strategy focused organization, as described by Kaplan and Norton (see Chapter 2).

Incentive compensation is used much less extensively in the public sector than in a commercial setting (not surprising as the latter has a clear profit or loss equation with which to base bonuses). It is also fraught with difficulties, not least there oftentimes being a backlash from employees against the very notion of "pay-for-performance" within a public sector setting. Nonetheless good examples from best practice companies can be found, and provide useful learnings.

Christchurch City Council case example

For example, consider our case organization, Christchurch City Council, New Zealand.[13] Peter Ryan comments; "We've made good progress in compensation. Fully 450 people (covering all the management layers – from the CEO, through department heads to team leaders) and forming about 1/8 of the workforce have the major portion of their incentive remuneration tied to scorecard results. In July 2007 we put scorecard related targets into all managers' individual performance plans."

"It's a very structured approach through which performance to scorecard targets drive a manager's performance review and determines their bonus," he adds.

The compensation link works this way. The performance assessment is weighted to highlight the council's scorecard priorities. Therefore in 2007 35% of the bonus was dependent on performance to the customer perspective, 20% was allocated to the financial perspective, people 15% and process 10%. The remaining 20% of the bonus was linked to individual development targets.

"This review and compensation link is based on performance to clearly defined measures and targets," says Ryan. "It is a lot more scientific than the ad-hoc discussion that often informs public sector performance reviews."

Christchurch's example is interesting in that the biggest single contributor to the bonus is organization performance to customer-facing objectives – more so than for financial results. Moreover, the approach is much less individualistic than would typically be found within a commercial organization.

As two further examples, consider the US Postal Services and the Civil Service College, Singapore – both of which are case studies in the work "Developing a Public Sector Scorecard."[14]

US Postal Service case example

The giant US Postal Services (which has 750,000 employees) has a version of the Balanced Scorecard that comprises just five strategic objectives; "improve service," "generate revenues," "enhance performance-based culture," "Seek reform (President's Management Agenda)" and "manage costs." (See Figure 9.2)

For incentive compensation the Balanced Scorecard framework has weightings that are configured to local needs. For example, a corporate level goal that supports the overall "improve service" objective is

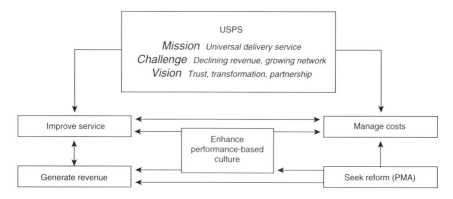

Figure 9.2 **Balancing Goals and Objectives**

"timely, reliable delivery." This is measured by percentage of first-class mail delivered on time – for overnight, two day and three day deliveries. At the functional department and operating unit level where they are responsible for managing the logistics of the network, they'd have more weight on the three-day target. At the Post Office level, their weight would be on overnight first-class mail.

"The scorecard would be narrowly defined for a supervisor, and more expansive as it is applied up the organization through postmaster, district level manager, area manager or vice president level," says Kent Smith, Manager, Strategic Business Planning. "Essentially we've abolished the old civil service approach where employees receive time-served rises irrespective of performance. What we do is put that money into a pool and through the National Performance Assessment Program – which converts goals and targets into individual performance goals and targets – employees get bonuses based on how well they achieve certain goals. We have the corporate goals that account for a certain per cent, unit goals account for a certain per cent and there are individual goals. The percentage weighting changes as it goes down the organization and becomes more specific to units and individuals, but all goals roll back up to the corporate goals."

He says that: "Being a public sector organization, the bonuses aren't big by private sector standards but are still enough to motivate." The compensation link extends as far down as supervisory levels, but it does not apply to the unionized workforce."

Civil Service College, Singapore case example

At the Civil Service College, Singapore, incentive compensation works at three levels though a tiered system: if the college performs well against its overall scorecard targets there is a percentage multiplier for strategic business unit bonuses. These, in turn, are translated into a multiplier at the individual level. This means that an individual employee's bonus depends on their personal, their unit's and the college's overall performance.

Says the college dean Brigadier General Yam: "For the first time people are seeing that they are remunerated directly to outcomes, so this is like running the organization as a commercial company with the full rigor of financial disciplines and not as a typical public service organization, but retaining the public sector ethos and values."

"Tying remuneration to outcomes is not without its challenges, especially as employees are generally not used to such an approach, but the pay/performance link was deemed critical if a cultural shift to a more business mindset was to take root."

Singapore is a nation that is renowned for the excellence and efficacy of its public sector organizations. Of course, it is also where we find the origin of the famous saying: "No money, no honey."

Non-incentive rewards

Typically, however, incentive compensation will not be used within public sector organizations. But even so, other non-financial incentive systems can be used as ammunition in creating a performance-centered culture. Indeed, research has also shown that non-financial rewards can be even more effective and powerful than monetary rewards. Here are some ideas from other government and not-for-profit organizations:

- One senior executive in a federal government agency regularly writes and sends handwritten personal notes to employees who deserve recognition.
- Time off – the chief executive of one local government body gave everybody a day extra holiday after they achieved a momentous performance turn-around.
- The chief executive of a major charity regularly sends a bouquet of flowers to the employees who have demonstrated performance-driven behavior.

- One government agency regularly holds "performance parties" with free coffee and cookies for the departments or teams who performed well.

However, the most powerful recognition and reward is the one we tend to forget too often: to say thank you! Please don't underestimate the power of a "thank you." If said in earnest by managers or senior leaders a simple "thank you" can clearly outstrip the impact of a pay rise.

Below we have compiled a few tips of how to reward and recognize people in order to create a performance driven culture:

- *Celebrate success*: Most government, public sector and not-for-profit organizations we have ever worked with are not very good at celebrating success. We need to do this much more often!
- *Reward effort, not just success*: When we reward and recognize people we don't have to wait until a major outcome objective has been reached. We can reward them for the right efforts, whether they led to success or not.
- *Reward straight away*: Studies show that if a person receives a reward immediately after they have done something well, then the effect is greater. The effect decreases as duration between performance and reward lengthens. If you can, don't delay the reward.
- *Don't create habits*: If we regularly reward similar behavior the rewards become a habit and lose their power. We need to avoid the routine-like rewards which people will just take for granted.
- *Don't "hard-wire" measures with compensation system*: A big mistake is to link the performance of a number of specific measures with rewards. This mechanistic link based on proxies can drive many dysfunctional behaviors.
- *Balance rewards for individual and corporate performance*: We need to avoid rewarding only individual performance as this can lead to increased competition and decreased team work. We need to balance individual performance with the performance of the team, groups, departments and corporate organization. There should be a three-way split between individual performance, departmental or group performance, and corporate performance.
- *Use the whole spectrum of rewards and recognitions*: There are other rewards than financial – we need to use these more often and start saying "thank you."

Linking reward and recognition to performance sends a clear and unambiguous message to the organization that performance management and improvement matters.

Managing poor performance

But if performance management and improvement matters, then public sector organizations must become better at managing "poor performers." Unlike much of the commercial sector, a massive problem is that in many public sector organizations, underperformance oftentimes doesn't have any real consequences.

As a result many public sector organizations carry "dead wood," that is people who have no commitment to their job or the organization and have no interest in performing. From our field observations, we have seen many examples of organizations that have created jobs with no responsibility and accountability just to transfer incompetent or indifferent people. As some of these jobs (called lemon rooms) are very well paid their existence compromises the hard work that public sector bodies must put in place now to drive efficient and effectiveness gains in these difficult economic times.

To be blunt public sector organizations have two options when faced with continued underperformance: help individuals to improve or fire them. Although this might sound harsh to some we will stress that there is nothing more demoralizing than seeing incompetent and blatantly lazy fellow workers who are focused on, and get away with, doing nothing. As Andrew Wileman rightly says: "Getting rid of underperformers lets an organization breathe. It removes a burden of cost and wasted time. It raises morale. A few weeks after you do it, the people who were saying it would destroy team spirit are asking why you didn't do it sooner."[15]

However, the preferred option is to help people improve through coaching, mentoring and a change of job in which they are more comfortable and competent (but without lemon rooms).

THE OFFICE OF STRATEGY MANAGEMENT

Thus far in this chapter we have essentially explained how to create a culture of learning and improvement, by describing some of the interventions that should be used and attitudes and approaches that should be avoided. Yet, even when the cultural underpinning is firmly in place, this does not guarantee the long-term survival of a strategic performance management framework such as the Balanced Scorecard.

Over the history of the Balanced Scorecard it has not been unusual for the framework (even when it has proven outstandingly successful) to be a relatively short-lived phenomenon. Oftentimes, the scorecard is dismantled when the scorecard champion (especially when it is the CEO) departs the organization. This has been common in both public and commercial sector organizations. The problem has often been that the Balanced Scorecard effort has been seen as implementing a specific program and not, as it should be, about inculcating a core organizational competence, or capability in strategy management. In essence, strategy management should become a capability that informs the structure, systems and culture of the organization.

In creating this capability/competence, Kaplan and Norton have, over recent years, evolved the concept of the Office of Strategy Management, which was fully explained in their fifth book *The Execution Premium: Linking Strategy to Operations for Competitive Advantage*.[16]

Led by a Chief Strategy Officer, the theory has it that the OSM integrates and coordinates activities across functions and business units to align strategy with operations. Kaplan and Norton state that the OSM can be viewed as the designer of an intricate watch, keeping all the various planning, execution and control processes synchronized despite their running at various frequencies. The OSM keeps all of the diverse organizational players – executive team, business units, regional units, support units (finance, human resources, information technology), theme teams, department, and ultimately the employees aligned, and executing the enterprise's strategy in unison, with each component playing its distinctive part.

Interestingly, although most private sector organizations do not have someone in charge of performance management (and therefore the OSM is something brand new) this is not the case in the public sector, where there are directors of performance, performance managers, and performance analysts. Indeed there is a whole raft of people with performance in their title. As examples from our case study organizations, Peter Ryan is Manager, Planning and Performance and NWCCA's Michelle McCusker, is Manager, Business Performance. At HMRC's IMS, Richard Ryder is Head of Planning and Performance and Kay McNeil is Head of Performance Improvement, Finance and Performance.

The problem is that most people holding such positions (and this obviously does not apply to our cited case examples) are just data collectors – just producing reports mainly for external audience. Very little happens with the reports and they are not linked to strategic objectives. Such departments therefore could well learn from the broader and more strategic role of an OSM.

Office of Strategy Management: Roles and responsibilities

The OSM has 12 core roles and responsibilities, which can be described through three lenses: architect, process owner and integrator.

Architect

The OSM ensures that all of the planning, execution and feedback processes are in place.

1. Define the strategy management framework and conventions

The OSM is the designer of the frameworks and processes for a single, integrated, closed-loop strategic and operational execution system. Its tasks include introducing the missing strategy execution processes and bringing order to what is otherwise a fragmented collection of management processes.

2. Design the strategy management process

The OSM creates the design for the sequence and linkage of strategy execution processes, ensuring the business unit and support unit strategic cycles are aligned in support of that of the enterprise.

Process owner

On an ongoing basis, the OSM should have primary ownership of the following strategy execution processes:

3. Developing the strategy

Typically, strategy development processes are the responsibilities of an existing strategic planning unit. But developing strategy should not be a one-time annual event. After all, performance measures, such as those supplied by the Balanced Scorecard, provide continual evidence about the validity of the assumptions underlying a company's strategy. The executive team, at its monthly strategy review meetings, discuss the assumptions and can fine-tune the strategy, strategic measures, or strategic initiatives as needed.

Rather than put an artificial distinction between strategy development and strategy execution, it is recommended that processes for developing strategy and executing strategy be performed within one group in the organization: the OSM. This will typically be an expansion of the strategic planning department into a more comprehensive office of strategy management that has responsibility for facilitating both strategy development and its execution.

4. Planning the strategy

By owning the scorecard process, the OSM ensures that any changes made at the annual strategy planning meeting are translated into the company's Strategy Map and Balanced Scorecard. Once the executive team has approved the objectives and measures for the subsequent year, the OSM coaches the team in selecting performance targets on the scorecard measures and identifying the strategic initiatives required to achieve them.

The OSM also standardizes the terminology and measurement definitions throughout the organization, selects and manages the scorecard reporting system, and monitors the integrity of the scorecard data. The OSM also serves as the central scorecard resource, consulting with units on their scorecard development projects and conducting training and education on building strategy maps and scorecards.

5. Aligning the organization

The OSM oversees the processes to cascade strategies and scorecards vertically and horizontally throughout the organization. It validates whether the strategies and scorecards proposed by business and support units are linked to each other and to the corporate strategy. In this role, the OSM helps the enterprise realize the gains from corporate synergies.

6. Review and adapt the strategy

At the strategy review meeting the executive team reviews strategic performance and adjusts the strategy and its execution. Managing this meeting is a core function of the OSM. It briefs the CEO in advance about the strategic issues identified in the most recent score-card so that the agenda can focus on strategy review and learning, rather than on a short-term financial performance review and crisis management.

The OSM, at the beginning of the meeting, provides a brief report on the progress of each action plan recommended at earlier meetings, records all of the recommended action plans, and follows up with the assigned manager or department to ensure that the actions are carried out.

The leadership team tests and adapts the strategy. The meeting requires a new input into the annual strategy meeting in addition to the traditional external and competitor analysis produced by the planning department. The company's internal competitor analysis should now include analytic studies of the existing strategy's performance. These studies use tools such as activity-based cost analysis of product line, customer, channel, and regional profitability, and statistical analysis that estimates and tests a Strategy Map's causal linkages.

Integrator

A variety of existing management processes must be informed by and aligned with the strategy, such as budgeting and operational planning and those to do with human resources and information technology.

7. Linking strategy to financial resource planning and budgeting

The OSM integrates with finance to ensure that business unit profit plans, resource capacity planning, and performance targets are aligned with strategic objectives. In addition to business and functional unit budgets, the corporate financial plan needs to incorporate the authorized spending (Strategy Expenditure – or StratEx) for cross-functional strategic initiatives.

8. Aligning plans and resources of important functional support departments

In addition to coordinating the linkage between strategy planning and finance, the OSM ensures that the plans for other functional departments are consistent with executing the strategy. The OSM plays a consulting and integrating role with these functional departments to help them align their strategies and plans with enterprise and business unit strategy.

9. Communicating the strategy

The OSM actively promotes understanding of the company's strategy and the scorecard to all business unit and support functions. If the strategy communication task is assigned to an existing internal communication department, the OSM plays an editorial role, reviewing the message to see that they communicate the strategy correctly. If a corporate communications group does not exist or if the group has little knowledge of or focus on strategy, the OSM becomes the process owner for communicating both strategy and the scorecard to employees.

10. Managing strategic initiatives

When the organization uses theme owners and theme teams to manage selection and management of strategic initiatives, the OSM monitors the process, soliciting information about initiative status and performance and reporting this information to the executive team in advance of the strategy management review meeting.

For organizations that do not use theme owners and theme teams, the OSM is the default mechanism for running the team process to select and rationalize strategic initiatives. The OSM assigns responsibility to an appropriate unit or function for those initiatives that already have a natural home. The OSM manages initiatives that cross unit and functional lines, ensuring that they get the financial and human resources they need.

11. Linking strategy to key operating processes

Strategy is also executed through business processes. The Strategy Map identifies the processes that are most important to the strategy and that must be analyzed, redesigned and managed. The OSM works with the theme teams, local line management, and the quality management department to see that necessary resources and organizational support have been provided to improve the performance of the strategic process.

12. Sharing best practices

The OSM needs to ensure that knowledge management focuses on sharing the best practices that will be most beneficial to the strategy. At some companies, learning and knowledge sharing are already the responsibility of a chief knowledge or learning officer; in those cases, the OSM needs to coordinate with that person's office. But if such a function does not exist, the OSM must take the lead in transferring ideas and best practices throughout the organization.

The OSM team

It is also important that time and attention is spent in creating the right OSM team. They require specific skills such as facilitation, analytics, multi-disciplinary background to take the corporate map and challenge top level team on strategy and communicate performance to people in the right manner, and get the right analytics, and then help cascade into the organization. As an example, although the term OSM is not used, Audit Scotland ensures that the scorecard is closely managed on a day-to-day basis, and this is the responsibility of Director of Corporate Services Diane McGiffen and a small team from corporate reporting that is skilled in data analysis.

FBI case example

The USA's Federal Bureau of Investigation (FBI) has seven people within its OSM. The FBI has 14 cascaded scorecards and the OSM helps focus on sustaining these scorecards. "They provide expertise to the organization and each area has mini OSM with full time or part time individuals," explains Palladium's Patricia Bush, who has been consulting on this project. "They then use the central OSM as a resource tool and for implementing and sharing best practice, doing analysis across the organization and identifying trends across the division," she says.

   We are not suggesting that organization implement an OSM that strictly adheres to the Kaplan/Norton description, or that it is called an OSM, but putting in place a central organization that makes strategy a core competence and is focused on the identification and sharing of performance best practices will certainly help in creating an organization which has a culture that is laser-focused on learning and improvement.

Ministry of Finance, Indonesia case example

As another OSM example, the Ministry of Finance (MoF), Indonesia is creating an office that is housed within its Centre of Policy Analysis and Harmonization. Presently it has a team of key performance indicator managers who are being transitioned to being a fulltime team of Balanced Scorecard managers to signal that their role is much wider than data collection. "The OSM will play an important role in getting buy-in to the scorecard throughout the ministry and for making the scorecard central to the way we manage performance," says Adi Budiarso, MoF's Head of Department, Centre of Policy Analysis and Harmonization.

The Ministry of Works, Bahrain, case study

Finally consider the Ministry of Works, Bahrain, which was perhaps the first organization in the Arab world to build an OSM (which it calls a Strategic Planning Section – SPS). The SPS was launched in early 2007 because: "We recognized that effective strategy management was so critical to the MoW's success that we needed to ensure that it became an internal capability," says Raja Al Zayani, Chief of the SPS, who adds that the SPS has now become the center of expertise for strategy management and the Balanced Scorecard.

Such is the level of importance attached to the SPS that Raja reports directly to Minister of Works His Excellency (HE) Fahmi Bin Ali Al-Jowder and not through an intermediary executive. HE Al-Jowder has also encouraged the introduction of the Balanced Scorecard in the Ministry of Electricity and Water, for which he also has ministerial responsibility. The SPS at the Ministry of Works has overall facilitative responsibility for the strategy formulation, implementation and learning process.

HMRC IMS case example 2

As we have stated, it is not uncommon to find the word "performance," in a public sector job title. In a similar vein, performance functions exist that might broadly deliver some, or all of the responsibilities of what we now know as an OSM. For instance, with the Information Management Services department of the UK-based HM Revenue and Customs, Kay McNeil leads a seven strong performance improvement team.[17] Although the team collates all of the information for the monthly performance sub-committee meeting and also uses the results from the business units scorecards to inform and update the IMS scorecard, McNeil stresses that the team's role is much more than simple data collection and reporting, however important that might be. "The team reviews the scorecard and will challenge back if required." She says, "The team talks to each coordinator to discuss how their unit's KPIs are impacting those in other

Business Units and we hold monthly meetings with the coordinators to discuss progress and share best practices." To explain, within each business the leader with responsibility for the scorecard is supported by dedicated performance coordinators, who are tasked with pooling together all of the information at the business unit level and to deliver this to McNeil's team by the eighth working day of the month.

CONCLUSION

This chapter has explained that "getting the culture right," is a critical aspect of a Balanced Scorecard implementation. In times of funding shortfalls, employees must be fully informed as to the intentions of the organizations, especially in regards to the efficiency saving goals that will typically appear on a Balanced Scorecard. Indeed, without the inculcation of a culture of trust and honesty, the scorecard will likely fail in such an economic climate.

We also outlined the critical importance of inculcating a culture of learning and improvement, that this is how step-change performance improvement is achieved. As part of this we explained that performance improvement should be a two-way dialog between those at the top of the organizations and those at the front-line of the enterprise, who must make strategy happen.

Finally, we explained that concepts such as the Office of Strategy Management are important as mechanisms for ensuring that strategy management becomes a core organizational capability of the organization, and therefore ensures that the Balanced Scorecard becomes more than a short-term project.

In the next chapter we describe the key learning points from this book, and provide an action template for implementing a Balanced Scorecard and Lean thinking within a public sector organization.

10

CONCLUSION AND KEY STRATEGIC PERFORMANCE QUESTIONS

May you live in interesting times.

Ancient Chinese proverb

INTRODUCTION: THE CURSE OF LIVING IN INTERESTING TIMES

The ancient Chinese proverb "may you live in interesting times," was coined as a curse, the belief being that only unstable, uncertain and very challenging times can be described as "interesting." Therefore, if you were living in "interesting times," you were living in difficult and even dangerous times.

The end of the first decade of the third millennium was certainly an "interesting time." The credit crunch and the resulting economic downturn caused great pain and uncertainty to people, organizations and countries across the world. In preparing this book, the world was starting to gradually move out of recession into what for most will be a slow and sluggish recovery – and hopefully a much less interesting time.

However, as we enter the second decade of the millennium, we might safely argue that public sector organizations are about to enter into their own version of "interesting times." The fact that the great economies of the world avoided the cataclysmic disaster of a depression (which many economists view as the economic equivalent of The Black Death) was almost exclusively the result of the trillions of dollars that central Governments made available for recovery packages – to save the banking sector from collapse and to stimulate spending by commercial organizations and consumers alike.

Although future economic historians might congratulate national Governments for their swift and effective interventions, they will also reflect on how the bill for this support was repaid. With tax hikes always a politically hot potato, it is now certain that the greater chunk of the bill will be paid by making deep and prolonged cuts into public sector budgets. As we explained in Chapter 1, a report by Audit Scotland has found that there will be a shortfall in the Scottish annual budget between 7% and 13% in real terms by 2013–2014. Put starkly, the report warned that "severe spending constraint is on the way."[1] Such severe spending constraints will be the norm across nation states. It will likely be some time before the public purses of national Governments are healthy again. Such economic realities pose challenges for public sector leaders that are complex as they are "interesting."

FIVE PRINCIPLES FOR RECOVERY

In the opening chapter of this book we listed the ten principles of good performance management in public sector organizations as demonstrated by those that exhibited superior performance. These principles were uncovered in the Advanced Performance Institute (API) research project, *Strategic Performance Management in Government and Public Sector Organizations – a Global Survey*. Conducted in 2008 and with more than 1100 responses this report is the largest and most comprehensive global study of government and public sector Performance Management to date.[2] In the chapters that followed, we used these ten principles as an empirically proven foundation for the guidance and advice provided to the leaders of public sector organizations for the driving of efficiency and effectiveness performance gains.

The authors of this book certainly hold firm on their recommendations that public sector leaders use these ten principles as a checklist for making step-change improvements to their strategic performance management practices and processes. However, given that the credit crunch and the subsequent economic downturn came hard on the heels of the publication of that research report, in 2009 API published a white paper that took the findings from the global survey and distilled them further into five principles for sustainable recovery.[3] These five principles took into consideration the new priorities of public sector organizations as they set out to contend with the "interesting" challenges of the new economic climate.

1. More Strategic Clarity
2. More Partnership and Synergies
3. More Intelligent Indicators

4. More Integration and Alignment
5. More Serious Appointments.

We will now summarize each point.

More strategic clarity

Reduced public sector budgets will mean less in the way of resources on which to operate. This will mean that public sector organizations will have to be absolutely clear about:

- Their core responsibilities and intended outcomes
- Their priorities in terms of internal processes and core activities
- The key enablers, such as resources and competencies, required to drive performance.

In order to achieve strategic clarity, it is crucial to understand the cause-and-effect relationships between overall aim, outcomes, outputs and enablers. As we explain in this book, to achieve this understanding many organizations are creating Strategy Maps in order to depict what outcomes and outputs they intend to achieve, and by which means they intend to deliver them.

More partnership and synergies

Over the past years, many Governments, most notably in countries such as New Zealand and Scotland, have realized that closer collaboration between public bodies could generate significant cost savings and create more citizen- or customer-centric services. Different initiatives by Government bodies have attempted to create closer collaborations between public sector organizations.

In the coming years there will be an even greater expectation on Government to create partnerships between the different public organizations at all levels, in order to generate efficient savings through synergies and at the same time deliver better services through a more cohesive service delivery (the efficiency/effectiveness balance that is the core focus of this book).

But strategic clarity is needed for partnerships in the same way that it's required within a single organization. The recommendation here is to also make use of strategy mapping tools to create joint plans

214

with identified aims, outcomes, outputs, and enablers when creating local partnership strategies.

More intelligent indicators

There are generally two main reasons why Government organizations collect data:

- To transparently demonstrate that public money was spent responsibly and that the agency has complied with regulation (efficiency)
- To gain insights that are used internally to inform better decision-making, leading to performance improvements (effectiveness)

As they gradually move away from an output-based tick-box mentality, many Governments are beginning to ask public bodies to only specify the key outcomes they intend to deliver, while providing organizations with more scope to develop their own controls to manage that delivery. In addition, organizations also need individualized internal management information to ensure that they are best managing their performance enablers (that will deliver those outcomes). By using approaches and techniques such as Key Performance Questions (KPQs – see below) public organizations can make the most of the new autonomy to create meaningful local sets of indicators.

More integration and alignment

In order to gain maximum benefits from their performance management initiatives, public sector organizations need to ensure that they align and integrate processes (including financial planning and budgeting; project and program management; people management and rewards; performance reporting; risk management; as well as business intelligence and analytics). State-of-the-art software systems can help with this, by creating an integrated solution to deliver total performance insight through performance management, performance measurement and business intelligence. These systems allow budgets and forecasts to be created and updated on the fly, based on a continuous inflow of both financial and non-financial data. Because such a system allows business units to feed in much of that raw data and market intelligence directly, it makes operations managers part of the planning-and-forecasting process. Integration enables an organization to leverage trend data and target setting to help cross-functional teams align agencies and improve collaboration.

More serious appointments

It is now generally agreed that to make performance management work requires a dedicated team of people to facilitate it. In order to embed the processes into the organization and ensure that the right measures are collected, analyzed and reported, time and resources are required, both of which tend to be in short supply in any organization. What is required to move forward is a team of highly skilled individuals who can act as performance advisors and who have the necessary skills to challenge the organizations on performance with a focus on performance improvements.

Many organizations have demonstrated that they are serious about performance management by creating teams and appointing people with the right skills. For example, US President Barack Obama has, for the first time, created a White House role of Chief Performance Officer (see Chapter 1). The position, which Obama has described as one of the most important in his Administration, is aimed at identifying areas for performance improvement (effectiveness) and efficiency gains. Other organizations have also up-skilled their in-house team from data collectors and performance reporters to internal performance analysts who spot trends, identify areas for improvements and generally challenge the organization to improve.

Recovery conclusion

Pulling together these five principles, the API white paper concluded: "The effects of the economy and the constantly changing landscape mean that every Government needs to adopt solid performance management programs, to increase accountability and performance improvements and to create the results needed for sustainable recovery. The key building blocks to achieve this are clear strategies for organizations, in the form of Strategy Maps, partnerships, better performance information guided by clearly articulated information needs, closer alignment between performance management and other key management processes, and the creation and up-skilling of a dedicated team to implement and manage the process."

KEY STRATEGIC PERFORMANCE QUESTIONS

To assist the reader in their quest to instill a robust and fit-for-purpose strategic performance management framework, we have put together 20 key strategic performance questions (based on API's KPQ innovation) that serve as an overall summary of the key observations and learnings within this book. Answering these questions will also go some way to helping the reader's organization to navigate the stormy economic waters that lie ahead.

Chapter 1: Both efficient and effective, the new Public Sector Performance Agenda

This chapter set the scene for the rest of the book by describing the new economic reality that public sector organizations are facing. We explained that this will lead to public sector organizations being forced to provide "more value for less money." Key strategic performance questions here include:

1. To what extent is my organization ready to operate with reduced budgets

As public sector budgets come up for renewal – and knowing they will be reduced, in real terms at least – leaders must systematically review their processes and activities to identify and drive out inefficiencies. Organizations must figure out how to cut costs and become leaner and more efficient. A thorough audit of a public sector organization's major processes and activities will likely highlight where significant efficiency gains can be delivered.

2. How will my organization deliver efficiency gains without impacting the effectiveness of product/service delivery?

Public sector bodies are being asked to become more effective *as well as* more efficient. This will likely prove a complex challenge for many. The case study companies that we profile within this book are at the vanguard of standing up to the plate to deliver to both performance dimensions. For example, Audit Scotland, has created a Strategy Map and supporting KPQs, KPIs and initiatives to deliver to the following vision: "On behalf of the Auditor General and the Accounts Commission, we will provide assurance to the people of

Scotland that their money is spent appropriately and we will help public sector organizations in Scotland to improve and perform better."

This vision speaks directly to the efficiency (value for money) and effectiveness (performance improvement) strands of Audit Scotland's responsibilities.[4]

Chapter 2: Balanced Scorecards, the journey from measurement to strategic performance management

In this chapter we fully described the two major Balanced Scorecard frameworks being deployed today and that which we focus on throughout the book: the "classic" Balanced Scorecard as described by Harvard Business School Professor Robert Kaplan and management consultant Dr David Norton and the Value Creation Map and supporting KPQs, KPIs and initiatives as developed by API. We also explained how the concept of the Balanced Scorecard has developed from a narrow measurement framework to being the centerpiece of a full-fledged strategic performance management system. Key strategic performance questions here include:

3. In what ways is my organization transitioning its performance mindset from one that is focused on measurement and output targets to one that is more interested in strategy execution

Securing great results begins with (and is largely dependent on) a full and proper understanding of the organization's strategic context. With this knowledge organizations can then properly plan the interventions that will drive breakthrough performance gains, and indeed identify appropriate metrics. A key challenge for the leaders of public sector bodies is to convince their managers and lower-level staff to think less about performance to mandated targets (however important these might be) and more about what the organization has to achieve on a strategic level. For many organizations this will require a significant change in mindsets.

4. To what extent is my organization outcome-focused as opposed to output-focused?

We are beginning to witness a gradual shifting away from output to outcome based performance management and measurement within the public sector; or put another way from a narrow measurement/

target setting view to a broader strategic performance management perspective. As a leading example, consider the work being carried out within New Zealand, which has one of the most advanced approaches in the world for ensuring outcome-based strategic public sector performance management. As one sector example, local authorities are mandated to set community outcomes and supporting performance metrics that must be identified and agreed through an extensive, heavily participative and legally mandated consultation program with local residents and other groups. Our case study organization Christchurch City Council exemplifies an outcome-focused view of performance.[5]

Chapter 3: Using Lean thinking to improve strategic performance

This chapter introduces the concept of Lean methodologies, such as Six Sigma. We explained that such methodologies are extremely powerful for driving efficiency gains within the organization.

We also explained that "Lean" methodologies work exceptionally well as part of a Balanced Scorecard implementation. But we made clear that Lean interventions must be in support of the strategic objectives of the organization. We also stressed that most of the objectives that will be supported by Lean approaches will be found in a Strategy Map's process perspective within a "classic" Balanced Scorecard or alternatively within the "core activity" component of an API Strategy Map. This is appropriate as the internal process/core activity section represents the area of a Strategy Map "where work gets done," that is, where the process improvement takes place that delivers value to the customer, shareholder or stakeholder. Key strategic performance questions here include:

5. To what extent do we understand how "Lean" can be deployed within a public sector organization?

Lean was devised, developed and first deployed within a commercial, and more narrowly manufacturing, setting. As we explain within this chapter, Lean can be equally well deployed within a public sector setting, although case examples are much fewer and implementations less mature. Leaders must understand what "waste" means in a public sector and then focus on driving out these inefficiencies.

6. How will we ensure that Lean is used to support the delivery of strategic objectives?

We strongly recommend that public sector organizations deploy both a Balanced Scorecard system and Lean in the implementation of strategy and the realization of efficiency and effectiveness gains. However, this does not imply equality. Rather Lean must be deployed as a tool to help implement the strategy – which will likely be described within a Strategy Map. Therefore think "strategy" *before* thinking "Lean."

Chapter 4: Designing strategy maps to agree strategic priorities

This chapter served as the first in describing the mechanics for building and deploying a Balanced Scorecard system. As we stressed, the first step *must* be the development of the Strategy Map. Indeed each of our case organizations began the scorecard creation by first developing the Strategy Map, whether a "classic" Balanced Scorecard or a Value Creation Map.

It is noteworthy that the cited API global research found that of the ten principles of good performance management for Government and Public Sector organizations none was more critical than "create clarity and agreement about the strategic aims." The most powerful way to achieve this, the study noted, is through the senior team working together to create a Strategy Map – or a highly visible plan – that depicts the strategy, with all of its components on a single piece of paper. These immediately provide focus and direction, showing at a glance what the intended outcomes are, as well as the core activities and underpinning enablers that will lead to their achievement.[6] Key strategic performance questions here include:

7. To what extent have the leaders of my organization reached consensus as to our strategic priorities

One of the most powerful outcomes of building a Strategy Map is that it enables the most senior team, often for the first time, to come to together to debate and ultimately agree on the organization's strategic priorities. As Andrea Smith, Head of Strategy at our case organization International Baccalaureate rightly comments, "Creating the map provides an ideal opportunity to clarify and agree on what's important to the organization... this opportunity should not be wasted."

8. How aware is the senior team as to the critical few objectives that will really make a difference in driving ultimate strategic success?

Each of the case organizations within this book has been careful to keep the number of objectives that appear on the Strategy Map to the "critical few" – that is those vitally important capabilities and relationships that must be mastered if the strategy will ultimately be delivered. As a few examples, the Ministry of Works, Bahrain has just 19 objectives at the corporate level, the North West Commercial Collaborative Agency has 17, International Baccalaureate has 16, Belfast City Council has 13 and Audit Scotland just 11.

Keeping the number of strategic objectives/enablers to the critical few is important. However, given that public sector organizations must deliver to a wide range of stakeholder outcomes, there's a tendency to choose too many objectives – 40, 50 or even 60+ is not uncommon. The result is an organization map that describes everything the company does rather than a Strategy Map that homes in on the critical few objectives that will successfully deliver the strategy. When there are too many objectives the scorecard becomes unmanageable and the program eventually dies.

9. What will be the value of cascading the Strategy Map to lower levels of the organization?

One of the strengths of a Strategy Map is that an enterprise- or corporate-level map can be devolved deep inside the organization. But organizations must be crystal clear as to what will be achieved through a cascade. Too often organizations create a suite of Strategy Maps and scorecards from the top-to-bottom of the enterprise without carefully considering the value of doing so. A general rule is that if the organization is not complex then perhaps one map will suffice (although some KPIs and targets will change at lower levels). However an organization of 100 people with five units of 20 focusing on different goals will probably require five maps.

That said, most of our case organizations have cascaded the scorecard from the corporate level, with the express purpose to achieve "line of sight" from the work of lower level functions/groups to the strategic goals of the organization as expressed on the corporate Strategy Map. For example, Belfast City Council has cascaded the corporate map to 26 service units.[7]

As a further example, following the creation of the corporate map, cascaded maps and scorecards were created at sector and directorate levels (14 devolved scorecards in total) within the Ministry of Works, Bahrain. As with the corporate Strategy Map, each devolved map had to align to four strategic themes: public/private partnership, key planning player, quality service and leading professional organization.[8]

Chapter 5: Agreeing high level strategic outcome targets and key performance indicators

Within this chapter we explained the role that KPIs and their associated targets play in a Balanced Scorecard rollout. We stressed that KPIs must be in support of the strategic objectives that are housed within the Strategy Map. Too many organizations (and this is equally true of commercial as well as public sector organizations) think that a Balanced Scorecard is first and foremost a measurement system. This is an erroneous and dangerous belief. It is also more than a little worrying that a staggering 92% of respondents to the API global survey reported that many of the indicators were neither meaningful nor relevant. We provided a robust process for ensuring that KPIs are indeed meaningful and relevant. Key strategic performance questions here include:

10. To what extent will we use Key Performance Questions (KPQs) to help identify meaningful and relevant metrics?

A KPQ is a management question that captures exactly what managers want to know when it comes to reviewing each of their strategic elements and objectives. The rationale for KPQs is that they focus our attention on what actually needs to be discussed when we review performance and, most importantly, they provide guidance for collecting meaningful and relevant KPIs. Far too often we jump straight to designing indicators before we are clear about what it is we want to know. By first designing KPQs we are able to ask ourselves: "What is the best data and management information we need to collect to help us answer our key performance questions?" Starting with KPQs ensures that, by default, all subsequently designed performance indicators are relevant. In addition, KPQs put performance data into context and therefore facilitate communication, guide discussion and direct decision-making.

KPQs are used extensively by our case study organizations and are found to be of immense value. For example, International Baccalaureate's Smith notes: "The process of thinking about and designing key performance questions has proven extremely useful. We already had a set of KPIs in place, but when we looked at them through the lens of the KPQs we found that they weren't that useful. They were much more operational that strategic and it became evident that we didn't have any KPIs that were really tracking the long-term health of the organization."

She adds that. "The senior team is really focused on our strategic priorities and in really understanding what it is that we are trying to do. That is why it is important to get the questions right and to make sure that KPQs and KPIs work together in delivering to the map."

11. How aware are we of the difference between strategic and operational measures?

The KPIs that appear on a Strategy Map should be just that – strategic. Strategic measures are different from those required to monitor operational performance. While with operational measures, it is desirable to get closer and closer to "real time" measurement, for strategic measurement that is not even what you're striving for. Organizations don't monitor strategic measures day by day, and certainly not hour by hour. Strategic measures are more about monitoring progress toward achieving your new and different envisioned destination (as opposed to just doing things better); as a result they typically don't change that often.

12. To what extent are we extracting insights from measures?

The purpose of using metrics is to trigger performance improvement. Indeed the cited API report "Strategic Performance Management in Public Sector and Government Organizations,"[9] found that one of the ten principles of good performance management was "use indicators to extract relevant insights."

Once organizations have collected meaningful data, they must analyze it before they can work out what it means – e.g. how they may need to change things to improve success against key strategic goals.

"Performance Management analytics," provide tools and techniques that enable organizations to convert their performance data into *relevant* information and knowledge. Without it, the whole performance management exercise is of little or no value to the organization. Public sector organizations must also ensure that they have the skills to analyze data and the analytics support effective decision-making.[10]

Chapter 6: Selecting strategic initiatives

In this chapter we described the process for selecting the strategic initiatives that will support the strategic objectives, KPQs and KPIs. Although sequentially the selection of strategic initiatives is the final step in the scorecard creation process, it is certainly not the least important. Indeed, we would argue that in a hierarchy of importance it is trumped by only strategic objectives. This is because it is where the real work of strategy implementation takes place. We also explained the role that Lean plays in the selection and implementation of strategic initiatives, and highlighted the emerging concept of "Balanced Six Sigma" that aims to pull together the Balanced Scorecard framework with the Six Sigma methodology. Key strategic performance questions here include:

13. To what extent do the initiatives under way in my organization, or that are proposed, support the strategic objectives that appear on the Strategy Map?

In choosing strategic initiatives the overriding criteria is that they must link directly though to objectives on the Strategy Map. Simply, no initiative should be launched or funded unless this link is unequivocally proven. This is because the purpose of an initiative is to close an identified gap between actual and required levels of performance to achieve a strategic outcome. Indeed, if an initiative is deemed critical for the success of the organization and does not correspond to an objective, then it signals a failing of the Strategy Map. For example IB's Smith and her performance management team liaised with the organization's project management office to ensure that projects green-lighted by the organization were fully aligned to the Strategy Map. "Projects will be agreed by the senior team based on the strategic relevance and the needs of the map," she says.

14. To what extent are our strategic initiatives cross-cutting, or cross-organizational?

While it is true that the real work of strategy implementation takes place through the strategic initiatives that are selected and funded, it is equally true that it is typically the case that the projects that drive the most powerful, or breakthrough, performance improvements, are those that span functions – or impact end-to-end processes. When selecting strategic initiatives organizations should, wherever possible, look to select those that are cross-organizational and should appoint an end-to-end-process owner, possibly a Theme Team leader to ensure that process transformation takes place. Lean methodologies can be particularly powerful for driving efficiency and effectiveness gains at the process level.

Chapter 7: Aligning financial management with strategic goals

Within this chapter we explained the importance of aligning financial management processes and practices with the strategic goals and described how a Balanced Scorecard enables such alignment. Indeed, "Strategic Performance Management in Public Sector and Government Organizations,"[11] found that one of the ten principles of good performance management was "Align other organizational activities with the strategic aims outlined in the Performance Management system," which included financial management processes.

We explained that a historic problem with scorecard implementations is that as they are typically longer-term programs progress is oftentimes stymied by the demands of the delivering to the annual budget – when money gets tight, strategic initiatives get cut. In today's economic climate this must be of real concern to public sector leaders. Key strategic performance questions here include:

15. To what extent are we judiciously managing our financial resources while at the same time ensuring that we are capable of delivering to our strategic goals?

Perhaps more than any other this question gets to the heart of the efficiency/effectiveness challenges that public sector organizations are facing today. They must be very careful as to how they manage and deploy their financial resources over the short term while at the same time not compromising the delivery of longer-term strategic objectives. Public sector leaders must scrutinize their spending to ensure that this short-term/long-term balance is understood and managed properly.

16. To what extent can we safeguard longer-term strategic investments by the deployment of tools such as StratEx?

In the last few years the concept of StratEx has evolved as a mechanism for safeguarding longer-term strategic investments from the short-term demands of the budget. In short StratEx (which stands for Strategy Expenditure, so can be thought of in the same light as OPEX – operating expenditure – or CAPEX – capital expenditure) sets aside a pot of money for longer-term investments, and therefore cannot be cut as part of measures to reduce annual budgetary spend. Although challenging, organizations may well consider whether StratEx – or other similar approach – is an appropriate way to heighten the likelihood of delivering to the strategy in these financially restricted times.

Chapter 8: Keeping your eyes on the ball: Reporting and reviewing performance

As we explained in this chapter, most public sector organizations are still poor in reporting and reviewing performance. We explained that software can be useful in improving performance reporting and reviewing processes, while making it very clear that software is not in and of itself a scorecard solution. We also described how organizations should better present reports so that recipients are enabled to make better decisions. Key strategic performance questions here include:

17. To what extent will an automated solution enable us to drive better decisions from the scorecard program?

The importance of this question is that it ensures that the point of Balanced Scorecard automation is to better support decision-making processes, not as a way to simply collect and report data. When organizations rush to automate the scorecard it is often because they are simply looking to generate a report card. By doing so, organizations will not reap the full benefits of a Balanced Scorecard implementation. Note that all of case study organizations fully understood that software was an enabler of good strategic performance management and that it might be inappropriate to rush to automate. Raja Al Zayani, Chief of the Strategic Planning Section at the Ministry of Works, Bahrain says that although they have derived great value from their automated scorecard solution they waited more than a year before purchasing a software solution because they wanted to be careful that the Balanced

Scorecard did not become a technology-led framework – advice we would certainly endorse.

18. To what extent are we appropriately reporting and communicating performance information?

API research finds that unfortunately most information is not delivered to managers in a way that best enables their making good decisions. Reports are typically constructed in ways that fail to highlight the most important points and are extremely difficult to make sense of. In this chapter we provided a five-step process that can be used to makes sure that a) the reports are meaningful and b) strategically relevant. This process involves both graphical and textual visual display mechanisms.

1. Start with the Strategy Map
2. Frame the report with a key performance question (KPQ)
3. The KPQ should then be supported by appropriate and meaningful graphs and charts
4. Headings should then be used to capture the salient points of the report (or the key insights)
5. Narratives should be used to better tell the story and contextualize the graphics.[12]

Our case organization Audit Scotland was, at time of preparing the case study, in the process of redesigning its performance reports to bring best practice to the communication and display of information. Within these reports, headlines and narratives will be used to capture the key messages, using ideas and graphic/textual formatting from magazines and newspapers. As a further communication device, Audit Scotland is planning to create an A3 summary sheet/poster each quarter to disseminate the key strategic messages.

Chapter 9: Building a culture of strategic performance management

Within this chapter we stressed the absolute importance of ensuring that the culture of the organization is appropriate for succeeding with a Balanced Scorecard. The fact is that the implementation of any performance measurement or improvement system will typically face (oftentimes fierce) resistance from some managers and staff alike – who might be suspicious of the underlying motives. In an environment of significant "belt tightening," resistance to the introduction of a Balanced Scorecard should be both expected and planned for as many employees will see it as simply an underhand way to prioritize job slashing opportunities and initiatives. Even in good times Balanced Scorecards typically fail to do so because of cultural reasons – we can therefore expect larger numbers of failures when deployed in an economic downturn. Key strategic performance questions here include:

19. To what extent is our culture appropriate for the successful implementation of a Balanced Scorecard?

Implementing a Balanced Scorecard is a significant cultural challenge. Employees must trust that the organization is deploying the scorecard as a strategic performance management framework and not as a cost-cutting tool.

They must also believe that the scorecard is not primarily a "reward or punish" mechanism. Keep in mind that most people do not like being measured. If they have good reason to fear the measurement component of the scorecard they will resist its implementation. Moreover, employees are the ones who must implement strategies. The fact is, if you haven't got employees on your side, then no matter how elegantly you formulate the Strategy Map and the accompanying KPQs and KPIs, the scorecard will fail. End of story. Organizations might well benefit by running a cultural diagnostic before rolling out the scorecard, as this will highlight the scale of the cultural challenges ahead and help to identify appropriate cultural interventions.

20. To what extent is our culture appropriate for learning and improvement from performance information?

Staying with the culture theme, note that the API research found that "create a positive culture of learning and improvement from performance information," was one of the ten principles of good performance management. Alongside "create clarity about the strategy with agreements on intended outcomes, outputs and necessary enablers," this principle had the strongest impact on performance improvement. The implication is clear – gain agreement on the strategic goals and ensure that the culture is geared toward learning and improvement culture then the likelihood of step-change performance advancements is heightened.

FINAL WORDS

As we move through the first years of the second decade of the third millennium, the leaders of public sector organizations across the globe are grappling with extraordinary challenges. Only time will tell how many will have the ability to deliver the "more value for less money," proposition that will be demanded of them. Those that properly build and deploy Balanced Scorecards and support this with appropriate Lean methodologies and other intervention tools will be well placed to do so and successfully meet the needs of various stakeholder groups – from Ministers to the man on the street, from suppliers to internal employees. There is no doubt that many will find the test too stretching. But others will succeed and those that do will become celebrated and benchmark case studies for many years to come. They will become the heroes of "the interesting times."

NOTES

Chapter 1   Both Efficient and Effective: The New Public Sector Performance Agenda

1 The official website of the American Recovery and Reinvestment is www.recovery.gov.
2 Barack Obama, "Efficiency and Innovation," Weekly Address, April 18, 2009, White House, Washington D.C. USA.
3 See www.scotland.gov.uk.
4 The original Balanced Scorecard study took place in 1990 and included companies such as Cigna, Hewlett Packard and Analog Devices – the term "scorecard" came from work that was being done within Analog Devices.
5 "Strategic Performance Management in Government and Public Sector Organizations." A research paper by Bernard Marr, *The Advanced Performance Management*, co-sponsored by CIPFA Performance Improvement Network and Actuate, 2008, UK. Copies of the study can be downloaded for free from www.ap-institute.com.

Chapter 2   Balanced Scorecards: The Journey from Measurement to Strategic Performance Management

1 The saying "What gets measured gets done," is usually attributed to Peter Drucker but the actual origin is obscure.
2 "Strategic Performance Management in Government and Public Sector Organizations." A research paper by Bernard Marr, *The Advanced Performance Management*, co-sponsored by CIPFA Performance Improvement Network and Actuate, 2008, UK. Copies of the study can be downloaded for free from www.ap-institute.com.
3 As 2.
4 Bernard Marr and James Creelman, "Outcome-Based Performance Management: Christchurch City Council Drives Toward a Long-Term Strategic Horizon," Advanced Performance Institute, 2008. Available for free download at www.ap-institute.com.
5 Dr Robert S. Kaplan and Dr David P. Norton, *The Balanced Scorecard: Translating Strategy into Action*, Harvard Business School Press, Boston USA, 1996.

6 Dr Robert S. Kaplan and Dr David P. Norton, "The Balanced Scorecard: Measures that Drive Performance," *Harvard Business Review*, Boston, USA, January–February 1992.

7 Dr Robert S. Kaplan and Dr David P. Norton, *Strategy Maps, Converting into Tangible Outcomes*, Harvard Business School Press, Boston, USA, 1996.

8 James Creelman, *Building and Implementing a Balanced Scorecard*, Business Intelligence, UK, 2008.

9 Dr Robert S. Kaplan and Dr David P. Norton, *The Strategy-Focused Organization: How Balanced Scorecard Companies Thrive in the New Business Environment*, Harvard Business School Press, Boston, USA, 2001.

10 Dr Robert S. Kaplan and Dr David P. Norton, *Alignment: Using the Balanced Scorecard to Create Corporate Synergies*, Harvard Business School Press, Boston, USA, 2006.

11 Dr Robert S. Kaplan and Dr David P. Norton, *The Execution Premium: Linking Operations to Strategy for Competitive Advantage*, Harvard Business School Press, Boston, USA, 2008.

12 Bernard Marr, *Strategic Performance Management: Leveraging and Managing Your Intangible Value Drivers*, Butterworth-Heinemann, 2006.

13 Bernard Marr and James Creelman, "Using a Strategy Map to Build External and Internal Accountabilities: The Case Of Audit Scotland," Advanced Performance Institute, UK, 2010. Available as a free download from www.ap-institute.com.

14 Bernard Marr, Ronan Cregan, Emer Husbands and Gerry Millar, "Measuring and Managing Performance in Local Government, Belfast City Council," Advanced Performance Institute, UK, 2007. Available as a free download from www.ap-institute.com.

Chapter 3   Using Lean Thinking to Improve Strategic Performance

1 http://www.lean.org/WhatsLean/.

2 Dr Robert S. Kaplan and Dr David P. Norton, *The Execution Premium: Linking Strategy to Operations for Competitive Advantage,* Harvard Business School Press, USA, 2008.

3 Dr Robert S. Kaplan and Dr David P. Norton, *The Execution Premium: Linking Strategy to Operations for Competitive Advantage,* Harvard Business School Press, USA, 2008.

4 James Creelman, *The Finance Function: Achieving Performance Excellence in a Global Economy*, Business Intelligence, UK, 2009.

5 Bernard Marr and James Creelman, "Management Case Study: Outcome-based Performance Management: Christchurch City Council Drives Toward a Long-term Strategic Horizon," Advanced Performance Institute, 2008. Available as a free download from www.ap-institute.com.

6 Bernard Marr, James Creelman and Mark Ranford, "Management Case Study: Creating and Implementing a Balanced Scorecard: The Case of the

Ministry of Works, Bahrain," Advanced Performance Institute, 2009. Available as a free download from www.ap-institute.com.

7 See www.ogc.gov.uk.

8 Dr Zoe Radnor, Paul Walley, Andrew Stephens and Giovanni Bucci, *Evaluation of the Lean Approach to Business Management and Its Use in the Public Sector*, Scottish Executive, UK, 2006.

9 Naresh Makhijani and James Creelman, *Achieving Breakthrough Performance with Six Sigma*, OTI Indonesia, 2010.

10 Dr Zoe Radnor, Paul Walley, Andrew Stephens and Giovanni Bucci, *Evaluation of the Lean Approach to Business Management and Its Use in the Public Sector*, Scottish Executive, UK, 2006.

11 For more see the W. Edwards Deming Institute at http://deming.org/.

Chapter 4   Designing Strategy Maps to Agree Strategic Priorities

1 Bernard Marr, "Strategic Performance Management in Government and Public Sector Organizations," Advanced Performance Institute, co-sponsored by CIPFA Performance Improvement Network and Actuate, UK, 2008. Available as a free download from www.ap-institute.com.

2 Christopher D. Ittner and David P. Larcker, "Coming Up Short on Nonfinancial Performance Measurement," *Harvard Business Review*, November 2003, USA.

3 Bernard Marr and James Creelman, "Management Case Study: Implementing a Performance Scorecard in a Global Organization: Creating a Roadmap for the International Baccalaureate," Advanced Performance Institute, UK, 2010. Available as a free download from www.ap-institute.com.

4 Bernard Marr and James Creelman, "Building a Strategy Map to Drive External and Internal Performance Accountability and Improvement: The Case of Audit Scotland," Advanced Performance Institute, UK, 2010. Available as a free download from www.ap-institute.com.

5 Bernard Marr and James Creelman, "Management Case Study: Implementing a Performance Scorecard for a Collaborative Commercial Agency: Involving all Employees in Mapping, Managing and Monitoring a Pathway to Success," Advanced Performance Institute, 2009. Available as a free download from www.ap-institute.com.

6 Bernard Marr and James Creelman, "Outcome-Based Performance Management: Christchurch City Council Drives Toward a Long-Term Strategic Horizon," Advanced Performance Institute, 2008. Available as a free download from www.ap-institute.com.

7 A case study on Royal Canadian Mounted Police can be found in James Creelman, *Creating a Strategic Balanced Scorecard*, Business Intelligence, London, 2003.

8 Bernard Marr, Ronan Cregan, Emer Husbands and Gerry Millar, "Measuring and Managing Performance in Local Government, Belfast City Council," Advanced Performance Institute, UK, 2007. Available as a free download from www.ap-institute.com.

9 Bernard Marr, James Creelman and Mark Ranford, "Creating and Implementing a Balanced Scorecard: The Case of the Ministry of Works, Bahrain," Advanced Performance Institute, UK, 2000. Available as a free download from www.ap-institute.com.

10 For more information please see: http://www.albawaba.com/en/countries/Bahrain/237843.

11 James Creelman and Naresh Makhijani, *Mastering Business in Asia: Succeeding with the Balanced Scorecard*, John Wiley & Sons, Asia, 2005.

12 Bernard Marr, "New Directions for Government: Five Principles for Sustainable Recovery," The Advanced Performance Management, Actuate, 2009, UK. Available as a free download from www.ap-institute.com.

Chapter 5   Agreeing High Level Strategic Outcome Targets and Key Performance Indicators

1 Bernard Marr, *Managing and Delivering Performance: How Government, Public Sector and Not-for-Profit Organizations Can Measure and Manage What Really Matters*, Butterworth-Heinemann, UK, 2008.

2 A case study on Brisbane City Council can be found in James Creelman and David Harvey report, *Developing a Public Sector Scorecard: Achieving Breakthrough Results in Service Delivery and Performance*, Business Intelligence, UK, 2003.

3 See www.thepalladiumgroup.com.

4 Bernard Marr, "Strategic Performance Management in Government and Public Sector Organizations," Advanced Performance Institute, co-sponsored by CIPFA Performance Improvement Network and Actuate, UK, 2008. Available as a free download from www.ap-institute.com.

5 For a full description see Bernard Marr, "What are Key Performance Questions," Management White Paper, Advanced Performance Institute, UK, 2008. Available as a free download from www.ap-institute.com.

6 Eric Schmidt, CEO, Google Inc. in an interview with Jeremy Caplan for TIME, October 2, 2006.

7 Bernard Marr and James Creelman, "Building a Strategy Map to Drive External and Internal Performance Accountability and Improvement," Advanced Performance Institute, UK, 2009. Available as a free download from www.ap-institute.com.

8 Bernard Marr, Jane Watters and Maria Weir, "Measuring and Managing Intangibles: The Scottish Intellectual Assets Centre, Management Case Study," Advanced Performance Institute, UK, 2007. Available as a free download from www.ap-institute.com.

9 Bernard Marr and James Creelman, "Management Case Study: Implementing a Performance Scorecard in a Global Organization: Creating a Roadmap for the International Baccalaureate," Advanced Performance Institute, UK, 2010. Available as a free download from www.ap-institute.com.

10 See http://www.resultsaccountability.com.

11 Bernard Marr, "Strategic Performance Management in Public Sector and Government Organizations," Advanced Performance Institute, co-sponsored by CIPFA Performance Improvement Network and Actuate, UK, 2008. Available as a free download from www.ap-institute.com.

12 For a step-by-step process for turning data into meaningful and action-able knowledge see Bernard Marr, *The Intelligent Company: Using Evidence-Based Management to Turn Data into Actionable Knowledge*, John Wiley, UK, 2010.

13 Bernard Marr, James Creelman and Mark Ranford, "Creating and Imple-menting a Balanced Scorecard: The Case of the Ministry of Works, Bahrain," Advanced Performance Institute, UK, 2009. Available as a free download from www.ap-institute.com.

Chapter 6 Selecting Strategic Initiatives

1 Bernard Marr, "Strategic Performance Management in Government and Public Sector Organizations," Advanced Performance Institute, co-sponsored by CIPFA Performance Improvement Network and Actuate, UK, 2008. Available as a free download from www.ap-institute.com.

2 Bernard Marr and James Creelman, "Management Case Study: Implementing a Performance Scorecard in a Global Organization: Creating a Roadmap for Better Education at the International Baccalaureate," Advanced Per-formance Institute, 2010. Available as a free download from www.ap-institute.com.

3 Bernard Marr, Mark Ranford and James Creelman, "Management Case Study: Creating and Implementing a Balanced Scorecard: The Case of the Ministry of Works, Bahrain," Advanced Performance Institute, 2009. Available as a free download from www.ap-institute.com.

4 Bernard Marr, Ronan Cregan, Emer Husbands and Gerry Millar, "Manage-ment Case Study: Measuring and Managing Performance in Local Govern-ment: Belfast City Council," Advanced Performance Institute, 2007. Available as a free download from www.ap-institute.com.

5 See http://en.wikipedia.org/wiki/Big_Dig.

6 Bernard Marr, Mark Ranford and James Creelman, "Management Case Study: Creating and Implementing a Balanced Scorecard: The Case of the Ministry of Works, Bahrain," Advanced Performance Institute, 2009. Available as a free download from www.ap-institute.com.

7 James Creelman, "Understanding the Balanced Scorecard: An HR Perspec-tive," *HR.Com*, Canada, 2002.

8 James Creelman, David Harvey, *Developing a Public Sector Scorecard*, Business Intelligence, UK, 2004.

9 James Creelman, *Reinventing Planning and Budgeting for the Adaptive Enter-prise*, Business Intelligence, UK, 2006.

10 http://www.lean.org/WhatsLean/.

11 Naresh Makhijani and James Creelman, "Achieving Breakthrough Performance with Six Sigma," *OTI Thought Leadership Series*, Volume 2, Issue 1, 2010, OTI, Indonesia.

12 "Report of the Review of NHS Pathology Services in England," An Independent Review for the Department of Health, UK, 2006.

13 "Reducing Turnaround time in Pathology Using Lean Thinking," www.institute.nhs.uk.

Chapter 7   Aligning Financial Management with Strategic Goals

1 Bernard Marr and James Creelman, "Using Performance Management to Transform a Failing Organization: The Improvement Journey of NE Lincolnshire Council," Advanced Performance Institute, 2009. Available as a free download from www.ap-institute.com.

2 Lori Calabro, "On Balance," an interview with Dr Robert S. Kaplan and Dr David P. Norton, CFO Magazine, USA, February 2001.

3 See www.bbrt.org.

4 James Creelman, *The Finance Function: Achieving Superior Performance in a Global Economy*, Business Intelligence, UK, 2009.

5 James Creelman, *Reinventing Planning and Budgeting for the Adaptive Enterprise*, Business Intelligence, UK, 2006.

6 The most recent of the research series is "Planning for Economic Survivability: Linking Strategy to Action," The Hackett Group 2009 Book of Numbers Research Series, The Hackett Group, USA, 2009.

7 "Planning for Economic Survivability: Linking Strategy to Action," The Hacket Group 2009 Book of Numbers Research Series, The Hackett Group, USA, 2009.

8 "Performance Metrics and Practices of World-Class Finance Organizations," The Hackett Group 2007 Book of Numbers Research Series, The Hackett Group, USA, 2007.

9 Bernard Marr, James Creelman and Mark Ranford, "Creating and Implementing a Balanced Scorecard: The Case of the Ministry of Works, Bahrain," Advanced Performance Institute, UK, 2009. Available as a free download from www.ap-institute.com.

10 Bernard Marr and James Creelman, "Outcome-Based Performance Management: Christchurch City Council Drives toward a Strategic Horizon," Advanced Performance Institute, UK, 2008. Available as a free download from www.ap-institute.com.

11 James Creelman, *The Finance Function: Achieving Superior Performance in a Global Economy*, Business Intelligence, UK, 2009.

12 Bernard Marr, Ronan Cregan, Emer Husbands and Gerry Millar, "Measuring and Managing Performance in Local Government," Advanced Performance Institute, UK, 2007. Available as a free download from www.ap-institute.com.

13 James Creelman, *Reinventing Planning and Budgeting for the Adaptive Enterprise*, Business Intelligence, UK, 2006.

14 Dr Robert S. Kaplan and Dr David P. Norton, *The Execution Premium: Linking Operations to Strategy for Competitive Advantage*, Harvard Business School Press, Boston, USA, 2008.

15 Bernard Marr, "Strategic Performance Management in Government and Public Sector Organizations," Advanced Performance Institute, co-sponsored by CIPFA Performance Network and Actuate, UK, 2008. Available as a free download from www.ap-institute.com.

16 Bernard Marr and James Creelman, "Information Management Services, HM Revenue and Customs, Management Case Study," Advanced Performance Institute, UK, 2010. Available as a free download from www.ap-institute. com.

17 See www.bbrt.org.

Chapter 8   Keeping Your Eyes on the Ball: Reporting and Reviewing Performance

1 Bernard Marr, *The Intelligent Company: Five Steps to Success with Evidence-Based Management*, John Wiley, UK, 2010.

2 Bernard Marr, "Strategic Performance Management in Government and Public Sector Organizations," Advanced Performance Management, co-sponsored by CIPFA Performance Improvement Network and Actuate, UK, 2008. Available as a free download from www.ap-institute.com.

3 Bernard Marr, James Creelman and Mark Ranford, "Creating and Implementing a Balanced Scorecard: The Case of the Ministry of Works, Bahrain," Advanced Performance Institute, UK, 2009. Available as a free download from www.ap-institute.com.

4 See http://www.thepalladiumgroup.com/about/hof/.

5 Bernard Marr and James Creelman, "Outcome-Based Performance Management: Christchurch City Council Drives Toward a Long-Term Strategic Horizon, Management Case Study," Advanced Performance Institute, UK, 2008. Available as a free download from www.ap-institute.com.

6 Bernard Marr, "Selecting Balanced Scorecard Software Solutions," Advanced Performance Institute, UK, 2007. Available as a free download from www.ap-institute.com.

7 Bernard Marr, "Strategic Performance Management in Government and Public Sector Organizations," Advanced Performance Management, co-sponsored by CIPFA Performance Improvement Network and Actuate, UK, 2008. Available as a free download from www.ap-institute.com.

8 Bernard Marr and James Creelman, "Building a Strategy Map to Drive External and Internal Performance Accountability and Improvement: The Case of Audit Scotland," Advanced Performance Institute, UK, 2009. Available as a free download from www.ap-institute.com.

9 Dr Robert S. Kaplan and Dr David P. Norton, *The Execution Premium: Linking Strategy with Operations for Competitive Advantage*, Harvard Business School Press, USA, 2008.

10 Bernard Marr, Ronan Cregan, Emer Husbands and Gerry Millar, "Measuring and Managing Performance in Local Government: Belfast City Council," Advanced Performance Institute, UK, 2007. Available as a free download from www.ap-institute.com.

11 Bernard Marr and James Creelman, "IMS HM Revenues and Customs case study," Advanced Performance Institute, UK, 2009. Available as a free download from www.ap-institute.com.

Chapter 9   Building a Culture Focused on Strategic Performance Management

1 Dr Robert S. Kaplan and Dr David P. Norton, *The Balanced Scorecard, Translating Strategy into Action*, Harvard Business School Press, USA, 2006.

2 Edgar Schein, *Organizational Culture and Leadership*, Jossey-Bass Publishers, California, USA, 1992.

3 James Creelman, *Driving Corporate Culture for Business Success*, Business Intelligence, London, 1999.

4 See www.thepublicmanager.org.

5 Hubert Saint-Onge and Charles Armstrong, *The Conductive Organization: Building Beyond Sustainability*, Elsevier-Butterworth-Heinemann, USA, 2004.

6 Culture and Change Management, a survey of 236 organizations commissioned to support the report "Driving Corporate Culture for Business Success," James Creelman, Business Intelligence, 1999.

7 Bernard Marr and James Creelman, "HMRC IMS management case study," Advanced Performance Institute, UK, 2010. Available as a free download from www.ap-institute.com.

8 Bernard Marr, Ronan Cregan, Emer Husbands and Gerry Millar, "Measuring and Managing Performance in Local Government, Belfast City Council, Management Case Study," Advanced Performance Institute, UK 2007. Available as a free download from www.ap-insitute.com.

9 Bernard Marr, "Strategic Performance Management in Government and Public Sector Organizations," Advanced Performance Institute, co-sponsored by CIPFA Performance Improvement Network and Actuate, UK, 2008. Available as a free download from www.ap-institute.com.

10 As 1.

11 Hubert Saint-Onge and Charles Armstrong, *The Conductive Organization, Building Beyond Sustainability*, Elsevier-Butterworth-Heinemann, 2004.

12 Hubert Saint-Onge and Charles Armstrong, *The Conductive Organization, Building Beyond Sustainability*, Elsevier-Butterworth-Heinemann, 2004.

13 Bernard Marr and James Creelman, "Outcome-Based Performance Management, Christchurch City Council Drives Toward a Long-Term Strategic

Horizon," Advanced Performance Institute, UK, 2008. Available as a free download from www.ap-institute.com.

14 James Creelman and David Harvey, *Developing a Public Sector Scorecard: Achieving Breakthrough Results in Service Delivery and Performance*, Business Intelligence, London, UK, 2004.

15 Andrew Wileman, *Driving Down Cost: How to Manage and Cut Costs Intelligently*, Nicholas Brealey Publishing, London, 2008.

16 Dr Robert S. Kaplan and Dr David P. Norton, *The Execution Premium: Linking Strategy to Operations for Competitive Advantage*, Harvard Business School Press, Boston, USA, 2008.

17 Bernard Marr and James Creelman, "HMRC IMS Management Case Study," Advanced Performance Institute, UK, 2010. Available as a free download from www.ap-institute.com.

Chapter 10   Conclusion and Key Strategic Performance Questions

1 See www.scotland.gov.uk.

2 "Strategic Performance Management in Government and Public Sector Organizations." A research paper by Bernard Marr, The Advanced Performance Management, co-sponsored by CIPFA Performance Improvement Network and Actuate, 2008, UK. Copies of the study can be downloaded for free from www.ap-institute.com.

3 Bernard Marr, "New Directions for Government: Five Principles for Sustainable Recovery," The Advanced Performance Management, Actuate, 2009, UK. Available as a free download from www.ap-institute.com.

4 Bernard Marr and James Creelman, "Using a Strategy Map to Build External and Internal Accountabilities: The Case of Audit Scotland," Advanced Performance Institute, UK, 2009. Available as a free download from www.ap-institute.com.

5 Bernard Marr and James Creelman, "Management Case Study: Outcome-Based Performance Management: Christchurch City Council Drives Toward a Long-Term Strategic Horizon," Advanced Performance Institute, UK, 2008. Available as a free download from www.ap-institute.com.

6 Bernard Marr, "Strategic Performance Management in Government and Public Sector Organizations," Advanced Performance Institute, co-sponsored by CIPFA Performance Improvement Network and Actuate, UK, 2008. Available as a free download from www.ap-institute.com.

7 Bernard Marr, Ronan Cregan, Emer Husbands and Gerry Millar, "Management Case Study, Managing and Measuring Performance in Local Government: Belfast City Council," Advanced Performance Institute, UK, 2007. Available as a free download from www.ap-institute.com.

8 Bernard Marr, James Creelman and Mark Ranford, "Creating and Implementing a Balanced Scorecard: The Case of the Ministry of Works, Bahrain,"

Advanced Performance Institute, UK, 2009. Available as a free download from www.ap-institute.com.

9 Bernard Marr, "Strategic Performance Management in Government and Public Sector Organizations," Advanced Performance Institute, co-sponsored by CIPFA Performance Improvement Network and Actuate, UK, 2008. Available as a free download from www.ap-institute.com.

10 For more information see Bernard Marr, *The Intelligent Company: Five Steps to Success with Evidence-Based Management*, by strategic performance management expert Bernard Marr (2010).

11 Bernard Marr, "Strategic Performance Management in Government and Public Sector Organizations," Advanced Performance Institute, co-sponsored by CIPFA Performance Improvement Network and Actuate, UK, 2008. Available as a free download from www.ap-institute.com.

12 See also: Bernard Marr, *The Intelligent Company: Five Steps to Success with Evidence-Based Management*, by strategic performance management expert Bernard Marr (2010).

INDEX